"How does my therapist do it? Every patient has wondered how their therapist, sometimes idealized, sometimes scorned, manages her love life, raises his children. This useful and unusual collection pulls back the curtain on that second question. With warmth, depth, and beautiful writing we learn what a psychoanalytic sensibility offers parenting in the digital age."
—**Sherry Turkle**, Professor of the Social Studies of Science and Technology, MIT; Affiliate Member, Boston Psychoanalytic Society

"This is a rare and special book, first hand reports of parenting in the face of how hard it is to become a person in the unsettling changes of our modern world. Some are happy and others painfully anguished, but all are touchingly wise. In these personal stories, nothing is "as if" or second hand. All have the evocative power of good fiction, yet all carry contributions advancing understanding as valuable as any academic text ... perhaps more so, since here insights come *in vivo* rather than *ex cathedra*. Conceptually educational and helpful? Absolutely. Emotionally powerful and moving? Definitely. Their memories linger on."
—**Warren S. Poland**, author of *Intimacy and Separateness in Psychoanalysis*

"This is a book not just for parents, not just for clinicians, but for all of us. In moving, personal, well-written essays, highly trained psychotherapists and child development specialists allow themselves unusual vulnerability. They reveal that even with all their clinical sophistication, they were neither perfect parents nor graced with perfect children. Paradoxically, we are reassured when we see that even "the experts" reveal the same uncertainties, sorrows, worries, joys and hopes familiar to parents everywhere. Highly recommended."
—**William S. Meyer, MSW**, Departments of Psychiatry and Ob/Gyn, Duke University Health System, USA

Psychoanalytic Reflections on Parenting Teens and Young Adults

Psychoanalytic Reflections on Parenting Teens and Young Adults explores the rich, multi-layered parent-child interactions that unfold during the period of separation and launching. While this is a necessary transitional time, parents inevitably experience feelings of loss and longing for the past as well as hope for the future.

With honesty, humor, and originality, the book brings together the voices of psychoanalysts, speaking frankly, and not just as professionals, but also as parents grappling with raising young adults in today's fast-paced world. The contributors reflect on the joys, regrets, and surprises as well as the challenges and triumphs they experience as their children reach the threshold of young adulthood. They address a wide range of topics relevant to parents and practitioners alike – indeed to all those who are closely involved with the growth and maturation of today's youth. Offering both a broad perspective and an intimate look at present-day parenting dilemmas, the chapters focus on five main areas of interest: raising youth in the digital age, developmental difficulties, evolving gender norms, social concerns, and finally, the building of resiliency.

Psychoanalytic Reflections on Parenting Teens and Young Adults offers an alternative lens to consider the complex challenges parents face in raising today's teens and young adults, replacing the customary notion of "failure to launch" with the concept of "holding on with open arms." The explorations in this book advance the idea that in the end, these struggles are essential for growth, buoyancy and wisdom. It will appeal greatly to psychoanalysts and psychoanalytic psychotherapists, as well as family therapists.

Anne J. Adelman is a clinical psychologist and psychoanalyst with the Contemporary Freudian Society and the Washington Baltimore Center for Psychoanalysis. She is a faculty member of the New Directions Writing Program and maintains a private practice in Chevy Chase, MD, USA.

Psychoanalytic Reflections on Parenting Teens and Young Adults

Changing Patterns in Modern Love, Loss, and Longing

Edited by
Anne J. Adelman

Routledge
Taylor & Francis Group

LONDON AND NEW YORK

First published 2018
by Routledge
2 Park Square, Milton Park, Abingdon, Oxon OX14 4RN

and by Routledge
711 Third Avenue, New York, NY 10017

Routledge is an imprint of the Taylor & Francis Group, an informa business

British Library Cataloguing-in-Publication Data
A catalogue record for this book is available from the British Library

Library of Congress Cataloging-in-Publication Data
A catalog record for this book has been requested

ISBN: 978-1-138-57908-8 (hbk)
ISBN: 978-1-138-57910-1 (pbk)
ISBN: 978-1-351-26276-7 (ebk)

Typeset in Times New Roman
by Apex CoVantage, LLC

For my mother, Mary Adelman

Contents

Contributors

Anne J. Adelman, Ph.D., is a clinical psychologist and psychoanalyst with the Contemporary Freudian Society. She is the co-author of *Wearing My Tutu to Analysis and Other Stories* (2011) and co-editor of *The Therapist in Mourning: From the Faraway Nearby* (2013), both with Columbia University Press. She is a faculty member of the New Directions Writing Program and maintains a private practice in Chevy Chase, Maryland.

Devra Adelstein, LISW-S, is a clinical social worker and child psychoanalyst who serves on the faculty of the Hanna Perkins Center and the Cleveland Psychoanalytic Center. She consults with schools on issues of child and adolescent development and maintains a private practice in Cleveland Heights, Ohio, working with children, adolescents, adults, and families. She is a graduate of the New Directions Writing Program.

Hemda Arad, Ph.D., is a psychoanalyst. Her Seattle-based private practice spans more than 20 years of work with individuals, couples, and groups. She has served on the faculty of the Northwest Center for Psychoanalysis and New Directions in Psychoanalytic Thinking. She is a member of the International Association for Relational Psychoanalysis and Psychotherapy (IARPP) Advisory Council since its early days and has worked with the China American Psychoanalytic Alliance as a psychoanalyst and supervisor of psychoanalytic candidates.

Mary Collins is an associate professor of creative writing at Central Connecticut State University. She has published several books, including, most recently, *American Idle: A Journey Through Our Sedentary Culture*, which won the Grand Prize in Nonfiction at the Indie Awards in 2010. Her essays have won several national awards, including Best Essay from the American Society of Journalists and Authors.

Nancy J. Crown, Ph.D., is a clinical psychologist and psychoanalyst. She maintains a private practice in New York City, where she works with adults and children. Dr. Crown is an assistant clinical professor at the Albert Einstein College of Medicine and a faculty member in the Child and Adolescent

Psychotherapy Training Program of the William Alanson White Institute. She presents, teaches, and publishes on various topics, including developmental disabilities.

Karen Earle, LICSW, is a psychotherapist in private practice in Shelburne Falls, MA. Her clinical focus includes learning difference, trauma, and relational difficulties. She has ongoing interests in attachment theory and family systems. A recent graduate of the Massachusetts Institute for Psychoanalysis Postgraduate Fellowship Program, she is on the faculty of New Directions: Writing with a Psychoanalytic Edge, a division of the Washington Center for Psychoanalysis. She taught writing for many years and served as the director of the Writing Lab at the Bryn Mawr College Graduate School of Social Work. She offers writing workshops in memoir and journaling and has published poems in a number of literary journals, including *The G W Review, Chaffin Journal, Chaminade Literary Review, The Hudson River Valley Echoes,* and *The Denver Quarterly.*

Michelle Flax, Ph.D., is a psychologist/psychoanalyst in private practice in Toronto, Canada. She is on faculty at the Toronto Institute for Contemporary Psychoanalysis and is a board member of the Advanced Training Psychoanalytic Psychotherapy Program. She has written on a wide variety of topics, ranging from dealing with erotic transference to aspects of treatment.

Noah S. Glassman, Ph.D., is a graduate of the New York University Postdoctoral Program in Psychotherapy and Psychoanalysis and is a member of its Psychoanalytic Society. He has published articles and chapters on gay parenthood, adoption, and HIV/AIDS, as well as research on transference. He is in private practice in Manhattan.

Ann V. Klotz lives in Shaker Heights, Ohio, where she heads Laurel School. She holds a B.A. in English from Yale College and an M.A. in the individual study of drama from the Gallatin Division of New York University. She has worked in girls' schools as a teacher and administrator for more than thirty years and is devoted to the social and emotional development of girls. Klotz frequently blogs for *The Huffington Post* on the intersection of motherhood and school leadership. Additionally, her work has appeared in *Literary Mama, Mothers Always Write,* the Good Mother Project, *Mutha Magazine, Independent School Magazine,* and *Community Works Institute Journal.*

Irene Smith Landsman, Ph.D., is a clinical psychologist in private practice. She has written about the psychological consequences of loss and trauma, and in particular the problem of making meaning in the wake of life-changing events. More recently, as part of the New Directions program of the Washington Center for Psychoanalysis, she writes personal essays and is working on a memoir.

Kerry Leddy Malawista, Ph.D., is a training and supervising analyst in the Contemporary Freudian Society and is in private practice in Potomac, Maryland, and McLean, Virginia. She is on the permanent faculty at the Contemporary

Freudian Society and the Washington School of Psychiatry. She is the coauthor of *Wearing My Tutu to Analysis and Other Stories* (2011) and coeditor of *The Therapist in Mourning: From the Faraway Nearby*, both with Columbia University Press. Her essays have appeared widely, including in *The New York Times*, *The Huffington Post*, *The Washington Post*, *The Account Magazine*, *Zone 3*, *Washingtonian Magazine*, and *Voices*, alongside many professional chapters and articles.

Lizbeth A. Moses, Ph.D., is a clinical psychologist and a member of the International Psychoanalytic Association and the Contemporary Freudian Society. She is a teaching analyst at CFS and a guest instructor at the Washington, D.C., program of the Case Western Reserve School of Medicine. She has a private practice of adolescent, adult, couples, and family psychotherapy and psychoanalysis in Bethesda, Maryland.

Billie A. Pivnick, Ph.D., is faculty member and supervisor in the Child and Adolescent Psychotherapy Training Program at the William Alanson White Institute, Columbia University Teachers College, and the New Directions Program in Psychoanalytic Writing. In her private practice in New York City, she specializes in treating children, adults, and families confronting difficulties resulting from adoption. She has also written numerous articles on adoption.

Christie M. Platt, Ph.D., is a psychoanalyst and clinical psychologist in Washington, D.C. Her private practice encompasses a diverse population including university students, adult professionals and veterans of both the Iraq and Afghanistan wars. Her writings on intersubjectivity, issues of race and ethnicity, and the arts have been published in various publications including the *American Journal of Psychoanalysis*. She is a teaching analyst at the Baltimore Washington Center for Psychoanalysis.

Elizabeth Trawick practices psychoanalysis and psychotherapy in Birmingham, Alabama. She is a training and supervising analyst in the New Orleans Birmingham Psychoanalytic Center. She taught at the New Center for Psychoanalysis in Los Angeles, where she was also a training and supervising analyst at the Psychoanalytic Center of California. As a participant in the New Directions program of the Washington Psychoanalytic Center, she has worked to learn to write meaningfully of the unmentalized.

Preface

This book explores the demands and stresses of contemporary life that influence young adults and their parents during the protracted period of separation from their families of origin. That this period of separation is somehow unique in the current world is questionable. Each generation wonders, "What makes life today different from life in previous generations?" Today, dramatic advances in technology, medicine, social discourse, and climate provide ready answers. But my focus here is an exploration of how these differences impinge on how young adults separate from their families. In this volume, I have invited a group of authors to look beneath the surface – not just at what is different in the modern world but at how these transformations affect the internal lives of adolescents and young adults as they transition to adulthood.

This book grew in part out of changes in the consulting room I have observed over the last twenty years working with children, adolescents, young adults, and their families. During this time, I realized I was hearing more and more about the impact of technology on adolescents and their parents, and challenges families were facing as a consequence. I recall the first time I really understood just how different things were. In the early '90s, a young man came to see me because he was arguing with his parents over his decision to move to another state to live with his girlfriend.

"What is it about your decision that is giving them trouble?" I asked.

"Well, they just don't get it," he said slowly.

"Just don't get what?" I replied. "I'm not sure I understand."

"They think it's strange that we haven't met in person, but it's not! We love each other!" he declared. "See, we met in cyberspace, and we've been dating online. My parents just don't understand that kind of thing."

"Me either!" I thought to myself.

The young man continued, "They think it has to be the way it was for them, but it's just not like that anymore! And I can't get them to understand." I told him I could see how difficult it might be for his parents and him to understand one another, but perhaps there would be a way for them to learn to listen to each other's points of view.

I came to recognize that what I was hearing from this young man presaged dramatic changes in how people form intimate bonds, close connections, and new relationships in light of rapidly growing advances in technology. Just as two geographically separate individuals could now forge an intimate connection, this same technology has allowed all sorts of isolated individuals and diverse groups to connect in ways previously unthinkable. Indeed, the very writing of this book and the collaborations between the invited authors and myself has been rendered vastly more feasible with today's technology.

In the realms of human development, human psychology, and neurobiology, advances in technology have provided us with a deeper knowledge of neuronal connectivity and have begun to flesh out the complex relationships among brain, behavior, emotion, culture, environment, and society. Understanding human development and psychology from a psychoanalytic point of view, however, retains a fundamental core unchanged by technology. However much the modern world evolves around us, the responsibility of the psychoanalyst remains the same: to listen to our patients with depth, empathy, patience, and open-ended inquiry. Changing circumstances demand re-examination of previously held assumptions; we must avoid making premature judgments or drawing conclusions that may ultimately short-circuit our capacity to more fully understand our patients and help them to more fully understand themselves. Psychoanalytic listening entails paying attention to the meanings that lie beneath the surface and bringing them to the foreground.

As a clinician, I see teens and young adults every day who, along with their families, struggle to gain ground in a fast-paced, stressful, and demanding world. What I am struck with most is the profound resilience with which these families confront challenges and gracefully work through them. Successful families, with ever-growing acceptance, learn to adapt in the face of often overwhelming difficulty. I have worked alongside parents and children as they developed a greater capacity to tolerate uncertainty and ambiguity, to contain anxiety and restore its function as a useful signal, to work through differences, and to make sense of their feelings of emotional distance, in their efforts to deepen intimacy. This process allows families to develop a more genuine sense of interpersonal connectedness and internal aliveness.

In this book, we explore the capacity of ordinary children and families to negotiate the developmental dance of holding on and letting go in the context of the exceptional demands of today's world. We are looking at how parents help today's young adults to navigate the complex social and emotional landscape that modern innovations have begun to transform. We want to examine how we can gather up our children with open arms, no matter how close to or far from us they have landed. Ultimately, the stories that appear in this volume are stories of personal struggle, profound resilience, and meaningful change, both internal and interpersonal. As such, they are resonant because they are deeply human.

Acknowledgments

The reflections in this book are inspired by the patients I see each day in my office. They – along with my own children – have opened my eyes to the challenges of navigating the complex terrain of modern life, all the while building resilience and gathering strength, wisdom, and insight. I thank them for entrusting me with their lives and stories.

My gratitude goes out to the authors whose work appears in this volume, for sharing their insights, for being honest and reflective, and for demonstrating courage, commitment, and determination as both parents and clinicians. These authors include my dear colleagues at New Directions in Psychoanalysis, whose vibrant voices can be heard throughout these pages. Working with these individuals is a privilege.

Special thanks to Kerry Malawista, who helped set this project afloat. I am ever grateful for her thoughtful edits and cherished friendship.

My thanks to Kate Hawes and Charles Bath at Routledge for their guidance during the course of this project. Heidi Fritschel's calm, steady presence throughout provided much appreciated assistance. Ruth Taswell's exquisite eye for detail and astute commentary imparted invaluable refinement. This book would not have been possible without the unwavering support of Eric Taswell, who spent many hours patiently reading these pages, offering compelling ideas, perceptive comments, and boundless encouragement. I benefited enormously from the delight, support, and vast education about social media that my daughters provided. The gift of parenting them has taught me much about myself and has helped me become a wiser parent and clinician.

To all of the adolescents and adult children whose stories light up these pages, I am forever enriched by your humor and intelligence, and your profound courage and optimism for what lies ahead.

Introduction

Anne J. Adelman

A couple of years ago, I was at a family wedding with my teenage daughters, where we met a friend of the groom, a young woman in her late twenties whose father was a psychiatrist and whose mother was a psychoanalyst. When she learned that my daughters shared a similar plight, she began to regale them with her own stories about being the child of mental health professionals. We laughed at her tales of dinner-table conversations about feelings and Freud, the existence of the unconscious, and the nameless people who came to see her parents for secret meetings about which they could divulge nothing.

"Things were never normal in our house," she told us. "My father was always delving deeper, wondering what I really *meant*, no matter what I told him." I watched both of my daughters nodding emphatically, getting into it with relish.

"I know, whatever I say, they have to say, *How do you feel about it?*" my younger daughter replied, mimicking my voice perfectly. I held back my protests, listening.

"They always want to *talk about everything*. It's so annoying!" she added. I felt a bit piqued.

"Come on," I objected laughingly. "I'm not so bad!" But my feeble protest went unheard as the conversation rolled forward, with rising hilarity among the small group and another quip from their new friend: "And whenever I hang out with friends, they say, *Think about what you're doing and how you're going to feel if this happens, or that . . . .* And when I'm mad? – I get the *Let's talk about it* routine. I used to just say to my dad, 'Please get out and leave me alone now, Dr. Freud.'"

As I laughed, I conceded the truth of what they were saying. They recognized one another as kindred spirits, or allies belonging to a peculiar tribe. By articulating the strange intersection between psychoanalysis and parenthood, they declared themselves members of the Offspring of Psychoanalysts Club. They clearly spoke the same language.

Then, they became Facebook friends. These are modern times.

* * *

In this book, psychoanalysts draw on their experiences as parents and professionals to consider what has changed and what has stayed the same for parents raising young adults in modern times. As technological innovations and sociological and political trends have catapulted our culture into a changed universe, parents face fresh challenges and dilemmas. As the Internet and social media have created opportunities for new connections to be forged, new ideas shared, new possibilities imagined and realized, they have also triggered many unknowns.

Take, for example, the situation of many parents today, raised before the Internet era, who lack a template for how to assess and manage the dangers of technology. While cell phones and other digital devices offer many advantages – the security of immediate access to one another when we need it, an infinite amount of information at the tips of our fingers, and a complex web of interpersonal connections – they also pose risks and safety concerns that alarm parents. Loss of privacy, cyberbullying and cyberstalking, shaming, overexposure to negative and dangerous information, among other hazards, have become commonplace. But adolescents and adults increasingly rely on digital devices – for education, for information, for social communication. Still, "Put away your phone!" has become nearly every parent's battle cry.

Such changes reflect contemporary trends. It is not that digital technology alone has changed the world, but rather that it represents a seismic shift in how we engage with the world and with others around us. Parents and practitioners alike are obliged to develop new approaches to the task of parenting teens and young adults, who are often tethered to their devices, stressed by the demands of a multitasking world, or struggling with anxiety and depression heightened by such pressures. Confused by shifting norms, parents may alternate between overindulgence and hypercontrol, between intrusion and a laissez-faire attitude. Clinicians confront similar challenges in the consulting room, where families seek guidance about how to help their adolescents and young adults flourish while balancing the ever-present lure of social media.

The writers whose work appears in this volume have thought deeply about raising young adults in modern times, and offer their reflections as both parents and psychoanalysts. As parents, we articulate experiences with our own children. And in sharing these stories here, we each capture some essential feature of what all parents may at times face in this modern era. As analysts, we draw on theories of development, personality, internal conflict, unconscious fantasy, sexuality, and attachment. We examine the transition of today's young adults from dependency to separation and autonomy.

What makes this volume unique is that the stories shared are personal. Drawing from our own experiences as parents first, professionals second, we offer an intimate look at the process of parenting, and at the multilayered interactions between parents and children.

We recognize that there is a wide range of topics relevant to parents and practitioners involved with twenty-first-century young adults on the cusp of separation. Some of the topics we address are not necessarily new to our time; we aim to understand them, however, through a novel contemporary lens. Our focus is on uncovering the underlying dynamic themes that define the modern youth's transition to adulthood – the emotional and psychological currents essential for parents and children to work through while building resilience and establishing independence.

Specifically, this collection of essays explores developmental delays, new understandings of gender identification, social challenges, and resiliency in the face of loss. We look at intrinsic patterns common to young adults, balancing what is unique to each individual family with shared threads that run throughout this transitional period. With the advantage of analytic insight, we flesh out an understanding of how to navigate the challenges of parenting young adults. By bringing together our lives as both parents and professionals, we ask how best to stay steady and loving in the face of children's often unexpected and sometimes confusing developmental trajectories.

* * *

Important disclaimer: Psychoanalysts do not make better parents. On the contrary, being a psychoanalyst means being painfully aware of every pitfall, every mistake made as a parent. Psychoanalysts know what not to say, sometimes even as the words are spoken. They may understand why they inadvertently repeat the very dynamic from their childhood they swore would never recur, or why they can't simply be a friend, rather than a parent, to their own offspring – even as the clear boundary they just set gives way to the wish to avoid conflict, and they opt instead for the warm satisfaction of a cozy cuddle-up.

Psychoanalysis lends a framework within which to think about parenting – what we do, who we are, and how we live. Psychoanalysis also provides a structure for understanding development, family dynamics, and what is important for children as they grow. As psychoanalysts, we cannot leave these ideas at the door when we are at home with our children.

For many parents, raising children is a transformative experience. You may discover parts of yourself you didn't know existed. You may have felt inextricably bound to your children when they were young, while at the same time preparing yourself for their eventual passage to adulthood. Parenting involves unwrapping the tendrils, bit by bit, and taking back the parts of yourself that you had put on temporary hold while you were out on loan to your children – allowing them to grow into individuals with their own separate lives.

This can be a delicate process for psychoanalyst parents, whose children, born with a lifetime membership in the Offspring of Psychoanalysts Club, may receive mixed benefits. On the one hand, our background and training in development, unconscious processes, and the internal workings of the mind heighten our awareness of developmental issues in both the young adult and in the parent. On the other hand, this same background and training likely infiltrate if not the overt content, then at very least the style of our parenting. Because of our training, we may think we understand what our children are experiencing, yet we may also be blinded by our own presumptions.

Members of the Club inevitably feel the weight of this. Try as we may to keep our psychoanalytic selves in our consulting rooms, we can't help but think dynamically about the psychological well-being of our offspring.

Parenting is a layered experience for all parents, buffeted by various internal and external forces that invariably shape how you raise your children: how you were parented yourself, who you are with your partner, who you are in your own family of origin, what your professional life is like, what your support system is like, how much stress you experience, how stressed or anxious your child feels, and who innately your child is becoming, among other factors. But for psychoanalyst parents, an inclination toward self-reflection, self-analysis, and the search for meaning magnifies the process.

* * *

But what of writing about our children, as we do here in this volume? Writing about ourselves as parents and about our own families shares issues with writing about our patients.

Writing about patients is complicated. There are ethical issues to consider and confidentiality measures to adhere to: Do we discuss with our patients our desire to write about our work with them? Do we share what we've written? Invite their feedback? Do we disguise them to preserve their confidentiality, even if the disguise alters certain facts of their story? Can there truly be informed consent when a therapist asks permission to write about a patient?

Judith Kantrowitz (2004) has studied the importance of balancing a duty to protect patients' privacy and the integrity of their treatment with the need to learn from colleagues and deepen our understanding of the critical function of psychoanalysis. She acknowledges, "Writing about patients is like walking in a minefield." Nevertheless she urges clinicians to "not stop writing about patients but to face and struggle with the conflict it creates as honestly as possible."

As parents and clinicians, we have drawn from these ideas as the bedrock of writing about our own families. We write honestly and intimately about our children in this book, sharing personal reflections, struggles, joys, and sorrows, because they are relevant and a fundamental part of who we are.

While all authors have discussed their chapter with their children, and many shared the writing with them, writing about our own families still raises complicated concerns and feelings. If an adult child did not want to be written about, he or she was not. And if certain details felt too personal or off-limits, they were omitted.

Ultimately, however, the stories in this book are not about our children but about ourselves – about how we, as parents and as professionals, have striven for clarity, for openness, for an ever-deeper capacity to fulfill our roles as mothers and fathers in the most authentic and caring way we can.

* * *

This volume adopts a multifaceted approach to exploring the challenges facing parents and families in today's fast-paced world.

The first section of the book, entitled "Parenting in the Digital Age," offers an overview of contemporary trends facing today's adolescents and young adults. In particular, the section examines the tension between parents' desire to hold onto the past and the need to let go and move forward, to lean in toward adolescents as they ready themselves to step over the threshold to adulthood.

Here, we examine what has changed dynamically for today's youth, with special consideration of the impact of social media on the process of growing into adulthood – and on the process of parenting. Parents and children find that social media can act as an omnipresent third party in their relationship, raising new challenges related to social connectedness and loneliness as well as to family relationships.

How can young adults develop the ability to be alone with their thoughts and feelings when they are virtually never alone? At the same time, social media risks heightening feelings of isolation and encouraging dependence on a constant virtual feed, impeding the process of separating and achieving autonomy.

The second section, "Developmental Concerns," delves into common themes and emotional complexities facing the families of young adults with developmental difficulties. The medical, social, and cognitive challenges that are addressed here – such as autism and cognitive delays – are not unique to our time, but the ways in which such difficulties are understood and addressed have evolved significantly. Such delays can interfere with or derail a young adult's capacity to consolidate his or her development and reach greater maturity. We examine how parents may best meet the needs of their particular young adult as they shepherd him or her toward independence – how long to hold on, how to let go while still staying within arm's reach, how to stay steady in the face of their young adult's need to engage and disengage with parents as they strive for autonomy.

The third section of the book, "Unbound: New Definitions of Gender," is devoted to examining our evolving understanding of gender and sexuality. New technologies, new medical possibilities, and deeper knowledge about gender identity have increasingly allowed some of today's young adults to live their lives more openly than in the past. In some areas of our country and the world, we are better equipped to appreciate the needs of teens and young adults as they begin to explore their gender identification and sexual orientation.

We still have far to go in bridging the many divides that continue to stand in the way of understanding and accepting sexual diversity and gender fluidity. Many continue to hold false or inaccurate assumptions about the spectrum of gender identity and sexual orientation: they misunderstand adolescents' efforts to find common language to communicate their shared experience, or they "misgender" them or lack the desire or ability to understand a realm of diversity that is strange or confusing to them.

Nonetheless, continuing to work toward achieving mutual understanding and respect is essential, as is supporting young adults' efforts to communicate openly with one another and with their families. In this section, we explore how families grapple with changing norms, shifting language, and emerging adaptations, both in themselves and in their adult children. We look at how parents learn to embrace such change, and how they mourn what feels lost even as they celebrate what has been gained.

The fourth section, "Social Topics," addresses several psychosocial challenges that affect young adults in our modern world, including adoption, alcoholism, trauma, and immigration, among others. While all of these challenges have affected families throughout the generations, here we shine a light on how we can best understand their impact on today's young adults in particular. We consider how parents can approach such issues with understanding and forbearance, making themselves available to support their young adult child through difficult experiences.

The final section, "Building Resilience," speaks to the capacity within families to gather together despite strife or adversity and emerge stronger, closer, and often with greater appreciation for one another. This section explores the ways in which families regain strength, balance, and a new equilibrium after a traumatic experience.

The capacity to develop resilience rests on a number of factors, including the ability to draw support from the community, to offer support and empathy in return, to represent and remember the lost loved ones, and to restore hope, faith, humor, and internal flexibility. Each family member needs to find internal solace and, at the same time, nurture one another through grief. Ultimately, we strive to understand how families mourn, and gradually come to grips with events that shatter the security of the world they knew.

We offer these stories as a way to explore how both contemporary and long-established trends influence the way families move through the child's transition to adolescence and young adulthood. Doing so in the current era of technological, social, and political change calls for a blend of insight, resolve, and empathy. Informed, thoughtful, and flexible parenting can help youth acquire the perseverance and determination needed to master the risks, setbacks, and turmoil they may encounter in an ever-changing world.

With this book, we seek to launch a fresh, lively conversation about parenting today's youth – when to stand up for what is in the child's best interest, when to step out of the child's way, how to stay right alongside as they move through their own development, sometimes faltering and at other times flourishing. We hope to inspire reflective dialogue for all those involved in guiding and supporting today's youth – parents and practitioners alike – to create the space for new understanding and genuine curiosity, and to foster greater flexibility in considering the broad developmental spectrum of young adulthood. Most significantly, we hope to deepen our understanding of family resilience, maturational processes, and the developmental achievement of autonomy that is the hallmark of young adulthood in the modern age.

Reference

Kantrowitz, J. L. (2004). Writing about patients: I. Ways of protecting confidentiality and analysts' conflicts over choice of method. *Journal of the American Psychoanalytic Association*, *52*(1), 69–99.

Part I

Parenting in the digital age

In the age of Facebook, Instagram, and Snapchat, children are virtually tethered to their peers as they were once psychologically tethered to their parents. Technology bypasses the struggles and challenges of learning to be alone. Parents often struggle with feeling abandoned or being rendered obsolete in their teen's social world. In their interactions with their children, they constantly contend with the presence of social media, which creates a "virtual third" in the relationship. This section explores the various dynamics of how the parent-child relationship weathers these developmental changes: when it works well, and when it gets derailed.

Anne J. Adelman's chapter examines the impact of social media on the inner lives of adolescents and on the contemporary relationship between parents and their young adult children. When children are small, parents form the center of their fast-growing universe. Parents are involved in every aspect of their life and care, including the development of their social world. As children develop, they naturally turn their attention outward, away from the security of their family and toward the tantalizing new and complex world of social connections. At school age and into adolescence, friendships become the playing field for identity formation, the development of moral values, decision-making, separation and individuation, and often the exploration of risky behaviors. For parents, this can be a challenging terrain to navigate. How does the mother of a teen forever surrounded by virtual friends navigate her wish to still belong inside the magic circle of friendship from which she is now appropriately excluded?

Christie M. Platt's chapter explores how the advent of new technology can, on the one hand, keep teens and young adults tethered to their parents and unable to fully separate and, on the other, allow for a delicate yet vital connection that can carry them through difficult times. As a young adult, Platt traveled far from home, with little hope of connecting with her family until her return. She compares this period of her life to her experience as a parent of a son who also ventured far from home. Finding himself in the midst of a military coup in a far-flung land, he was still able to communicate through modern technology that allowed both mother and son to feel anchored during a transcontinental upheaval. Platt examines how digital connectivity may alter the nature of the parent-child bond, at times facilitating and at other times impeding emotional maturation.

What is lost, what is gained in the digital age

Anne J. Adelman

When my older daughter was born, in 1997, I don't remember if I owned a cell phone yet. With her strapped to my chest in my blue denim Baby Bjorn, we walked around in our own bubble.

By the time my younger daughter was born two and a half years later, I already had a Blackberry, given to me when I went back to work after my first maternity leave. I got my first iPhone when my daughters were in elementary school. As my daughters were growing up, so too was the digital era. Among the other middle-school parents, the standard conversation was about cell phones: Does your daughter have one yet? When are you getting her one? What rules do you have in your house about the phone? Do you know her password? Check her texts? Shut it off at night? Allow her to keep it in her bedroom? No one seemed sure, and everyone wanted, desperately, to get it right. One thing seemed universal: parents were eager to show that they were in charge, that they had control over their child's use of technology, and that the rules in their house were ironclad.

For my older daughter, quiet and bookish, the phone and its allure were muted. She was nearly out of middle school before our family even discussed getting a phone for her, and then only because she was riding the school bus home and would be home alone until her little sister arrived back from the local elementary school. When she did get her phone, social media had not quite entered her sphere, so her usage was minimal.

Not so her little sister. It was as if my two girls, born just two and a half years apart, belonged to different technological generations.

My younger daughter got her first phone when she was twelve. The norms, incredibly, seemed to have already shifted. Most of her friends were getting them at the same time. The driving force behind my daughter's first cell phone was swim team. She was a competitive swimmer, and it was difficult for me to find her when we were at large swim meets. If I looked down on the deck from the bleachers far above, where parents sat together to watch their children's races, all I could see was a sea of latex-covered heads and fish-eyed, goggled faces, making it nearly impossible to figure out which swimmer was mine. The heat schedule sheets were often sold out, or I had forgotten to put a couple of dollars in my pocket to buy one, so texting became the only way I'd know for sure not to miss her swim. "I'm going on deck!" her text would chirp. "Lane 7!" And I'd rise from my seat and cheer alongside the rest of the parents till the race was over and I'd see her climb out of the pool, dripping and panting. At the end of the meet, my phone would ping again, "I'm going to the parking lot," followed by the inevitable, "Can we get Chipotle?" Then, at one especially chaotic meet, she lost her phone. After a delicate discussion of whether she was truly ready for such a hefty responsibility, we relented and got her a new phone – fortunately we'd paid the insurance so there was no replacement fee.

I had no idea then that we had unwittingly invited into our relatively low-key family a stealthy, skulking beast, hungrily waiting to swallow up my chatty daughter and spit out a distracted adolescent, vaguely detached from the real-life experiences the rest of us were having at home.

Growing up in the age of social media

Across the ages, parents have grappled with the complexities of raising adolescents and launching them into the world. In Joseph Stein's *Fiddler on the Roof*, the beloved musical adaptation of Sholem Aleichem's stories, Tevye, a hardworking milkman, a husband and breadwinner, a philosopher and a Jew, a good friend and neighbor, is first and foremost a parent. Beset by the demands of changing times, poised on the threshold of launching his young daughters into adulthood, Tevye struggles to keep up with his daughters' strivings toward independence. Tevye, too, must change, as he prepares for his daughters to take leave of the family home and begin their own lives. His oldest daughter, Tzeitel, begs his permission to marry for love instead of accepting the marriage her father had arranged for her. Tevye finds he must bend his own internal rules and traditions to come to terms with the marriage, letting go of his dream of a comfortable union with a wealthy man for his eldest daughter. His second daughter, Hodel, requires him to stretch further, falling in love with and marrying a radical revolutionary who defies tradition and challenges the old way of life. With his third daughter, Chava, Tevye's ability to bend and stretch is tapped out – allowing his daughter to marry outside of his faith is a line he cannot cross. He declares her dead to him.

Tevye's story, set in Russia in 1905 and unfolding against the backdrop of the approaching revolution, is the quintessential story of all parents of young adults. In the face of his daughters' desires to break with tradition and follow their own path, Tevye's heartbreaking dilemma still rings true today. The task of any parent of a child getting ready to launch is to keep up with the pace of change while holding firm to family values and to the organizing principles that guide parenting decisions and actions. How far, as parents, can we adjust to keep alongside of our children as they inevitably make their way into the world of their own devising? And how can we build the resilience necessary to integrate new information, accept the inevitable separation that is the developmental imperative of young adults, and come to terms with the unique adults our children will become – young adults with their own dreams, desires, experiences, and knowledge that may challenge, defy, or surpass our own?

Even now, having watched *Fiddler on the Roof* dozens of times, I am still heart-sick when Tevye draws the line at Chava's marriage. The audience bears witness to not only his pain as a parent but also to the sorrow of his daughter, who loves her family but must follow her heart. Although we understand and empathize with Tevye's decision, it nonetheless represents, in part, a breakdown of a primary parental function. As Chava's choice reveals to her father, sometimes a child's pathway diverges from what the parent might have wished for, imagined, or even dictated. In order for a child to successfully separate, a parent must find a way to come to terms with the child's efforts to establish a clear border between herself and her parent. A parent must learn to tolerate the child's desire to take control over her own life, even when it carries her to places that a parent cannot readily understand. In some ways, this developmental process presents the parent with what can seem like a narcissistically injurious task: to hold steady even as the child turns away, needs less (and, paradoxically, more at the same time), and begins to forge a brand-new pathway. Could Tevye have had a different response? By the end of the play, he does, imploring his wife to tell Chava, "God be with you" – his way of conveying to his daughter, *I still love you and care for you, yet I am struggling to make peace with who you are becoming.*

Launching young adults is a monumental achievement at both ends of the developmental spectrum, requiring a shift for both children and their parents. For many parents, this shift is accompanied by a nostalgic mourning. The parent must somehow find a way to let go of how things were when the child was small, and to let go, too, of their own fantasies, wishes, and fears of who their child would be, as they simultaneously celebrate the adult she is about to become. Raising children inevitably evokes memories of parents' early years. While some parents are dedicated to ensuring that their children not suffer the painful childhoods they had, others long to replay their past, which seems rosier than what today's world offers. At some point, most parents find themselves musing aloud about how things were when they were young, often drawing an unflattering comparison with their own child's attitudes toward life. They worry that their children take their good fortune for granted, or fail to appreciate their origins – and in doing so, they may unconsciously reject their child's nascent efforts to find their way into the adult world. Parents are torn between an obligation to uphold traditions and values of the past and the desire to encourage children to grow into themselves, to reach beyond their parents' achievements.

As it was with Tevye, so it is today: as parents of young adults, it is our developmental imperative to keep up with the pace of change. Each generation brings changes previously unimaginable. We marvel at modern creations and simultaneously feel nostalgia for what came before. Across the ages, parents have always guarded against generational advances that render them suspicious and fearful. While the younger generation embraces the future, their parents step on the brakes, unwittingly impeding or denying inevitable developmental advances. The span of time between young adulthood and middle age seems to stretch and bend like an accordion, drawing out long notes of wistfulness and, in staccato haste, the rapid beat of time flying by.

Today, technology has profoundly altered our sense of time. In Tevye's village of Anatevka, news traveled fast, from the milkman to the butcher to the rabbi and back to the townspeople. Now, news travels at the speed of lightning. We think something is wrong if our Internet connection doesn't respond within seconds. We constantly scan our phone for messages and wonder why we haven't heard back within minutes. We reply to emails at all hours of the day and night. And technology has introduced a different sort of elasticity to time. In the analog world, time progresses forward. With modern technology, time can stretch forward and backward: a photo can be reworked or perfected in Photoshop, a performance can be digitally altered, advanced, or slowed. With a typewriter, a word can be whited out and retyped; on a laptop, sentences can be endlessly deleted, changed, rewritten, leaving no trace of what may have been on the page before. Unlike analog time, digital time is infinitely malleable.

Our children's sense of time is even more elastic. Technologically speaking, they function daily on a multidimensional plane, with several sources of incoming information available to them at any given time, from Facebook and Instagram to Snapchat and YouTube, among others. With such rapid shifts in technology, the span of a digital generation shrinks as well – for instance, the technology used by current college students will be obsolete by the time today's high schoolers reach college themselves. Technology is just one example of the shifting times, but it is such a prevalent, consuming one – one that simply cannot be ignored even though we may at times wish it away – that it serves well to illustrate the developmental issues in launching today's young adults. How do we parents learn to navigate this new terrain with our adolescents and young adults? What psychological changes arise from the current norms that are transforming the way we live?

The globalization of information affords many more opportunities for today's youth than in the past – whether to their benefit or detriment is a persistent dilemma. At its best, the Internet opens up young minds to new ideas and new ways of thinking; at its most perilous, it can be dangerously overstimulating. It is important that we try to parse out the potentially damaging effects of technology and the ordinary changes of adolescence, cloaked in the trappings of a new digital world.

The Internet has given voice to a multitude of like-minded groups who can now connect, feel less isolated, find common ground, and integrate into mainstream culture. Learning, growth, innovation, and development unfold at an increasingly rapid clip. In college seminars, you may find students not only raising their hands the old-fashioned way, but also simultaneously tweeting remarks and finding relevant articles on Facebook or other online news sites to post on a whiteboard in front of the class. Words like "multitasking," "googling," and "texting" have become so much a part of our modern-day parlance that we barely remember a time when they didn't exist.

Before the Internet age, parents, teachers, and other adults were the primary source of information about the world, influencing and shaping their children's viewpoints and values. As children developed and gained new experiences of their own, these ideas could be challenged and reworked. Now, children must digest and integrate a virtual kaleidoscope of information often before their brains have the developmental and neurological capacity to evaluate, reason, or make sense of the rapid-fire deluge of data they are exposed to. Along with technological advances, the social lives of teens and young adults move at high speed. For instance, it seems that many teens start drinking younger, and drinking more, than in the past – it is hard to find a college campus where drinking is not present at most social gatherings. The same is true with substance use, sexual behavior, and other risk-taking behavior. Furthermore, because of social media, it is harder for teens to maintain control over their private information, so their experiences and exploits are available for all to see. For example, if a teen is sexting, she may quickly find her nude photos disseminated throughout her school and beyond. Risk-taking behaviors are by no means new to the 21st century, but they do occur with greater frequency and urgency. It is as if the young adult brain is in a perpetual state of hyper-drive. The faster the world seems to move, the hungrier their brains grow for more stimulation.

Although today's youth are educated early on about using the Internet safely and taught to recognize and avoid risky situations, their relative technological sophistication is offset by their adolescent neurological development, which is actively unfolding and rapidly changing during the teen years. Still impulsive, they lack the judgment and life experience necessary to make careful, well-informed choices. Thus, their use of the Internet remains subject to reckless errors. Parents may be shocked and angry when they get bills for hundreds or sometimes thousands of dollars spent on an online game, or when their teenage daughter is cyber-bullied. In turn, teens and young adults may be unprepared for the online problems that may befall them, such as privacy violations or other threats to their reputation.

Social media and loneliness

Perhaps the most significant issue facing adolescents in the digital age is the frequently solitary nature of technology. Whichever sites children and teens are exploring on the Internet, they are often doing it alone, without the mediating presence of the important adults in their lives. Even when they are overwhelmed, titillated, confused, frightened, or guilty, they may not quite recognize that such reactions are meaningful. They may simply assume that, since what they are looking at is available to the public, they should be able to handle it on their own. If my friends aren't bothered by it, they might reason, then why should I be? In light of this, they learn to ignore inner signs of distress, conflict, or shame, thereby losing touch with their internal experience. And often, things move so fast that teens are on to the next thing before they've truly processed the last. Their brains are kept in a state of chronic, invisible-to-the-eye irritability. It is like consuming foods that upset our digestion – for instance, with an unknown gluten allergy, we may not make the connection between gluten and stomach cramps at first, but we find ourselves perpetually uncomfortable and ill at ease.

Paradoxically, although screen time is a solitary pursuit, it simultaneously allows an adolescent to virtually connect with a host of friends and acquaintances. Many youth keep themselves forever yoked together in cyberspace. Through social media, teens can experience a sense of connection to their virtual world at any time of day or night. This cannot help but change something fundamental about the nature of the inner life of the child and adolescent. Constant access, through social media, to our friends and families, to news and information, to what's hot and trending, has taken up residence in the space that used to be occupied by an aspect of internal life that can best be described as yearning.

Is it possible that yearning is an experience that will soon be extinct?

Looking back, I vividly remember, when I was a teenager, pining for my friends during the endless weeks of summer vacation. The accordion of time stretched out unbearably long. I would write detailed letters, place them in the mailbox and put up the red flag before I got on the camp bus in the morning, and rush to see who had written me back when I hopped off the bus at the end of the day. I just wanted an end to the social exile that was my summer. I remember my thirteenth birthday, when nestled in the back of the mailbox was a small, bulging envelope. Inside it, I found five silver star studs. The boy I loved at the time had taken them off his jean jacket, the one I always borrowed, and sent them to me with a note that read, "Five stars for my star. Happy birthday." That was enough to spark pleasure that thrilled me and left me longing for the end of summer, aching to hasten the excruciating span of time.

Yearning creates a fertile space for the inner life and the imagination to grow. In longing, we necessarily turn inward, summoning an internal image of the other for comfort. Longing is linked to the development of the capacity to mentalize, that is, to hold in mind a living image of another significant person. By invoking our internal representations of the loving presence of the other, we learn to self-soothe, to quiet our distress, and to temper loneliness. Yet, when the yearned-for other is always virtually available – even when absent in a literal sense – then the space for mentalizing, for imagining, for summoning to mind one's internal objects, starts to collapse. In her 2011 book *Alone Together*, Sherry Turkle offers an in-depth exploration of the loneliness of teens in the digital age. As Sonia Sukenick (2012) writes in her review of the book:

> Turkle describes how being constantly "tethered" – to one's device, to social media, to incoming data – has the effect of rendering teens more alone, not less so. She informs us that, on line, the self is flattened out into personae. Privacy is gone. . . . Turkle asserts that the continuous connectivity afforded to us by our machines does not bring us to a place of communion with each other, but rather further isolates and distances us. As we constantly relate to our "machines of connectivity", we actually create a digital cocoon around us. . . . Being virtually connected with one another has the consequence of causing us to be less than fully present, and, at times, needlessly aggressive (as in the case of adolescent cyber bullying), and most importantly, somewhat dissociated in our lives.

Being tethered online can give rise to a self that is fragmented, heightening feelings of aloneness. For many teens, face-to-face contact increasingly gives way to device-driven connections. Turkle describes how a teen's sense of self can split into components of self-states – the self a teen may want to show the world, the self that is at the receiving end of social media posts, where everyone else's life looks like the idealized version of what that teen may yearn for, the self that is exposed and the private self that is kept so hidden from view that it begins to feel illusory. Attention is divided, and teens are less present at any given moment. As Turkle explains, when teens live their lives online, they can begin to feel lonelier and more isolated even as they distribute themselves more widely among their virtual friends, whether on Facebook, Instagram, or through an online game or chat room. To make matters more complex, parents' efforts to intervene are often frustratingly thwarted, intensifying the generational digital divide, one aspect of the larger pattern of disconnection.

This, then, is the vicious cycle of the digital age: in spite of being continuously plugged in via social media to one's peers, teens suffer from heightened feelings of isolation. And loneliness then drives the desire for even more online contact. It's as if there is no being alone for today's young people, who can always count on a cyberspace ally to immediately respond. For instance, when an insecure teen seeking validation posts a photo, she counts the number of "likes," virtually satisfying her needs for affirmation with a liberal sprinkling of thumbs-ups. Checking her social media accounts, she closes the emotional distance by creating a feeling of being together even when apart. The virtual presence of all her friends living their lives online can comfort her. Alternately, seeing online posts of friends who look as though they're having the time of their lives without her gives rise to "FOMO" – fear of missing out on the fun. Either way, it's like carrying your internal life on an external hard drive – you're never far away from it, yet it doesn't reside fully in your mind or imagination.

Even when teens are together, their phones are never far from view. They may share photos, look at each other's Twitter feeds or Instagram accounts, or prepare to post their best photos with the input of their friends. While unaware of how divided their own attention might be, teens nonetheless are unsettled when their friends spend more time looking at their phones than at the person they are with, or pay little attention to the conversation. This leaves them feeling disconnected and unheard. Sometimes they themselves tire of the constant intrusion of their phones. For example, out to dinner, they may play "Phone Pile," putting their phones in the middle of the table at a restaurant. The first to reach for the phone pays the bill. In this game is the implicit recognition that it is hard to be the only one to unplug.

Parenting in the presence of the "virtual third"

If the developmental trajectory of today's teens is digitally mediated, how does this impact the parent-child relationship? In small ways and large ones, digital technology also double-helixes its way into the already complex patterns of relating between parent and child. A simple instance is when a parent receives a Facebook notification that her child has posted a new photo. Curiosity gets the better of her and she clicks on it. *Oh, nice photo*, one part of her mind thinks, while another part thinks, *"What? At 2:00 am? I thought you were asleep. . . ."* Already boundaries have shifted. Information has come through a third party, as it were, not directly from the child. Now the parent has to contend with the information: What has she seen about her child online? What does she know, why does she know it, how did she learn it, what should she do about it? It's not unlike seeing a patient with an overeager relative, interested in filling the therapist in on the latest exploits, trials, and travails of the patient. Having information supplied by an external source can likewise sit uncomfortably with parents – what are they supposed to do with it? They may mention to their child that they saw the Facebook post, so that it's out in the open and can be discussed. Nonetheless, the child didn't choose to share it directly with the parent, and that changes how parents understand what they saw. It has entered the arena of the parent-child relationship through a back door and now must be dealt with.

Navigating the ambiguity and uncertainty of the digital world with a child can put a strange twist in the parent-child relationship. Parents, having had no prior childhood digital experience of their own to draw on, struggle with how best to handle their child's use of technology. Some parents check their children's phones often, closely monitoring their child's online activity and setting strict limits, others never check at all, and some just muddle through the quandary of what to do. They experience themselves as helpless to intervene in the face of what they perceive as a powerful dependence on digital access. They feel an uncomfortable pull to limit their child's exposure, often describing their child as "addicted to their phone" or "perpetually plugged in." Indeed, there is a growing body of literature and research available about the effects of technology on teens and their families. Many have described how technology interacts with the brain much the way drugs and alcohol do, by stimulating the dopamine receptors of the brain. Technology seems to have a built-in addictive component that really does affect the adolescent's ability to disengage.

In this way, digital technology acts as a "virtual third" in the relationship between parent and child, affecting the relationship in a myriad of ways. For many parents of teens, it is as if they can never be fully alone with their child – there is the constant ghostly presence of their child's online "friends," literally numbering in the hundreds or thousands, along with friends of their friends and *their* friends, and so on.

To be fair, adults have their own online lives, which can preoccupy them and lead to an exquisite dance of missed connections. Once, I was sitting in a doctor's office, and across from me sat a mother and daughter, both on their phones. I noticed first one, then the other, glance away from the phone and turn toward their companion, but they never seemed to look up at the same time. Each time one looked up, the other had turned her gaze away, so the pair never made eye contact. It was a striking sequence of reverse hide-and-seek, an excruciating and never-finished game in which neither could experience the reassuring feeling of being found – nor even recognize the desire to be found.

The unending intrusion of cell phones is the same with infants and toddlers. On a recent visit to an urban hospital, I looked around the waiting room and noticed every young child was holding an electronic device – there were no books to be found. Beside me, a mother was holding her two-year-old boy on her lap and had propped a bottle against her shoulder. Above her breast, she had placed her cell phone with the screen facing out, toward the boy. While the child gulped milk from the bottle, he was also drinking in the screen, while the mother gazed absently into the distance.

Such moments underscore Sherry Turkle's notion of loneliness in the digital age. The intrusion of the "virtual third" casts an invisible, divisive shadow that disrupts the real-life opportunities for moments of intimate, genuine face-to-face contact. In the first years of a child's life, there are literally hundreds of thousands of parent-child interactions that are woven into the child's development and that lay down a template for the parent-child relationship as it unfolds over time. It is impossible not to wonder what effect it has when a mother's gaze is turned away, checking her email or texting a friend, or when the child's attention is absorbed by the glow of the screen instead of "the gleam in the mother's eye" (Kohut, 1966, p. 252). Does that template become one of mixed attention, of missed connectivity – a Swiss-cheese, disjointed pattern of mutual engagement and disconnection? And how might that affect the child's experience of herself and others over time, into adolescence and young adulthood?

At this pivotal developmental transition, it is typical for adolescents and young adults to return psychically to an earlier phase of separation and individuation, reworking primary themes of self and other, of holding on and letting go. Just like the toddler taking her unsteady first steps, the young adult wobbles more or less into independence, the tether to the parent now as fine yet sturdy as an invisible nylon thread. What becomes of the child whose internal interpersonal world is marked by interruptions in connectedness, where the "virtual third" has created a landscape speckled with pixilated interactions?

The perpetual presence of the "virtual third" has an impact on the parent as well, who, as the child gets older, feels increasing competition for the child's attention, engagement, and responsiveness. Indeed, it is hard to vie with the "dopamine drip" that social media and digital data provide, especially to the young, dopamine-hungry brains of adolescents. Parents may struggle with feeling abandoned or even rendered obsolete in their teen's social world.

Before the age of digital media, it was implicitly understood that a certain level of secrecy was the code of adolescence. In Robert Paul Smith's classic 1957 volume, *Where Did You Go? Out. What Did You Do? Nothing.*, he writes: "It was our theory that the grown-up was the natural enemy of the child, and if any father had come around being a pal to us we would have figured he was either a little dotty or a spy. What we learned we learned from another kid" (p. 3). He writes with humor and great affection about the lost art of neighborhood play, where what matters most is not who is the marble champion of the world, an example of adults co-opting children's play, but who is the marble champion of the block you live on, and how do you get to be as good as him, so you can beat him and claim his winning marble for your own. Decades ago, adults were beginning to mourn the simple, unstructured pleasures of being a child before adult "spies" took over and started to infiltrate children's play with structure, competition, and a trophy for all. Children's freedom to play, to let their imaginations roam, and to establish their own secret lives away from their families, was curtailed by an emphasis on achievement, structured competition, and close parental supervision.

Today, the secret lives of children are online and ever-present. The trend of helicopter parenting has met its match in digital technology: social media effectively creates a firewall between parents and children. Parents who have grown accustomed to the psychological bonds that tie their children to them now experience their teens, in their transition to adulthood, virtually tethered to their peers instead. As Smith's decades-old book reminds us, it is appropriate and healthy for parents to be extruded from the social lives of their teens. However, when the virtual tether to online life tugs constantly at their attention and demands to be reckoned with, it changes the nature of the very process of separation. The parent-child relationship exists in a sort of shimmery landscape. Parents can peek in to their child's online world; sometimes they may indeed be invited in, but other times, they find themselves on the outside, waiting for permission to engage. The contradiction of the virtual third is that it produces children who, in some ways, have prematurely sought to separate from their parents while on the other hand they are maturationally ill equipped to individuate from their peers. Precocious or puerile? It's hard to say.

Social media through a developmental lens

Technology has undoubtedly massively altered the psyche of the digital generation. However, not everything that is developmentally important is necessarily lost. Digital technology, as mentioned earlier, has also brought about significant positive advances. How profoundly is normative adolescent development affected by modern life? Just as in 1957, when Smith lamented the loss of childhood innocence and freedom, today's parents are shocked at the changes they observe in their own teenagers. Yet there is something recognizable and enduring about the behavior of today's adolescents, even with their brains steeped in technology. Perhaps we parents are also struggling more than we know with our own difficulties in adjusting to the changing times.

As a parent, I have been grappling with these same questions since my own two daughters entered the digital arena.

As my daughters matured, I learned to listen to my intuition most of the time. I felt comfortable knowing when they were ready to cross the street by themselves, or go downtown with a friend, or stay out past 10 in the evening. They both started to drive as soon as they were old enough to get their permits, and I could see they were conscientious and careful. But somehow, my intuition seemed to fail me when it came to technology. There was no roadmap of experience to guide me in parenting my way through the digital world. As soon as I read one article or heard a lecture, I'd make up my mind to follow that guideline, but when I tried it out, it slipped though my fingers like silvery fish.

I understood the importance, especially for my younger daughter, of maintaining her close relationships to her peers. She has a knack for getting along with everyone. Her sympathetic ear, her sense of humor, and her spirit of adventure draw people to her, and she thrives on social interactions. As a younger child, she was always the one to run away and hide under the bed with her friend when a play date was over and I showed up at the door to pick her up. Every afternoon she'd spend with a friend would stretch out into the evening, and likely as not turn into an overnight at one or the other's house. It was natural that she would be drawn to social media. She seemed to maintain a reasonably moderated online presence. She didn't bring her phone to the dinner table or engage in risky online behaviors.

But gradually, I became aware of a subtle, almost ineffable shift in how it felt to be together. She and I always had a particularly warm and easygoing bond. We liked the same things, and we laughed at the same jokes. But unlike me, she grew up in a time when social media took off. By the end of middle school, she was absorbed by it. I remember when she asked me if she could open an Instagram account. "It's like Facebook, but with only photos," she told me. "It's just a way to see stuff my friends are doing." "Hmmm," I said innocently, "sounds harmless enough."

When Snapchat launched, we had another discussion about it. She used it liberally. Little by little, I noticed that her cell-phone habits were starting to change. As she entered high school, her real-life circle of friends grew at a healthy rate – but her online community ballooned. It was as though she was living life on two planes, and sometimes I felt that her online life was taking over.

I saw that my daughter was enlivened and energized by her active social life, and I was glad she seemed well adjusted. But I noticed how rarely she spent time reading a book by herself or relaxing at home or hanging out in the kitchen while we made dinner. Pretty soon, the phrase "Put away your phone" became a constant refrain. It began to feel like she was only half-present. We'd talk about it often, but to little avail. She seemed neither able nor willing to curb her appetite for her digital diet. She was hooked.

The phone became a constant companion in our lives. Driving carpool home from swimming or soccer practice, the once-lively chatter of the girls I'd known for years started to die down. Glancing in the rear-view mirror, I saw four or five bright-eyed girls, gaze glued to their phones. Sometimes they'd even be texting one another in the car while I drove in silence. I felt powerless to break the digital spell. It was as though communication had acquired another dimension, and I felt flattened. I was like a New York City cabdriver, separated from my passengers by bulletproof plexiglass. At times, I'd imagine what it would be like to be part of such a gaggle of girls, with their perpetual yet invisible system of communication. I wondered what they were seeing on their phones as they laughed, tossed their hair, or nudged one another and showed each other their screens. Who was talking to whom, what plans were being made, what gossip shared? It was dizzying.

One day, driving home from a soccer game in the heat with four silent, phone-bound girls, I felt particularly irritated, left out, and frustrated. The game had been won, the girls had played well, and I wanted to celebrate their win, to turn up the radio and sing out loud together, to talk about their play. But every foray was met with a grunt, and when I turned up the radio, my daughter growled, "That's too loud, can you turn it down?" I'd thought it was a pretty good song, but I turned it down, miffed. I tried to peek over her shoulder as I drove but, as unsafe as it is to drive while texting, it's even less safe to look at someone else's phone. The car was silent, except for an occasional "Oh, that's funny" or "did you see this?" while they showed one another their phones. I wondered, *What are they all looking at?*

Then a memory surfaced. I was a freshman in high school. Sitting on my friend's bed, along with six or seven other girls, we were all laughing and talking. I felt happy, at ease, one of the gang. Most of these girls had been in school together since kindergarten, and had a close-knit, easygoing friendship. Having moved to the school only recently, I was still a relative newcomer. I yearned to be part of the group, and, gradually, I gained acceptance. I knew a few of these girls better than others – the other West Siders who would take the public bus to school with me in the morning, the girl who had a house near mine up in the country, the girl I sat next to in biology who shared my lab dissections and notes. Because I had moved schools and skipped grades, it hadn't been easy to settle into a steady friendship group. I wanted in. Sitting in my friend's room, surrounded by happy chatter, I thought I had found it.

Then, out of the corner of my eye, I saw two of the girls whispering to each other. In that self-conscious way of the new girl, I feared that they were talking about me. Another girl joined the whisper, then spoke out loud, with a sidelong glance, "So are we all going to Evan's party?" Awkward silence. The phrase "are we all" seemed to hover in the air for an instant, while I wondered if *I* was one of *us*. Party? It was news to me. Were they inviting me to join them? Was I supposed to play along, or wait till someone included me? I felt the color rise in my face. The girl sitting at my side glanced at me, then away, murmuring "Maybe you didn't get the invitation. . . ." A silent, invisible door shut, and I feared I was on the wrong side of it.

I have no recollection of what happened next. Maybe I did go to Evan's party, in the end. But what stayed with me was the feeling of teetering on the edge, neither in nor out, with no clear idea of which direction I needed to tilt in order to assure my acceptance. I remember most vividly the sense of not being able to read the signals clearly. This group of girls, friends for so long, had established their own unspoken language, like a code. I know now that they were not necessarily trying to keep newcomers away. But for me, not having been initiated from the start, there was so much I had to understand and absorb before I would belong. And the painful part of that process had to do with the feeling that everyone else was in on a secret I didn't know. All I had was the tingling of my spider senses, telling me something was happening out of sight and I, for the moment, was on the outside of the magic circle.

I recognized, then, what I was struggling with in relation to my daughter. Maybe it wasn't that a digital leviathan had opened its great jaws and gobbled her up. Rather, the chronic presence of the cell phone meant that I was perpetually bearing witness to the typical social absorption of adolescence. When I was growing up, my social sphere existed outside of the house and away from my parents' scrutiny. Now, digital media shattered that boundary and brought it right into our home. I could see with my own eyes my daughter's comfortable engagement with her friends, and her preference to live in that world – a preference that was developmentally appropriate. Yet the immediacy and omnipresence of that world overwhelmed me, and I feared that I had lost her attention. I felt acutely left out. I wanted "in," just as I had with my circle of friends so many years ago, and I was having trouble letting go.

I can say with some measure of certainty that my own mother never felt that way. What was different, I suspect, was that for me, social life was something that happened when I was "out" doing "nothing." My parents didn't exist in my social world, and when I got home at the end of the day I'd have to wait till the next day to re-immerse myself with my friends. I was prohibited from calling them on the phone, because, as my father reminded me daily, the telephone was for "communication, not for conversation." In contrast, because of ceaseless online and cell-phone activity, my daughter never had to suspend that social tether, and I, unlike my mother, got to see it play out, leaving me on the outside of her magic circle of friendship. Of course I was on the outside – that's where I belonged. But watching her daily absorbed with the virtual third had re-evoked, in me, an earlier feeling of extrusion.

As my daughter has continued through high school, many of these concerns have eased. My misgivings have lessened, and alongside of that, my intuition has kicked back in. While I still worry about all the "lost" time my daughter spends on social media, I am no longer fearful. Maybe it's that I've gotten used to the omnipresence of the phone, both hers and mine; maybe it's that I've understood more deeply what is at stake for her. I recognize that easing separation is a fundamental aspect of parenthood. As an adolescent readying herself to leave home, she needs me to stay solidly in place so that she can safely move away, toward establishing her own world and defining its boundaries. This core developmental milestone remains as significant in the digital age as it was when a youthful Robert Paul Smith played marbles and other street games. I began to understand that my daughter's use of her phone has become another avenue for separation and individuation. And while some part of me may wish to return to an earlier time myself, I needed to let go. This was her time.

Conclusion

Clearly, digital technology has markedly changed the way we all interact in the world. We see teens who are never alone, yet who struggle with profound loneliness accentuated by a digitally driven world. I have no doubt that it has changed adolescent brains, shortened their attention span, deeply reduced the time they spend on other activities such as reading and playing outdoors, altered the nature of their relationships, created greater stress, and affected, for many, their moods and their ability to regulate them. The Internet can deliver misinformation, too much information, or at times frightening or risky information. But at the same time, it has opened minds; sown widespread awareness of a greater world beyond the familiar; inspired curiosity, generosity, and ingenuity. On the one hand, as Tevye was fond of saying, we have tradition and everything that comes with it; on the other, the beckoning of the future that the young adult is about to inhabit, and that the parent must learn to embrace.

Ultimately, we parents need to do our best to stay alongside of our teens, try to see the world through their eyes, and teach them to consume a healthy digital diet. Similarly, as psychoanalysts, we need to acknowledge that our theories, too, need to bend with the demands of the changing times. Our recognition, both as parents and as practitioners, of the changes we see in our consulting rooms and in our living rooms require that we stretch toward a new understanding of today's adolescents and young adults, one that incorporates both analytic tradition and contemporary theoretical advances. We must learn to reckon with the presence of technology in our consulting rooms, as well. Do we permit (or even invite) our adolescent patients to text us, and recognize that they feel trusting enough to want to communicate with us in their language? Can we balance our own online presence with our patients' needs for our relative anonymity and analytic neutrality – which must extend to our lives online? How do we understand the teen who, in session, wants to share with us something they saw on YouTube, or the parent who keeps her phone on during her session "just in case my kid needs me"?

How we view the inner life of today's adolescents and young adults must incorporate recognition of a seismic shift in the youth's experience of both solitude and attachment. In turn, this must also inform how we guide parents in building their resilience and flexibility in helping their young adult child to engage fully with the world, to launch across the digital divide and into adulthood with passion, confidence and optimism.

* * *

And the boy I loved? The one who sent me the stars? He broke up with me later that summer. It turns out he met another girl. I remember the typewritten letter he sent me:

Dear Anne,
I still like you but I'm spending more time with Roxanne . . .
Different technology. Same old story? Maybe the jury's still out.

References

Kohut, H. (1966). Forms and transformations of narcissism. *Journal of the American Psychoanalytic Association, 14*, 243–272.

Smith, R. P. (1957). *Where did you go? Out what did you do? Nothing.* New York: W. W. Norton.

Sukenick, S. (2012). Turkle, Sherry. Alone together: Why we expect more from technology and less from each other. *Journal of Analytical Psychology, 57*(1), 128–129.

Turkle, S. (2011). *Alone together: Why we expect more from technology and less from each other.* New York: Basic Books.

2

Growing up in a world of cell phone technology

Christie M. Platt

I was recently empathizing (I thought) with a successful thirty-something professional young man about his difficulty finding a mate in the great sea of online dating sites. He bemoaned the time and energy it takes to strike up an online conversation enticing enough to decide to meet in person. When and if this "date" takes place, both people know it is actually a "job interview" to determine whether the other person might be "relationship material." I murmured something about people meeting one another in a more natural, organic sort of way when I was young, musing that it had seemed much easier then. He did not feel comforted but rather affronted. "Now that we've determined that your childhood was so much better than mine, can we get on with talking about my life?" I was taken aback and forced to become aware of the assumptions I had been making about how much better things were when I was growing up. To use Bollas's (1987) wonderful phrase, "What exactly is my 'unthought known' about the world today?" Will we find ways to remember the open spaces that existed before cell phones? Just as we are trying to protect the untouched wild spaces of our national parks, I wonder if we need to preserve some of the untouched wild spaces of our internal worlds.

Today, I can only say with certainty that instant forms of communication have changed the ways we relate to one another and that they will continue to do so. This paper is an attempt to look at some of technology's reverberations as they affect relationships between parents and their children, particularly during adolescence and young adulthood. I am interested in how the experience of uninterrupted communication today affects the process of separation and individuation during this important phase. I will focus on the use of the smartphone, e.g., primarily texting and calling, but social media such as Facebook and Instagram are also relevant.

The notion of separation and individuation is associated with Margaret Mahler (1974), who first identified the way that toddlers practice going forth into the world: touching, tasting, and exploring. In a recent psychotherapy session, a young mother glowed as she described her child's growing ability to communicate. She marveled at his perseverance. When he acquires a new word he repeats it over and over again until it sounds correct to him and he feels he has mastered it. At 16 months the word he has been practicing is "More!" When I asked her how much he comprehends of her words, she told me that he seems to understand quite a lot, including her admonition, "Don't go where I can't see you." Then he looks at her, smiles mischievously, and (at least at this point) goes no further. In a few months, he will push up against these limits and both she and he will worry when the distance between them becomes too great. He will return to her, anxious until he is safely within her orbit. She will have to learn to tolerate his ever-expanding universe. In ten or twelve years' time, when he reaches puberty, they will repeat this dance on a whole new level. If all goes well, her son will be exploring the full range of his capacities, finding his place in the pecking order of his peer group, and evaluating his parents' world to determine what he will incorporate and what he will discard.

The example above suggests that there is a mutually satisfying sense of attachment between mother and child, but this feeling of confidence began much earlier. Winnicott's seminal article entitled *The Capacity to Be Alone* (Winnicott, 1958) suggests that babies learn a great deal about the world they will inhabit from their earliest experiences with the mother. If their caretaker is responsive when needed but not overly intrusive, the baby will develop a felt sense that it can survive in a universe in which its needs will be adequately met. I would add that if the mother feels successful in her efforts to nurture her child, she will also develop confidence in a secure bond between the two. This early attunement augurs well for their future connection.

Mary Ainsworth's 1970 study attempted to categorize the different attachment styles of mothers and their babies (Ainsworth et al., 1970). In this study, the baby is confronted by the introduction of a stranger, the loss of the mother, and the return of the mother. She found that babies and children who had a secure attachment to their mothers were sad when they left, subdued when left with a stranger, and happy when their mothers returned. Not surprisingly, she found that mothers who were securely attached to their babies were also sensitive to their needs. This would seem to further illustrate Winnicott's description of the mother-infant couple who are comfortable in one another's presence, neither under- nor over-involved with one another – as Goldilocks might say, "Just right." Such ease also suggests that object permanence has been achieved, usually at about eight or nine months of age. When a mother leaves the room, the child has come to realize that she will return; she has not vanished or disappeared. She still exists.

Peter Blos (1967) theorized that we might view adolescence as the second phase of separation and individuation. During adolescence, one has the opportunity to develop a more nuanced and realistic internal representation of oneself and one's parents. As we know, this is often a turbulent and destabilizing process, as idealization gives way to disappointment and finally to reality. In addition, one's own narcissistic preoccupations are similarly challenged as one tries to establish a place among one's peers. It is during this time that an adolescent must begin to metaphorically leave home and look outward to the world. Outbursts and oppositional behavior are the hallmark of this hormonally fuelled phase of development. But, how do instant and frequent communications with one's parents impact this process? The tether of technology may impede separation and maturation, when parents swoop in and intervene to rescue a child rather than leaving room for the child to work through feelings of alienation or disappointment on their own. In this way, though undoubtedly reassuring at times, parents may also interrupt important, often unconscious, efforts by the child to deal independently with the his or her own feelings.

In *Portrait of the Artist As a Young Man*, Joyce depicts the explosive, yet completely natural, feelings that Stephen Dedalus encounters within himself as he discovers and satisfies his sexual urges through masturbation and an encounter with a prostitute. He must reconcile these actions with his ensuing guilt and his efforts to reconcile his desires with the Catholic morality of his upbringing. The resolution of these conflicts allows him to mature and accept responsibility for his commitment to live his life as fully as possible, accountable finally to himself. His struggle, depicted in an almost blow-by-blow account of his internal dialogue over the course of an evening at a family event, is emblematic of every adolescent's need to find his or her own direction. Had Stephen Dedalus been encouraged or remonstrated with by the constant intrusion of his parents' well-meaning efforts to ease his turbulent emotions, he would have been stymied, if not prevented, from coming to his own hard-fought certainties about who he was and how he wanted to live his life. What if he had been receiving text messages from his parents during the dinner asking him to look more cheerful?

Until recently, parents and children were unable to communicate with one another throughout the day. Schools might have two or three telephone lines in a central office that could be used by administrators in the case of an emergency. When a child went to kindergarten and elementary school, it was assumed that the child's day would take place independently, away from the parents' gaze. For the length of the school day, children lived in a separate world of schoolmates and teachers. School was a private world, a discrete kingdom, whose nature could be disclosed or concealed almost entirely at the child's discretion. Parents did not intrude on this world, leaving the children to navigate their school world with relative independence. This also provided parents with an important respite from the responsibilities of parenthood while their children were under the jurisdiction of educators.

When my own children were born I mistakenly imagined that they would experience life from a vantage point similar to mine. I didn't anticipate that my childhood landscape would no longer exist. The feeling of uncluttered space I once took for granted is no more. Much of my out-of-school time was unprogrammed so I was left to my own devices. When I came home from school in the afternoons, I was told to "go play outside and come back at dinnertime." Accordingly, I would change into jeans and visit neighbors or take long walks in the country by myself. I was free to disappear for hours. By contrast, my children had two working parents and lived in an urban setting, so after-school activities had to be planned. In some ways their lives have been more constricted than mine, but they have also had stunning access to the world that lies beyond theirs, particularly through the Internet. By the time children have become teenagers today, they have already been blasted with dazzling images of what to wear, what to look like, and what to want. These messages have arrived via advertisements as well as sophisticated and often cynical kids' television programs larded with product placement. Just to put things in modern-day context, the American Psychological Association estimates that advertisers spend more than $12 billion per year to reach the youth market and that children view more than 40,000 commercials each year (Wilcox et al., 2004).

Today, lack of communication from a homeroom teacher is more likely to provoke a sense of unease for parents, who may wonder, *What is going on at school?* Parental involvement is idealized, so smartphones are always at hand, ready to receive any missive from school that might arrive. Mothers, and increasingly fathers, sit in business meetings, lunches, and therapy sessions with their phones perched next to them, always vigilant and always tethered. If a child has forgotten her homework or come down with a cold, parents must be on call to respond, this in a time when both parents are likely to be employed. If an email, text message, or phone call is missed, a parent may feel terribly guilty and feel that they have been neglectful. Parents who have children later in life may approach parenting their children with a degree of professionalism that inherently carries with it a high degree of anxiety. Such is the breeding ground of the helicopter parent.

Erik Erikson (1950) said that adolescence was a critical period for the development of a core sense of identity: Who am I in relation to my parents and to my peers? What do I like? Who do I like? How am I perceived by others? Although teenagers today have grown up in a world saturated with social media, the instant feedback may prove daunting. Social media confronts teens with regular postings about what friends (and not-friends) are doing, where they are going, who is included and who is left behind. One person posts an Instagram picture and within 15 minutes has 158 "likes" while another posts and anxiously waits for similar approval ratings. At a time when emotions can rise and fall in a matter of seconds, these comparisons can be devastating. Adolescents are trying to create a brand at the same time that they are trying to figure out what their brand actually is.

Living in an age of overwhelming Internet information makes for a lot of scrutiny of both parents and children by the ever-present media. Parents read parenting books and blog posts, and talk with their friends about the right way to raise their children. As a result, they are focusing on their children in a way that may deprive children of a certain degree of privacy. Privacy is feared because there are so many frightening stories about children and secret lives, particularly as they take place on the Internet. Discussions abound as to when children should have access to Facebook accounts. At what age should children be given a cell phone? At what age should they be able to have a smart phone? What restrictions should they have for the Internet? Parents must make so many more decisions on a daily basis at a time when there is a sense that the forbidden and the dangerous surround us all. Those parents who are perceived as being too lax are castigated for giving too much freedom. Some have even been arrested for being what are now called "free-range parents." Obviously, this has a significant impact on the separation-individuation process.

The unintended consequence of all this attention is that it may deprive children of the richness of having private worlds. Secrets are an essential component of a child's private life in which conflicts, worries, and excitement occur, all of which the child grapples with on her own. These are opportunities for cognitive and moral development that are part of the maturation process (Jacobs, private communication). When I set out to write this paper, I firmly believed that there was more to mourn about what has disappeared with the introduction of so much technology than there was to celebrate. In part, I have viewed these technological advances with a skeptical eye precisely because they seem to render my own childhood quaintly archaic. The slower-paced world I knew has given way to the age of instant information. The rate at which we receive information has increased exponentially with every passing year until it is like drinking from the proverbial fire hose. The long stretches of emptiness and thick swaths of boredom seem more remote and therefore far more idyllic to me now than they seemed at the time.

Perhaps it is the availability of things to do with one's various devices that most differentiates my childhood from my children's. With the advent of Game Boys, computers, and smartphones, children no longer grow up "with nothing to do." Harris says in his book *The End of Absence*, "I fear we are the last of the day-dreamers. I fear our children will lose lack, lose absence, and never comprehend its quiet, immeasurable value" (Harris, 2014). Like Harris, I have unconsciously mourned the loss of all that quiet, all that emptiness, and have idealized it as a bright and shining time.

Of course, it was never completely idyllic. When I was lonely or at odds with my family or just wanted to share something, I daydreamed about having my own personal telephone that I could carry with me at all times (but I never imagined that something as small as a smartphone could do all that *and* carry my record collection in it as well.) With such a marvelous invention, I would have called my best friend whenever I liked. I would have thought that loneliness could be fully banished from my life. I could not have imagined that there would be a time when the airwaves would be filled with messages, news stories, and photographs that would make me feel like it was actually impossible to feel caught up with one's friends, much less cultural trends, politics, and world events. How different is it for me than it has ever been for anyone who reminisces nostalgically about one's youth?

We live in a culture that almost fetishizes youthfulness. We have parents who are trying to stay young, kids who are trying to grow up, and a merging of generations. In the Sixties, everyone talked about "the generation gap." This described the gulf between teenagers and their parents. The music that made parents cringe back then is now listened to by parents and children alike, e.g., Neil Young and Bob Dylan (who just won the Nobel prize for literature). One of Dylan's first and most famous songs was aptly entitled "The Times They Are A-Changin'."

Today, adults tend to expose children to complex social situations at far earlier ages. One of the reasons for this is television. Children's shows are far more sophisticated than when I was growing up and much of the time grown-ups are not depicted in particularly respectful ways, e.g., *South Park* or *The Simpsons*. The current election cycle (2016) has produced so much sex, mudslinging, and name-calling that the quest for the Oval Office looked more like a playground rife with bullies than a platform for discussion among potential world leaders. As I sat in a museum café this afternoon writing, I was surprised to hear a lengthy discussion among a group of sixth graders about what their teachers were like this year. Suddenly, they switched topics and were speculating on the income differential between drug dealers who sold marijuana vs. those who sold cocaine. A conversation that had sounded so age-appropriate abruptly swung to what seemed preternaturally precocious for suburban middle-schoolers. Where had they gathered enough information about the ins and outs of dealing to be making such cool appraisals of the relative merits of selling one drug over another? How does a constant stream of such information distract them from a more immediate focus on their middle-school lives? With so much information, it is as if everyone, children and adults alike, have multiple smartphone applications running in the background, absorbing a certain amount of energy all the time.

By the time millennials graduate from college, they do not seem particularly intimidated by their elders. They no longer feel they have to "pay their dues" before they can find jobs with responsibility. After all, they are growing up in an age when technology has made billionaires out of their contemporaries. The commercialization of just about everything has instilled a sense of entitlement and expectation in the younger generation. At the same time, financial forecasting suggests that many millennials will not be able to enjoy the same standard of living as their parents did, with housing costs going up and so forth. So we find that more children are coming home to live with their parents after college. This "failure to launch" phenomenon is often ascribed solely to financial factors, but perhaps it may also be understood as failure to successfully complete the tasks of adolescence: separation/individuation and a sense of identity.

I would suggest that with every technological advance, we are producing children who process information far more quickly than their parents do. They are sophisticated without necessarily being mature. At a young age, they adopt the trappings of adulthood but often have no idea how to generate a satisfying lifestyle for themselves. With instant communication, adolescents and parents stay can stay in touch more regularly than they did when the means of communication were not as readily available. Should we expect that early attachment styles will prevail during adolescence? Perhaps the secure adolescent is the one who can go out in the world, make connections with peers and teachers, but requires only an occasional need for reassurance from a parent? And might this be expressed through the use of technology to stay in touch?

When my daughter was in high school, she participated in a life skills group that was supposed to encourage kids to talk about whatever was on their minds. Newly possessed of a mobile phone, she informed the class that her mother heard from patients that some grown-up children talk to their mothers every day, sometimes several times a day. She was surprised that anyone would want to do this, but her teacher quickly responded that she and her 30-year-old daughter spoke every morning as they each went to work. This story highlights the possibility of an almost instantaneous value judgment: is a relationship "better" if the two people involved speak more frequently, or is there some lack of independence exhibited by both mother and daughter if they do this? And *is* one better than the other?

When adolescents go off to college it is often the first extended physical separation they have had from their parents. While some have already visited friends or relatives, gone to camps, or experienced the absence of parents, it is clear when one packs off to college that the process of leaving home has begun in earnest. Suitcases are packed, dorm rooms furnished, and eventually parents take leave of their children, often with tears in their eyes once they are safely out of sight. The student goes off to explore a new world. Or perhaps the student sits in the dorm room, tentative about the exploration, subdued by the loss of the parents.

A student who seeks therapy early in their freshman year is clearly having some discomfort with the transition to college life. But this is not always the case. Sometimes a parent will anticipate that the child will be anxious or unsettled and make arrangements in advance for their departing child to receive immediate support. Such was the case with Rachel. Rachel was a tall young woman, although her full height was diminished because of her tendency to hunch her shoulders. She picked nervously at her cuticles and looked down at her lap through many of our sessions. Much of what she told me about herself was mediated by her mother's "presence" in the room, even though her mother was back in Chicago.

Before Rachel had even been accepted into college, her mother had been anxiously thinking about how to help her succeed. When Rachel was just beginning to talk to college counselors and friends about what college she might like to attend, her mother had already been thinking about it for months. She had accumulated dozens of brochures and created informal spreadsheets that indicated the strengths and weaknesses of each college as well as the application deadlines. Rachel's mother had clear ideas as to what Rachel needed in terms of the size of a school, its location, and what programs it would offer. With the best of intentions, she preempted Rachel's ability to formulate her own ideas. Rachel's mother was having trouble managing her own fears about Rachel's separation, and she was keenly aware that her anxiety could taint Rachel's ability to go off to college. In an effort to protect Rachel from her conflicted feelings about her daughter's leaving home, she pushed Rachel away. When Rachel called home, her mother would not pick up her phone and delayed responding to Rachel's text messages.

Rachel told me about her life at college and about her homesickness. Her mother's efforts to sever the umbilical cord between them resulted in feelings of confusion and anger for Rachel. Why wouldn't her mother answer the phone? Why wouldn't she let her come home for a long weekend during the fall semester? She longed to see her two brothers and found herself thinking about everything that she was missing at home, wondering what the family was doing and wishing she could pet the family dog. She carried her cell phone with her everywhere like a transitional object, hoping to hear from her family. This need to be reassured about her importance to her family generalized to a need to hear from her friends as well. No matter where she was, she was compelled to check her phone to see if she had heard from anyone at all until she received a signal that someone was thinking about her and that she hadn't been forgotten. It was as if she was uncertain whether her mother (and therefore everyone else in the world) would reliably keep her in mind, a sort of reverse mentalization. She hated this about herself but it had become an addiction for her. She made me think of the anxiously attached toddler who goes off to explore her environment and turns around, looking for her mother's smiling and encouraging face but finds instead that her mother has turned her back, or worse, that her mother has left. I wondered, then and now, whether she might have fared better had the cell phone not yet been invented. When letters and an expensive long distance call were the only means of communication, anxiety about whether one would hear from someone was restricted to a once a day mail drop or possibly a phone call on a public phone shared by many others.

When I went to college, most of my friends called home once every week or so, using the pay phones to make collect calls or feeding chunks of change into the telephone until they were gone. Although I went to school thousands of miles from home, my family expected that there would be a few weeks that would be difficult and that I would gradually make friends. The first weeks of college were considered to be a rite of passage that happened to everyone. The fact that it was assumed that we would all emerge alive and well shaped our expectations. I found less and less need to check in with my family. While I might have liked to tell my friends at other colleges more details about my college life in real time, it wouldn't have occurred to me to tell my family that I was walking across campus to my next class or that I had lost a school book and was worried about it. By the time my next phone call came around, I had most likely worked out any number of the everyday challenges presented in the course of a day. My new friends became increasingly important to me and I felt liberated by the opportunity to shape a new life for myself that was distinct from the life I had lived with my family. I do not hold up my own example as a shining representation of a secure attachment with my family. But I do think that when I went to college my family and I shared the belief that what I was doing was perfectly normal and like people who had gone to college before me, I would figure things out. There were countless times that I felt lonely and sad, homesick and insecure, but I believe that if I had shared all of that day by day by calling home, my adjustment to college would have taken far longer. Unlike Rachel, I had no expectation that my parents would call me on a daily basis and given the public nature of phone calls in the dormitory, I probably would have been embarrassed if I had to be summoned to the phone frequently to talk to my parents.

Another young woman, Elizabeth, described a different way of using her cell phone to stay connected to her family. She came from a tight-knit Italian family and had always felt close to them. However, just as she entered her freshman year of college, her parents sold the house where she had grown up and moved to another state. She was furious at them for what she perceived as a careless response to her need for the stability of a home base. She felt bereft without her childhood home. There she had spent hours in the kitchen doing her homework while her mother prepared dinner for the family. She found an ingenious way to recreate this experience by calling her mother on her cell phone. When her mother answered she asked her to place her phone on the kitchen table so that it was as if she were in the kitchen, with her mother, doing her homework as she had done during her high school years. The scene reminded me of Winnicott's concept of the capacity to be alone: Elizabeth was developing the capacity to be on her own in the virtual company of her mother. They weren't talking or interacting; they were just being together. Elizabeth gradually gave up these homework sessions. She had come to feel part of the new house where her parents lived and was able to relinquish the need for her original childhood home. These days, she is more inclined to call home to discuss her life and its ups and downs. Sometimes she will call home for bigger reasons, to discuss classes or vacation plans. At other times, she calls in a way I might describe as needy: "I can't decide what to wear! What should I buy for dinner?" The ease with which she can resort to the cell phone fosters a dependence that I think she could outgrow more easily if she couldn't call home so easily.

My work with both Rachel and Elizabeth led me to reflect on my own process of leaving home and heading out into the world. I felt far too influenced by the competing voices of my parents inside my head. My mother's voice was critical of my inability to conform to her expectations for me; she wanted me to be more refined in some way. I always felt her disappointment. On the other hand, my father clearly chafed at the confines of the world where I grew up. My own sense of what I wanted for myself, what I "wanted to be when I grew up," was confused. After my junior year of college, I still felt deeply uncertain as to what I wanted to do, or could do, when I graduated from college. I determined that taking a year off might allow me to figure some things out about myself. I had navigated the first two years of college with reasonable success so it seemed a natural transition to take a year off to travel with my college roommate. She desperately wanted to return to Africa where she had visited with her family. I had few preconceptions about Africa other than it was extremely far away from everything I knew. I imagined that being in such a completely different context would generate new ideas and aspirations. My parents were astonished when I told them but surprisingly unperturbed by either the destination or my wanting to go for an entire year. I think that I was (somewhat) unconsciously living out my father's desire to live a life that allowed for more uncertainty and seeking. My mother may have hoped that I would "get something out of my system" and that I would come back ready to take a more conventional approach to my life.

Years later, I found myself on my parents' end of the discussion, when my own son, now graduated from college, also left the country in search of adventure and self-knowledge. He chose Istanbul. Like my parents, I was not distressed by his decision to move so far away. As a history major, he had concentrated on the Ottoman Empire, and I applauded his wish to experience this part of the world. Unlike me, he was far more purposeful in his choice, but both he and I chose to travel in parts of the world where danger is always present in the background. We each stayed in touch with our families in very different ways, which I think of as reflective, at least in part, of how technology has changed the process of separation.

When I left home, I could a) write a letter, or b) make a costly overseas call at a payphone, or c) send a telegram. During the year I was gone, my correspondence took place through the mail and one overseas call on Christmas. I collected my thoughts and sent a letter home every two or three weeks, practicing my observational skills as I covered page after page of thin blue airmail sheets with my discoveries. Two weeks later, my parents would receive the letter with my best guess as to where they should next write to me, e.g., the American Express office in Johannesburg or Post Restante in Nairobi. They would send off their letters to me and with any luck, I would end up in the place I suggested they write and their letters would have arrived safely to the improbable Post Restante I had suggested in my last letter, by now at least three weeks old. I valued my entire year-long trip not least because I was traveling to places that no one else in my family had ever seen. They couldn't imagine where I was and I cherished this world I had entered all by myself. In my letters, I sought to share it, but for the most part it was mine alone. I now recognize how difficult it must have been for my parents to await my intermittent letters and non-replies to questions like: *How are you getting from place to place? Did you know that there have been uprisings in the country where you are*? And *where exactly are you?*

When my own son moved, I was to learn firsthand what my parents might have experienced during my own young adult travels. It must be noted that I never received one written letter from my son, who traveled by himself and whose cell phone was not programmed for world service. His father and I were at the mercy of his decisions as to when to call home, which he rarely did. Although he could have used the Internet to connect by way of video phone calls, his computer was stolen within two months of his arrival so a visual window to his life was shuttered. I had never traveled to Turkey and it was difficult for me to picture his life there: the place where he lived, the expat friends he met, and the students he was teaching. Because he lived in a poor Kurdish neighborhood, vague stories of tear gas and police filtered home. He brushed off our concerns and we could hear in his voice, on the rare occasions when he called, that his life was full. We felt happy and proud that he seemed able to adapt to such a foreign environment.

Six years later, the situation changed. Suicide bombings have occurred all over Turkey and within a 10-minute walk from his apartment. Explosions at the airport killed many people hours before he was due to return to the States for a summer visit. He and his girlfriend made it home, flying out by way of another airport.

On a sweltering summer afternoon, shortly after they had returned to Istanbul, I was just about to see my last patient when I saw that he had sent me a message, "I'm all right." Then a message from my husband, "Everything's all right." Why shouldn't it be? It took me a minute to register that something must have happened. A quick Internet search revealed that a coup attempt was taking place just at that moment. My last patient had recently visited Turkey that year and knew that I had been there as well. "God, so lucky we aren't there today!" he said. I agreed and tried to concentrate through that session, worry roiling through my mind.

When I got home, CNN was broadcasting the coup attempt live. My husband and I watched as tanks rolled down the streets near my son's apartment and over the bridge that crosses the Bosporus. We were able to call by means of Facebook messaging. My son and his girlfriend had been out for drinks at one of the many cafes overlooking the city. When they saw tanks, they assumed there had been some sort of terrorist attack. "Were the police telling you to leave the restaurant and go home?" I asked. "No, the *soldiers* were taking guns away from the police and arresting them." President Erdogan had fled and army jets were flying closely over the city, breaking the sound barrier to create the impression of bombs falling. There was the sense that Istanbul might look completely different by the next day. We were watching CNN in America and he and some friends were huddled into their kitchen together, watching CNN Turk, trying to figure out what was going on as well. As we watched in Washington, we would check in from time to time, also wanting to give our son the space to be where he was and, we hoped, not having to worry about us too much at the same time. Erdogan was able to return to Istanbul and send a FaceTime message to the people from his mobile phone, reassuring them that he was still in charge of the country. It wasn't a convincing medium to convey that he was in charge, but he was able to ask people to come out of their homes, take to the streets, confront the military, and demonstrate their loyalty to the current regime. Soon we were able to see small groups of people climbing on tanks and talking to soldiers. Images of soldiers with handcuffed police carrying assault rifles were also flashing. Suddenly, the images switched to CNN Turk headquarters. Soldiers were invading the studio and shutting everything down. Our lifeline to what was happening in Turkey was gone. Darkness. We called again and were grateful to find that the Internet had not been shut down. A Facebook post appeared from my son's girlfriend, like a William Carlos William poem:

> We have water, we have pasta and rice, we have Internet, we watch news, we hear the helicopters and jets, we make bad jokes, we get nervous, we read news, we talk to friends, we write to our families, we don't sleep. It's all fine – I eat gummy bears.

On that note, we were able to go to bed, restless and worried, waiting to tune into the news as soon as we could. When we awoke, order seemed to have been restored. The streets were calm. Thousands of people were being arrested and accused of disloyalty. Those being targeted were mainly Turks. I tried to reassure myself that my son would be safe.

Immediately afterward, my son and all his expat friends talked about if and when to leave Turkey. We imagined that it might be imminent, but as things settled into a state of apparent normalcy, it became easier for him to stay. His work is interesting as is his girlfriend's and they have a circle of friends from all over the world. Money stretches much further than it does in the States. And so he remains there.

A couple of months ago I was talking with a Vietnamese friend, whose earliest years were spent during in Vietnam while the war was still raging. I told her about my son in the gravest of tones, maybe even self-importantly. I was feeling touched by history, an ordinary person living in extraordinary times. She said plainly, "Don't worry about him. If you do, he will have to carry your burden as well. It won't help him." It was if I had been equating worry with love; the more I worried, the more I would be expressing my love. Like the fabled stranger on the road, she delivered a message that seemed to relieve me of my fears almost immediately. I have to be there if needed but in the meantime, I cannot worry – just as when he was a toddler and he needed a reassuring face as he went off to explore the world.

Would I be happier if I weren't exposed to the quotidian details of his life in Istanbul via news and his updates? I have to say, "Not at all." The possibility of being in touch as events unfold is deeply reassuring. When the Internet was threatened that night in July, I was terrified about what it would be like to rely on mail (unreliable in Turkey) or the telephone (expensive and also more unpredictable). I would venture to guess that it makes it easier for him to be in the situation he is in, knowing that he can get in touch with us in a variety of ways. If he had been living there for the past six years without benefit of technology, it would have been far more difficult for me to know him as his life has unfolded. Instead, he would have been immersed in a life about which I knew bits and pieces intermittently. I might have learned different things from letters; he might have given more thought to each letter, trying to provide a thoughtful portrait of his life – and I would have had those letters for posterity. Instead, I see his Facebook postings, and those of some of his friends who have become *my* Facebook friends as well. I can see their commentaries on current affairs as well as pictures that can range from a commonplace scene in the marketplace to a friend's wedding in Bulgaria. When one of his friends includes him in a post, I get insights into what outrages them and what makes them laugh.

When I was growing up, the expectations that were firmly laid out by my parents' generation resulted in a huge social movement to overthrow those conventions. It seems that my adolescence and that of many others required a greater revolt to establish a sense of independence than is needed today. We have come so far in our acceptance of the dignity of individual differences, in the eyes of the law and of each other. I desperately wanted to free myself from the expectations of my family and the community in which I grew up. As a parent, I find my own views about the world more closely aligned with my son's than mine were with my parents. He still did things that were ill-advised as a teenager, and I know that he had a life about which I knew absolutely nothing. But we did not tell him how to dress, how to think about things, or what sort of person he should marry. In order to understand myself and what I cared about, I needed to move beyond the gaze of my parents, to be in a world that they could not imagine and have experiences that belonged completely to me.

For many of today's youth, the Internet can serve the function of gaining access to the world beyond the familiar confines of home. With access to information comes power: this is a truism for a reason. Children grow up knowing that they can access information about anything in the world that is happening now, or that happened in the past, or that is trending in the future. For instance, the seemingly overnight increase in acceptance of transgender persons suddenly gained traction when people from the smallest towns in Alaska could connect with those persons living in the most liberal enclaves in America via the Internet. The feeling of isolation that has inhibited people from true self-expression has been radically reduced.

As adolescents discover their unique identities and separate from their families, it is possible to do this at a pace that is titrated for parents and children alike. Elizabeth, who still needed to feel connected to her family as she adjusted to her life in college, found a way to do that by having her mother leave her phone on the kitchen counter while she cooked dinner, thereby allowing Elizabeth to do her homework in the comfort of the kitchen, as it were. Gradually, these homework sessions were attenuated as she found the friends she needed at college who provided nourishing relationships in her new life. In the end, the way parents and children use the various technological means of communication has everything to do with the relationships they have formed prior to adolescence.

When I left on my long hitchhiking adventure to Africa, my father gave me a letter that I carried with me and still have to this day. I feel fortunate to have this letter, written on thick, vellum-like paper with his fountain pen. For me, he stated the most essential truth of what this period of leaving home is all about:

> *The realization finally has arrived that your life is going to progress independently of ours, which has to be, but it is a realization that is not easy. I look back on the last twenty-one years and cherish them. I look forward to the indefinite many, hoping that they will include much that we will be able to anticipate, and remember together.*

References

Ainsworth, M., & Bell, S. (1970). Attachment, exploration, and separation: Illustrated by the behavior of one-year-olds in a strange situation. *Child Development, 41,* 162–186.

Blos, P. (1967). The second individuation process of Adolescence. *Psychoanalytic Study of the Child, 22,* 162–186.

Bollas, C. (1987). *The shadow of the object: Psychoanalysis of the unthought known.* New York: Columbia University Press.

Erikson, E. (1950). *Childhood and society.* New York: W. W. Norton.

Harris, M. (2014). *The end of absence.* New York: Penguin Group.

Joyce, J. (1916). *A portrait of the artist as a young man.* United States: B. W. Huetsch.

Lanier, J. (2010). *You are not a gadget*. New York: Alfred A. Knopf.

Mahler, M. (1974). On the first three subphases of the separation-individuation process. *Psychoanalysis and Contemporary Science, 3*, 295–306.

Wilcox, B. L., Kunkel, D., Cantor, J., Dowrick, P., Linn, S., & Palmer, E. (2004). *Report of the APA task force on advertising and children*. Washington, DC: American Psychological Association. Retrieved from www.apa.org/pubs/info/reports/advertising-children.aspx

Winnicott, D. (1953). Transitional objects and transitional phenomena. *International Journal of Psychoanalysis, 34*, 89–97.

Winnicott, D. (1965). *The maturational processes and the facilitating environment: Studies in the theory of emotional development*. London: Hogarth Press.

Part II

Developmental concerns

The transition through adolescence and young adulthood requires a developmental shift on the part of both child and parent. At a time when children are stretching and flexing their muscles of autonomy, parents must play multiple and highly changeable roles for their children: a beacon of light for the vessel lost at sea, a steadying hand for the wobbly climber, a punching bag for the boxer in training – the ally and the alien, the doubted and the trusted. In turn, parents experience their adolescents as equally capricious, at times exhibiting wisdom and maturity, at other times seeming to revert to childlike behavior. This developmental dance can be heightened when a child's development takes an unexpected pathway. Then, the parent-child dance into adulthood requires a complex blend of ingenuity, patience, empathy, and insight, as well as the capacity to build resilience, on the part of both.

One way that social media has had a direct impact on developmental factors among young adults has to do with the ready accessibility of vast amounts of information about any and every concern. What parent these days hasn't stayed up late into the night surfing the web, trying to learn what they can about whatever seems to be ailing their child? There are enormous benefits to this technological advance in the dissemination of information. Young adults can find one another online and gather information, support, and encouragement from others going through the same things they are going through. Parents can readily get parenting tips, track down answers to complicated developmental questions, and find online support groups or like-minded communities. Yet, at the same time, it can be hard to tease out the nuances of a particular situation – the comfort of finding another person going through what you are going through is offset by the confusion and fear of your own reality. Grappling with a personal situation is very different from reading about another's.

The following chapters take a close look beneath the surface of developmental challenges, using a contemporary lens to examine how these difficulties affect young adults and their families.

Michelle Flax addresses the topic of how and when today's adolescents and young adults leave the home and set out on a pathway toward independence. She highlights an implicit expectation on the part of many that children are "due" to leave at a certain date, as though they have reached the end of their lease on childhood and moving out is an expectation or requirement. Instead, Flax shows how young adults can move fluidly between home and away, taking needed time to grow and consolidate their developmental achievements. This may vary for different children for different reasons, and Flax's approach as a parent is to find a way to "hold on with open arms" – that is, to be ready to catch adult children when they stumble but to release them when they are ready to fly away.

In Nancy J. Crown's moving chapter, we gain a glimpse into the rollercoaster ride of parenting a young adult with autism. Here, we see a young woman on the autism spectrum emerging into the adult world – one that can at times overwhelm her but that also provides her with ample opportunity for growth, contact, and maturation. Crown shines a light on the complexity of parenting a young adult with autism: when the parent has served as the outboard engine of the child's ego, how can she then learn to balance the autistic young adult's need for autonomy on the one hand, and guidance and support on the other? Crown explains that for the young adult on the autism spectrum, the more the parent can hold in mind her child's sensory processing differences, the more insight she will be able to gain into what her child needs. Ultimately, parents' task is to find a way to stay close at hand as their child progresses into adulthood.

In Lizbeth A. Moses's chapter about a young adult learning to manage his life-threatening allergies, we see how Matt moves from independence to autonomy by conquering a lifelong fear, one that has kept him relying on his parents' presence and care to protect him from danger. Now, on the threshold of leaving home, he discovers an inner strength he didn't know he had. In this way, Matt is able not only to take over his own care and safekeeping, but equally important, to internalize a sense of safety, self-integrity, and security. This allows him to develop the confidence, ego strength, and resilience necessary to navigate the demands of early adulthood.

For Devra Adelstein, the dual role of sister and parent she came to play for her own developmentally delayed sister explores the parallel developmental pathways of two young adults grieving their parents' untimely death. Here, one sister, hampered with cognitive vulnerabilities that have slowed her progression, endeavors to engage with the adult world while the other sister, a precocious young woman, becomes a substitute parent and guardian during a time when she still needs guidance and care from her own parents. Adelstein shows how a family's struggle to accept the reality of the developmental disability profoundly affected both sisters' transitions to adulthood.

Finally, Karen Earle's chapter explores in depth the attachment between a mother and daughter as it evokes previous experiences and the ghosts of earlier relationships, including her own early relationship with her mother. Earle, a therapist and poet, examines the long-term relational effects on her experience of parenting a premature infant. She offers a glimpse into the unconscious fantasies, conflicts, and fears of a mother still working through how she was mothered as a young child. Ultimately, Earle shows how these themes evolve and are reworked as both parent and child mature and are able to separate from one another in a developmentally healthy way, allowing both to thrive.

3

Holding on with open arms

Adult children living at home

Michelle Flax

I have two adult children living at home. My son is 26 and my daughter is 32. Let me say from the outset that I never imagined this would be the case. I was self-sufficient and married by 22 and had three children by the time I was 32. My husband's path was much the same. Is it always the case that we expect our children to be like us? The fact that my children are still at home is at odds with the fantasy I had of my life at this time. As is so often the case, I only became aware of my fantasy through its failure to materialize.

For a number of years, all three of our children were out of the house while they attended university. Our home was the empty nest we had expected. Before they left I felt anxious anticipating their leaving, and once they were gone I felt many a pang at having no children at home, but I surprised myself with how quickly I became accustomed to the quiet and the calm. It gave me space to recover from the intensity of the child-rearing years and to concentrate on my own ventures.

It is not uncommon these days for adult children to return home. Indeed, it was not long before both my daughter and youngest son came back. They are home for their own reasons; currently they have needs that the structure of family life at home helps fulfill. After suffering a devastating brain tumor, my fiercely determined daughter has spent the last few years in brain retraining pursuits. She is trying to establish a new path forward. While the family was in the midst of the crisis of my daughter's brain tumor, my youngest son was away at university. His studies suffered as he worked to deal with this family crisis alone, away from the family. He managed to graduate but returned home to have a stable base as he worked out how to shape his life.

While my particular situation may be unusual, I am far from alone in having my adult children at home. In fact, this is a widespread phenomenon – adult children stay in the home longer than they used to decades ago. Currently, the number of adult children residing at home is surprisingly high.[1] We see the living-at-home-while-adult phenomenon reflected back at us in a number of TV sitcoms and movies, which generally show adult children living at home in a tragicomic way (e.g., Howard in *The Big Bang Theory*, 2007, Matthew McConaughey's character in *Failure to Launch*, 2006).

There has always been a small subset of young adults who cannot leave home for their own (or their parent's) psychical reasons. However, the present socioeconomic conditions interact with psychical factors in such a way as to encourage a delay of adulthood.[2] The question arises: Are we to regard young adults as pathologically reluctant to embrace the role of adulthood? Is it the "prolonged adolescence" Bernfeld (1938) and Blos (1954) referred to many years ago, or a new phase, an "adultescence"?

These questions become particularly salient in our clinical work. As a therapist, I often work with young adults living at home, or the parent(s) of those young adults. I recently received a call from a mother of a 25-year-old who had returned home after her university studies. "Madison is living at home again and it's really thrown off all my plans for my own life," Madison's mother explained on the phone while setting up an appointment for her unemployed daughter. "I feel like I am at the airport and the plane has been delayed once again." I wondered aloud why Madison hadn't called to set up the appointment herself. "She would have," her mother explained sheepishly, "but I knew from your message to call you in the morning for an appointment, and Maddie isn't up yet."

Having my own adult children at home has made me (perhaps self-servingly) more sympathetic to both the parent and the adult child in this situation. Parents nod knowingly when talking to one another about their adult children living at home – or smugly, if their children have managed to leave the nest. Many parents recognize that we are dealing with something most of our parents did not encounter, and that we are caught in a new social phenomenon. Yet there can still be guilt and shame, not only for parents but also for the young adults if they live at home into their mid-twenties or beyond. I have mixed feelings about having two of my three children at home. While it makes sense right now for a number of reasons, and I regularly enjoy their lively company, there is a nagging doubt that perhaps I should have encouraged an earlier independence in some way. Many parents who contact me about their adult children living at home or returning home after having been away at school have a similar ambivalence. Generally, in my practice, parents who consult me are seeking help for their feelings of frustration, helplessness, worry, and parental guilt. They fear that they have been remiss in some aspect of parenting, given that their children have not yet found their full adult path. And for some young adults, staying at home can feel shameful, especially if they prefer the easier conditions of home. It is as if their dependency is writ large for all to see. I have heard more than one young adult say that they are reluctant to move on, because they fear that their best years would then be behind them, but they are also embarrassed that they are not where they imagine they should be at their age. Sometimes, children come back after a successful launch, either because of loss of employment or because of the breakdown of a relationship. When they do return home, they often revert to childhood ways, accentuating the potential discomfort of the situation. If they come back with their own kids, it adds another layer of complexity to the "crowded nest" (Shaputis, 2003) and can add to the young adult's sense that they have not successfully launched.

Socioeconomic considerations

So why do so many adult children currently live at home? One of the primary reasons is economic; many cannot afford to live on their own. The changed economic climate makes it harder for young people to find viable employment (Pew Research Center, 2013 [2012 census data]). Young adults are more likely to go to university today than they were in the past. Second degrees or diplomas are often required to build a career; this extends schooling and delays career starts. Initial experience in many fields is often unpaid or poorly paid (note the infamous "unpaid internship"). In addition, as some people retire later, young people may find themselves unable to advance in their chosen field. To add to this, in many places in North America, real estate has become so expensive that even renting can be unaffordable, leading young people to stay or return home to build up their funds.

Social considerations add to the economic factors. The phenomenon of later-age marriage delays moving out. The ease and comfort of living at home may also play a role, especially given the more lax attitudes around sexuality in some families. Changes in Western child-rearing practices over the past few decades have added to the issue. Parents' increased focus on fostering self-esteem in parenting Generation Y kids – people born between the late '70s and late '90s – may have inadvertently fostered failure avoidance. We put a high value on building and maintaining self-esteem. We told our children that they could do and be anything. Everyone was smart, everyone was a winner, and everyone was special. Few kids were held back in sports or school for fear it would damage their "self-esteem." More recently, "tiger parenting" privileged success-driven, overstructured childhood experiences over experiential learning. These failure-avoidance parenting styles may have contributed, along with other factors, to the phenomenon of adult kids staying home longer than in previous generations.

Psychological considerations

That it has become the norm for young adults to live at home through their twenties can mask how social trends interact with psychological factors. While there is certainly a "new normal" in terms of living at home longer, we must acknowledge that the young adult still needs to move toward full independence in order to claim a life of their own, distinct from that of their parent(s). This can be more difficult while living at home because a number of developmental tasks and internal crises can be accentuated and complicated. Examining the complex interaction between the current sociological conditions and the psychological considerations of the adult child and the parents can be helpful.

How are we to understand the psychological processes that occur as young adults and parents struggle with the challenges of this stage of life? Psychoanalytic theories of development, because of the emphasis on the influence of early child-rearing, have largely focused on the early stages. Ericson (1963, 1968) attempted to correct this bias by extending the notion of development processes to stages beyond childhood and adolescence. In Ericson's theory, adolescence is a time in which conflicts around identity are salient, while young adults struggle with the conflict between intimacy versus isolation. Blos (1962) spoke of a post-adolescent stage in which consolidation and integration of the personality take place through the establishment of a social role, courtship, marriage, and parenthood. Yet these early theories are not up to the task of talking to the particular situation of today, when so many young adults in their twenties and thirties still struggle with confusion over their roles and identities and may be caught in a delayed adulthood situation. The term "emerging adulthood" was coined by Arnett in 2000 and describes the period of time in the developed world between the ages of 18 and 25 or so, in which there is a distinct phase between teenage years and adulthood proper. Arnett insists that this stage is not merely a transition to adulthood but that it is a distinct phase of its own, with an emphasis on identity explorations, instability, and a prolonged self-focus. Arnett's paper has been influential in the fields of psychology and social work, and the term "emerging adulthood" has been integrated into the literature on development.

Separation, individuation, and attachment

In the usual course of events, children learn to separate and individuate from parents in early childhood, and then again in adolescence. Mahler (1979) introduced us to the idea of a separation-individuation child development phase in which the child increasingly distinguishes self from caregiver, and then slowly discovers his or her own will, individuality, and beginning identity. Blos (1967) talks about a "second individuation" that occurs as the later adolescent goes off to college or work and comes home less often. The successful adolescent moves toward a connection with the adult world as a psychologically separate individual who can manage in society at large. In their twenties and thirties, young people are working on the tasks of determining their future in terms of identity, occupation, and relationships. We might say that today a "third individuation" has to take place. Past successes with the ability to separate and individuate will help or hinder the young adult as they work on these processes.

A common theme in the development literature is that parents and their offspring eventually must take their leave of one another both psychologically and physically. But the emerging adult living at home must separate and individuate despite the external reality of living in a situation that (re)evokes their childhood position in the home, and the internal unconscious factors related to their attachment dynamics.

The ability of emerging adults to separate and individuate is influenced by their earlier attachment patterns, and we generally see a strong continuity of attachment patterns over time (Bowlby, 1969; Main, Kaplan, & Cassidy, 1985; Hamilton, 2000; Waters, Merrick, Treboux, Crowell, & Albersheim, 2000). Thus the adult child's living at home will likely be influenced by their early attachment patterns.

Insecure attachment patterns may play out in conflicts over independence, college adjustment, and career indecision (Lapsley & Edgerton, 2002), all factors that would influence how long a young adult may live at home. These patterns can be changed, but only when there is a full acknowledgment by the young adult that the experiences were negative (Waters, Weinfield, & Hamilton, 2000). This process is complicated when the adult child has a prolonged period of living at home. "Young adults who have not gained autonomy from their families of origin may find it too difficult emotionally and cognitively to acknowledge and explore poor treatment by a parent on whom they still depend" (p. 705). Thus those individuals who had earlier insecure and disorganized attachments may remain preoccupied with previous negative emotional experiences in ways that can compromise the process of becoming autonomous.

What is often under-recognized is that parents must be able to separate from adult children as much adult children need to separate from them. Embedded in the term "holding on with open arms" is the notion that the adult child's separateness of identity can be allowed and encouraged, even as this identity rubs up against dreaded fears and wishes in the parent's own mind. It involves moving away from the idea of superego parenting, with its notion of control over the child, to a more "arm's-length" style of parenting. This task is made more difficult when the adult child remains under the same roof. Watching one's adult child play video games in the basement while he or she ignores the dishes in the sink or the tasks involved in creating a career does not encourage arm's-length parenting. I find myself filled with anxiety when I notice that my adult daughter has not woken in time to get to her destination. To lower my aggravation, I must close the door on my adult son's messy room and unmade bed. Like so many parents, I find it both enticing and difficult to hand over responsibility to my children to manage their own lives. I project my own vulnerable, irresponsible child-self onto my children and then try to corral that child-self into place. I have to coach myself: "It is their life, let them live it."

I find myself giving this advice to parents within my practice too. Even as I gratuitously offer the advice, I am wary of it, as the story is so often more complex. Parents, in the "afternoon" of their lives,[3] are called on to manage the conflicts that arise out of having to juggle multiple roles, deal with aging, retirement planning, aging parents, and their own health concerns. The progress of their adult children often determines how parents feel about their own success and achievements. Partner relationships come into sharp relief as the chores associated with parenting decrease. Even as they consciously wish to support their child to move into adulthood beyond the home, parents may unconsciously strive to hold on to the status quo for their own reasons. Their own histories of separation-individuation and attachment issues play out in myriad ways. Often the presence of the adult child has come to be seen as essential for coping with attachment anxieties. Parents may fear that they will become irrelevant, or that the child's move away may signal their own dreaded aging, or that they will now be alone with a disappointing spouse. In my practice I see parents who cannot recover from their son's broken heart or their daughter's career difficulties. The parent must be able to separate and individuate in order to tolerate difficult affect states in themselves and their adult child.

James Hollis reminds us to turn "misery to meaning" in the passage of our middle years. All too often, that meaning centers on our children's passage. Parents have the task of working through their disappointments and getting on with their own lives even if their children are not progressing well (Adams, 2003). They need to reclaim aspects of themselves that they have projected onto their child and become aware that the complicated mix of feelings they feel in relation to their child's leaving or staying at home may arise from their own conflicted histories. "The paradox of individuation is that we best serve intimate relationship by becoming sufficiently developed in ourselves that we do not need to feed off others" (Hollis, 1993, p. 95). Parents are helped by recognizing that "holding on to" their kids only works if it is done with "open arms," allowing both their kids and themselves the room to find their own individuality.

Oedipal issues

The situation is further complicated because the adult child and parent are embedded within a family configuration. The child and two parents (or other family configurations, such as one birth parent and one stepparent) may form a triangular relationship, which contrasts with the earlier dual relationship of infancy. Internal psycho-dynamics related to oedipal situations continue to play out through the transition to adulthood. The adult child's ability to tolerate both love and hate for each parent or parent-substitute is a hallmark of the resolution of the ambivalent triangular relationship. Often, generational boundaries are unconsciously challenged. The oedipal relationship is seen in the laugh shared between a father and daughter at the expense of the "left out" parent, or in the comfort a son gives to a mother who is experiencing marital strife. It is seen in the mother who envies her daughter's easy life, when she herself at the same age was married and tending to a child, or the father who insists on demeaning rules for his adult son. It is seen in the anger of the brother who resents the "favourite" sister, who seems to bend the rules without consequence.

To successfully separate, both the adult child and parent(s) have to leave the extended triangular relationship and accept the boundaries inherent in moving away from relating as parent and child. One of the pressing problems of the adult child who lives at home is that the triangular structure can be maintained as an external reality, often infantilizing the young adult and re-stimulating childhood dilemmas of both the parent and the adult child. The regression that is so commonly seen when children return home is often due to the dynamics inherent in this triangular situation. The adult child frequently reverts to being the "child" again in a resurgence of the adolescent push and pull. Parents may be re-stimulated by their own unconscious oedipal dynamics, formed in their own family of origin, and find themselves playing out these dynamics within the present configuration. We see this in the parent who cannot accept any partner as good enough for their beloved son or daughter, or who will not let the adult child surpass them in any way. We see it in the competitive dynamics between father and son, mother and daughter.

The oedipal situation sometimes plays out in my own living situation. My adult daughter, who lives at home, does the shopping for our household, using our funds. She regularly buys too much. Our house tends to be overstocked. I find myself in an awkward spot. I want to show appreciation for the shopping, which saves me time and effort, but I also want to point out the concern I have about the quantities she buys. I speak tentatively, thanking her for shopping and adding that no more than three of the same item is ever necessary. She senses my tentativeness, my wish not to be too critical, and uses that space to enter into a conflict with me, stating that I appreciate nothing she does and that I criticize, instead of lauding the fact that she is now "running the house." In creating the conflict, she sets up a situation where I feel compelled to defend my right to assert myself in my own household, in order to right the internal wrong of her being the "wife."

Of course, oedipally tinged interactions regularly find their place in family interactions even after adult children have left home. But living at home accentuates and highlights these issues. While the internal family dynamics are regularly played out in situations where the adult child has left the home, extended "adultlescence" accentuates any lack of resolution of both unconscious and conscious conflicts related to triangular situations. This is particularly the case when the parents are in conflict or separated, or a parent has died, and the child steps in as the missing partner, either in the mind of the child or the adult.

Parents and young adults who consult with me often describe the conflict that pervades the home when adult children have not left the nest. "This is not what I imagined" is a frequent refrain I hear from parents. Sometimes, it is not quite what the young adult imagined either. Many parents admit to feeling envious of other parents whose children who are financially on their feet and/or getting married. Many young adults at home feel they are lagging behind their cohort. Disappointments often play out in tense exchanges between the parent and adult child. The ongoing dilemma is one in which the individual struggles between a "pushing away" versus a "holding on" (Blos, 1967). There can be issues all along the way as this dilemma is negotiated at each developmental stage. This process continues until the tasks of separation are more complete. Perhaps these conflictual processes can aid separation; we seem to need the promise of relief from the other's continued presence to help us separate. The fierce, primal investment of the parent in their child clashes with the ambivalent dependence/independence struggle of the young adult, and wild exchanges can result. Separating and becoming individuated away from the triangular relational configuration is thus never an easy matter for either the adult child or the parent(s), and it is clearly more difficult when the young adult lives at home for an extended period.

Clinical example

By way of example, let's return to 25-year-old Madison, whose mother called to see if I would see her. Her mother's concern was that she was doing very little at home besides sleeping and watching television. I agreed to see Maddie on her own to understand how she saw the situation. I learned that Maddie had finished her undergrad degree two years earlier – it had taken her 6 years to complete – and she was unsure what she wanted to do next. Her parents insisted she get a job. She had set up a few interviews for low-level jobs, but after she failed to get one of these jobs, she stopped showing up for scheduled interviews. Given that Maddie voiced a conscious wish to move out of the family home and to begin "her own life," I asked her about missing the interviews.

Maddie said that she had not done as well in her university schooling as she would have liked. She believed that since that her high school achievement was good with little effort, her university studies would be a "breeze," and she would be able to achieve anything she wanted to achieve. Her confidence was badly shaken over the 6 years of schooling. She was afraid to start anything new for fear that she would once again disappoint herself, especially as she was finding it so hard to get a job – even a low-level one. She said that had she secured a job early on, she would have been able to push through her lack of confidence, but her lack of success with even a low-level job scared her.

At first glance it seemed as if Maddie's decreased confidence was exacerbated by the current economic situation, causing Maddie to be part of the "new normal" wave of adult children living at home for an extended period. However, as we looked further into Maddie's world I began to see that the socioeconomic situation interacted with both Maddie's internal dynamics and the unconscious family patterns.

In her sessions with me, Maddie focused mainly on her concerns about her friendships. While her parents worried about Maddie finding a career path and moving on in life, Maddie was preoccupied with her sparse social world. As is so often the case with the older adolescent and young adult, peer relationships take conscious precedence over those with family. It became clear that Maddie had conflictual relationships with female friends. "They get too annoyingly close," she explained, even as she complained that she was lonely. It appeared that Maddie had some attachment-related anxiety and used strategies of avoidance and resistance to closeness to deal with these anxieties. Indeed, the early history showed that Maddie's mother had to be hospitalized for some weeks just as Maddie was born, and that Maddie had persistently refused to take the bottle for quite some time. Maddie described herself as a "self-sufficient" only child growing up. In first-year university Maddie had a falling out with a friend who chose to date a young man in whom Maddie had once expressed interest. The group of young women with whom Maddie lived in the university residence did not side with Maddie, and she was somewhat isolated. She perceived that her poor university performance was partially due to her ongoing social difficulties. Her earlier difficulties with competitive high school friendships suggested a troublesome friendship pattern born out of attachment anxiety and tinged with oedipal pathology.

As we explored further, it became clear that Maddie was spending her days at home sleeping or surfing various social media sites. Maddie grew anxious that time was passing, yet she felt no motivation to do much of anything. Slowly Maddie became conscious of her fear that she was like her mother, who seemed, to Maddie, to have given up on herself over the years. In her view, a difficult marriage had beaten down her mother and now the mother lacked a lively spirit. My patient watched her mother do little else but come home from a mind-numbing job and watch television by herself. Maddie's father, on the other hand, was driven to such an extent that his work fully occupied his attention. My patient now feared that if she did relinquish her paralyzed stance, she would discover that she was either like her mother, or like her father. She preferred to remain frozen rather than face that possibility, despite the fact that in so doing she was partially repeating her mother's behavior anyway. Maddie was afraid to leave her parents with no buffer between them, fearing that her parents' marriage would become even more conflicted if she were no longer at home. Furthermore, moving away from a frozen state might force Maddie to face her ambivalent attachments to significant others.

Maddie was having trouble separating from her family and individuating, or becoming her own person. There were a number of factors: she lacked confidence, her ambivalent attachments left her isolated, she feared becoming like either parent, and she did not wish to leave her parents alone in their unhappy state. The difficulty in being able to get a job and make good social connections accentuated her internal conflict. Ironically, her mother's view, communicated to me in the initial phone call, was that she was just waiting for Maddie to get a job and move out of her home so that she could feel free to separate from her husband and "begin her own life." Madison's continued living at home made both Madison and her mother feel locked into an unresolved dynamic between them.

It became clear to me that both Maddie and her mother had to work through attachment and oedipal losses in order to move successfully through this phase. Madison's continued living at home reinforced her idea that she had to facilitate the relationship between her parents and that she was part of the parental couple. Her reluctance to leave her parents to sort out their own marital relationship maintained a triangular arrangement. Over time it became evident that Maddie unconsciously "knew" that her mother planned to leave the marriage once she left. Her guilt about being the one to break up the marriage contributed to keeping her from actively pursuing her own life. As well, Maddie unconsciously sensed her mother's wish to be separate, causing a recrudescence of early maternal loss anxieties.

Her mother, while espousing the idea that she wished Maddie to leave so she could shape a new life for herself, overfunctioned for Maddie (as in booking her appointments), keeping Maddie in a childhood, triangulated position, and protecting the mother from being left alone in her marriage. The unconscious, oft-repeated patterns of relating within Maddie's family were affecting the ability of both Maddie and her mother to successfully separate and individuate, and consequently take their leave from one another.

Pathology or new normal? A therapist's dilemma

The living-at-home condition has to be seen in context. The therapist identifies both the earlier dynamics that impact the present condition and the current conditions that maintain this state. Are there attachment issues and thus difficulties in separating and individuating? What part is played by oedipal matters? What is the current parent-child dynamic? What are the socioeconomic conditions that prevent the adult child from moving out of the house?

The therapist will find it helpful to look at the trajectory of the adult child's life: is the individual's living at home likely to lead to a better outcome for their ongoing development? While an extended living at home may complicate and exacerbate any pre-existing conditions, on the other hand this "extended leave taking" (Loewald, 1962) can allow for the mourning of losses and the unconscious consolidation of identities for both the parent and the young adult, thereby facilitating successful developmental transitions for both. Perhaps the young adult's extended time at home allows them to build confidence, or better establish identity, or to achieve certain financial savings to make a moving out plan viable.

Maddie, for example, is now using her time at home to build her confidence and her skills so that she can begin to shape her own life, which might be similar in some ways to either her father's or her mother's but is, essentially, her own. Once she became aware in therapy that she was in a frozen state, and that even by remaining frozen she was making a decision, she began to risk new situations. She understood that she was not helping her parents' marriage by not moving forward herself, and that her parents' marriage was theirs to work out. Maddie began to look at her friendship patterns, seeing how she pushed away the very people for whom she cared. Slowly she began to risk more in relationships and to explore her passions. She tested herself out by doing volunteer work. She slowly built a more robust social world. Despite her fear, she went back to school and is now completing a second college degree. Staying at home is helpful to Maddie right now. Her mother has been able to step back from her concern about Maddie, knowing that Maddie is on a positive trajectory. Maddie's mother has come to the idea that her parenting role has changed from an overfunctioning, overprotective superego kind of parenting to an engagement that is closer to that of a consultant and partner in this life venture. She says now that she works on this by imagining that Maddie is the daughter of a good friend whom she is mentoring. She believes she has learned the hard way that unsolicited advice is seldom helpful. She and her husband have begun marital therapy to try to decide whether or not they will stay together.

While it is so often the case that parents can feel a great deal of frustration at having their adult children rely on the family resources, or crowd the space with their adult pursuits, what can be gained by having adult children at home can be very satisfying, particularly if there is relinquishment of the resentment on both sides. While parents can be close with adult children living away from the home, the presence of adult kids at home can bring a young energy. The young adults can be really helpful to parents in all kinds of ways, from carrying in parcels to technical computer help. And parents continue to be helpful to their adult children in ways that are not always acknowledged. I have been gratified to see how valuable it is to be around when my son or daughter has to complete a tax form, or make a medical decision. I am convinced that watching the business of the household from an adult point of view has been immeasurably helpful to both my adult children living at home.

Family configurations are heavily culturally and economically determined. Changing socioeconomic forces are currently shaping a new nuclear family in which adult children remain connected to their parents' support for extended periods. Blos (1967, 1979) points out that adolescent regression operates in the service of development. Remaining in the family in the current socioeconomic climate may extend the adolescent regression, yet it may also, under certain circumstances, be in the service of individual development and social advancement. While I could not have imagined that I would be dealing with my adult children living at home into their late twenties and early thirties, I can see the value of this arrangement in terms of their development. My two children live at home for very different reasons, yet I believe that both are on a positive path, and that their staying at home in their early adulthood has been helpful and will help them in the long run.

Sometimes as my family and I sit around the dinner table, laughing and discussing daily and world events, I am reminded how lucky I am to have their company. So often we feel we have too much or too little of the presence of our children. When they are young, in the primitive-needs stage or even at school age, it can feel overwhelming to deal with the demands. When our kids grow away from us, we so often lament their absence. When it goes well, adult children living at home can be that Goldilocks "just right" solution that is best to enjoy while it lasts. My son's recent admission to a professional graduate program in another city raises a myriad of feelings in me. I hadn't realized how much I had grown to love his messy presence in the home, and how much I will miss him when he is gone.

Notes

1 Well over half of younger adult children (ages 18 to 25) in North America live in the family home, or have boomeranged back. More than a third of 18- to 31-year-olds live at home in the United States; that adds up to over 21 million people – a steady and significant rise over the preceding decades (Pew Research Center, 2013). Canadian young adults are even more likely than their U.S. counterparts to live at home, with 42% of 20- to 29-year-olds residing in the family home (Statistics Canada, 2011).

2 This essay focuses primarily on affluent or middle-class adult children in our North American, Western, developed world. Cultural practices, financial circumstances, and disability issues heavily influence the length of time children may live at home.

3 *"Thoroughly unprepared, we take the step into the afternoon of life. . . .* The afternoon of human life must also have a significance of its own and cannot be merely a pitiful appendage to life's morning" (Jung, 1930, p. 787).

References

Adams, J. (2003). *When our grown kids disappoint us: Letting go of their problems, loving them anyway, and getting on with our lives.* New York: The Free Press.

Arnett, J. J. (2000). Emerging adulthood: A theory of development from late teens through the twenties. *American Psychologist, 55,* 469–480.

Bernfeld, S. (1938). Types of adolescence. *Psychoanalytic Quarterly, 7,* 243–253.

Blos, P. (1954). Prolonged adolescence: The formulation of a syndrome and its therapeutic implications. *American Journal of Orthopsychiatry, 24,* 733–742.

Blos, P. (1962). *On adolescence.* New York: The Free Press.

Blos, P. (1967). The second individuation process of adolescence. *Psychoanalytic Study of the Child, 22,* 162–186.

Blos, P. (1979). *The adolescent passage.* New York: International Universities Press.

Bowlby, J. (1969). *Attachment and loss.* Vol. 1., *Attachment.* New York: Basic Books.

Ericson, E. H. (1963). *Childhood and society* (2nd ed.). New York: W. W. Norton.

Ericson, E. H. (1968). *Identity: Youth and crisis.* New York: W. W. Norton.

Hamilton, C. E. (2000). Continuity and discontinuity of attachment from infancy through adolescence. *Child Development, 71,* 690–694.

Hollis, J. (1993). *The midlife passage: From misery to meaning in midlife.* Toronto: University of Toronto Press.

Jung, C. G. (1930). The stages of life. In G. Adler & R. F. C. Hull (Eds.), *Collected works of C. G. Jung. Volume 8, The structure and dynamics of the psyche.* Princeton, NJ: Princeton University Press.

Lapsley, D., & Edgerton, J. (2002). Separation – individuation, adult attachment and college adjustment. *Journal of Counseling Development, 80,* 484–492.

Loewald, H. W. (1962). Internalization, separation, mourning, and the superego. *Psychoanalytic Quarterly, 31,* 483–504.

Mahler, S. (1979). *Separation-individuation: The collected papers of Margaret Mahler* (Vol. 2). New York: J. Aronson.

Main, M., Kaplan, N., & Cassidy, J. (1985). Security in infancy, childhood, and adulthood: A move to the level of representation. In I. Bretherton & E. Waters (Eds.), *Growing points in attachment theory and research.* Monographs of the Society for Research in Child Development, 50 (1–2, Serial No. 209, pp. 66–104).

Pew Research Center. (2013). *A rising share of young adults live in their parents' home.* Retrieved from www.pewsocialtrends.org/2013/08/01/a-rising-share-of-young-adults-live-in-their-parents-home/

Shaputis, K. (2003). *The crowded nest syndrome: Surviving the return of adult children.* Olympia, WA: Clutter Fairy Publishing.

Statistics Canada. (2011). *Living arrangements of young adults aged 20 to 29.* Retrieved from www12.statcan.gc.ca/census-recensement/2011/as-sa/98–312-x/98–312-x2011003_3-eng.cfm

Waters, E., Merrick, S., Treboux, D., Crowell, J., & Albersheim, L. (2000). Attachment security in infancy and early adulthood: A twenty-year longitudinal study. *Child Development, 71,* 684–689.

Waters, E., Weinfield, N. S., & Hamilton, C. E. (2000). The stability of attachment security from infancy to adolescence and early adulthood: General discussion. *Child Development, 71,* 703–706.

4

It is hard to see the forest when the trees are too loud

Notes on autism parenting

Nancy J. Crown

"What makes me feel better is the way you understand me."

My young daughter and I were on a crowded bus returning home from running errands, including buying a gift for my mother-in-law. "Why we are getting Grandma a book?" she asked, her small face furrowing.

"Because when someone is sick, a present can help them feel better," I responded. "It says we are thinking of them."

"What makes me feel better is the way you understand me."

She said this almost to herself, but I've held it close ever since, a cherished heirloom, and I have reached for it in private many times over the years for comfort.

Fast forward: I am having my annual mammogram. The doctor asks if I have any concerns. My concern is that my daughter, who is now 30 years old and on the autism spectrum, will need a baseline mammogram in five years. For a million reasons, I can't imagine her ever tolerating this torturous procedure. My worry about her pulses constantly, winging through my mind on a loop.

Recently, the morning she arrived for a weekend at home, I woke up with a back spasm. We had agreed to a trip to a mall that sells Barbie dolls at a discount. The back spasm prevented me from driving, but she had a backup plan, and a backup for her backup plan. Barbies hold a very important place in my daughter's life. So, we went to a different mall, one we didn't have to drive to, and got the Barbie. The doll had styleable hair and came with miniature styling accessories, including the smallest curling iron you have ever seen. All the way home, we chatted about Barbies. At some point, I began to daydream about an ice pack and a cup of tea when my daughter piped up: "And when we get home, you can braid her hair and then . . ." "Whoa. I didn't sign on for Barbie hair styling." She was disappointed, I felt guilty, then resentful, and then – even guiltier.

My daughter has never been able to learn to braid. Her hands, as though they belong to some other person, refuse to obey her mind when it comes to tasks like braiding hair, fastening buckles, or swiping a metro card. When she speaks, her hands draw delicate pictures in the air accentuating her point, but they don't tie shoes. So, on this particular weekend, if I don't do the braiding, the Barbie remains un-styled.

My daughter also has a way of colonizing my mind. I have always thought there should be an item on the parent autism screening questionnaires asking whether your child ever uses your mind as though it was her own. Even now, she will assert something, for instance that the way the plant spills its shadow across the kitchen wall in the late afternoon is particularly beautiful, ask if I agree, and then ask me to explain why "I" think so. For me as her mother, to be in her presence is to have a large part of my mind on loan. This is exhausting: sometimes when she is home for the weekend, I catch a glimpse of myself in the mirror and realize I look like a pack of cats have had at me, or at the very least that I have styled my own hair with the kitchen blender.

And yet her intelligence, her kindness, her humor, her creativity, her abject goodness, and her readiness to forgive are always on hand. A butterfly or a pure shade of blue brings her joy. She will dismiss a shade with too much grey with the flick of an eye. She once sat next to an elderly arthritic woman on a plane. Between the two of them, they couldn't fasten a single seat belt. At the end of the flight, the woman turned to us smiling and said, "Well, she's a *lot* of company!" I have a friend who says that my daughter sprinkles fairy dust wherever she goes. It is true – she is effervescent in her joy, and her spark is contagious. The world, when my daughter describes it, seems like a better, brighter place. She has wound herself so thoroughly in and around my heart, but still, a person can only talk about Barbies for so long.

Autism and sensory processing

Autism is now widely described as a neuro-developmental spectrum disorder characterized by inborn problems with socialization and communication, and restricted cognitive and behavioral patterns. More than 90 percent of people with autism have difficulties processing sensory information, such as sounds, sights, and smells (Crane, Goddard, & Pring, 2009; Leekam, Nieto, Libby, Wing, & Gould, 2007). Sensory dysfunction often leads to confusion and dysregulation. For some, it triggers debilitating migraines. For others, it renders everyday interactions exhausting. For the rest of us, it makes the autistic experience quite foreign and therefore hard to keep in mind and to understand.

People with autism may experience perceptions in any sensory modality as too intense, too weak, or simply un-integrate-able. The pervasiveness of sensory dysfunction, and the profound and extensive nature of its consequences, would seem to implicate this processing difficulty in some of autism's other challenges. A child's sensory impairment renders the world, other people, and even aspects of the child's own self baffling and oftentimes overwhelming. In my view, this is also one of the central reasons parenting a child with autism is so challenging.

In an effort to cope, people with autism avoid, seek, or focus selectively on specific sensory information. For instance, sensory dysfunction means that the comforting touch of a caregiver may feel intrusive, a noise barely audible to you or to me might be unbearable, and the sight of a rose or a twirling object might elicit pure delight. The world perceived through autism-colored glasses is experienced in unique and bewildering ways, which can lead to excruciating anxiety, affect dysregulation, joy, rigidity, or what on the surface looks like a frank lack of feeling.

First-person accounts by autistic writers (see for example Adler, 2006; Shore, 2003; Simone, 2010; Willey, 1999; Williams, 1992) as well as research (see Happé, 1994) support the notion that autistic processing results in a unique experience of the relational, somatosensory, and physical worlds. One child highly attuned to music complained that he could not concentrate in school because his classroom radiator hissed all day "like a sad opera." A woman on the spectrum described the feel and sound of a fly buzzing in her ear "like an atomic bomb exploding" (Adler, 2006, p. 164). A mother explained she had to "divine" when her child was sick because his ability to register pain was so faint that he could have a raging ear infection without complaining. Another child spotted an olive pit from a distance of more than 30 feet and gagged at the sight. When my daughter was small, we assiduously avoided restaurants with blenders and public restrooms with hand dryers. The particular pitch of these appliances was painfully assaultive to her auditory system.

In what follows, I will detail this important aspect of the autistic experience – unique sensory processing – and I will discuss how this very common characteristic could play a role in many other features of autism, including aspects of cognition, socialization, and communication. I will outline how as a result, dealing with the world becomes chronically and intensely anxiety-provoking, frustrating, and exhausting. I will also illustrate how the child's distinctive perceptual processing system renders her experience quite foreign to neuro-typical parents and therefore presents a formidable challenge to our powers of understanding and empathy.

The good-enough autism parent

A fellow autism mom often looks after her friends' children along with her own. She is intelligent, funny, creative, and talented. She loves her child deeply and is so resourceful, sensitively attuned, and self-critical it would make your head spin. She said the following about autism parenting: "Just when you think, 'I've got this. I've *so* got this!' that's when you find yourself running in a fancy red full-length dress with a poodle under your arm screaming after two autistic kids." She had taken her autistic daughter, her daughter's friend, and the dog to an event, and somebody bolted from the car the moment the door opened. No one was lost or hurt, and yet just like that, she felt like a terrible mother – again.

At these moments, it can be helpful to remember Winnicott's concept of the "good-enough" mother (Winnicott, 1965a). That is, it is better for a child to have a "good-enough" parent than a "perfect" parent, because it is through our failures and reparations that we teach our children some of life's most important lessons – that it is okay to not be perfect, that relationships can survive ruptures, that we can endure disappointment and anger, how to forgive.

However, mothers of children with autism rarely feel good enough. The worry is ever present. When we get angry the guilt is crushing. So is the love. The vexing, unpredictable, tedious, uneven pervasiveness that is autism, and all the work it requires, exhausts the best of us. This is why I remind myself that my efforts to understand my daughter do make a difference. Even as I fail her in myriad ways – I couldn't prevent her from being bullied in fourth grade, I haven't been able to teach her to braid, and despite vowing not to, I run out of patience more times than I would like to admit – I try to remember that my struggle to understand my daughter's experience and to communicate that understanding to her have been crucial to her development. Of course, this kind of understanding is central to any child's development, but the difference when you are parenting a child on the autism spectrum in contrast to a typically developing child, is that your own experience oftentimes offers up so little to guide you. Parallel feelings of confusion and forever falling short unfortunately also plague the child with autism. She spends much of life mystified by the non-autistic world and "corrected" by (mostly) well-intentioned others who aim to smooth her way.

Thinking about the world from our autistic child's point of view is not a simple exercise – in fact it is highly challenging. Not only is our child's experience in many ways so frankly different from our own, but also, she often cannot help us to understand. Further, her very needs and behaviors take up a good deal of our energy and mental space, leaving precious little room for our own thinking. It can be hard to even calculate the tip for a taxi ride when you are being bombarded with Barbie drama.

While many people with autism struggle with theory of mind – that is, the ability to reflect on mental states in oneself and others (Baron-Cohen, 1985, 1997) – their parents, educators, and therapists must become theory of mind experts. For all human beings, the importance of being understood, seen, and recognized cannot be overstated (Winnicott, 1971a). My psychotherapy practice is filled with people who bring with them a childhood devoid of feeling recognized by important figures in their lives, and this is one of the most painful and debilitating aspects of their history. For many children and adults with autism, multiply this experience by infinity.

As children, when we are recognized and accepted, we come to know, accept, and value ourselves. We develop positive self-esteem, enhanced cognitive functioning, and an ability to self-regulate (Fonagy & Target, 2002; Gergely & Watson, 1996). Further, as parents, when we keep our theory of mind about us, we are able to notice and foster our child's unique strengths. A great deal is lost if we aim only to shape our child into a replica of a neuro-typical child. This is not to say we do not need to help her to navigate the neuro-typical world to the best of her ability. We do, but if this is all we do, we fail her profoundly. Not only do we strip her of necessary coping mechanisms (hand flapping, swaying, or time alone may be crucial at times for self-regulation), but we also miss out on what is unique about her and leave her, tragically, to the ravages of crippling anxiety and sensory sensitivities.

Only by trying to understand our child's experience (why are Barbie Dolls so important to an adult? Why is this special interest a useful one?), can we make sense of what, on the surface, may look like bizarre or unreasonable behavior. This understanding can then be communicated to the child (or adult) to help her better understand herself and the world. Understanding and the inherent acceptance it communicates can, in my daughter's words, "make [her] feel better."

Theory of mind and then some: mentalizing

Nothing is more painful as a parent than seeing your child suffer. Parenting a child on the autism spectrum requires a depth of courage, endurance, and resourcefulness that I am convinced can be marshalled only from the deep wells of the parent's love for and devotion to her child. Parents must rally and re-rally these resources, sometimes over years in the face of little evidence that what they are doing makes any difference whatsoever. The neuro-biological nature of the infant with autism means that as a social partner she is in many ways incapable of collaboration. As a baby, she may avoid visual or skin contact to protect herself from what she experiences as painful and disorganizing overstimulation. For the parent, this feels like rejection and failure. The heartache is unfathomable.

A central aspect of good-enough mothering rests on the parent's sound ability to accurately read, make sense of, and give back – or "re-present" – the baby's experience. In other words, babies have a fundamental need for their caregiver to mentalize (Fonagy, Gergely, Jurist, & Target, 2005), which means to practice theory of mind and then some. Mentalizing becomes an agonizing practice for the parent of an autistic baby who presents a confusing array of agitated, distressed, and/or withdrawn behavior. The baby's difficulty processing sensory input will frequently lead to her feel distressed and overwhelmed. As such, she will often be impossible to read. The mother-baby pair is headed for repeated experiences of intersubjective failure, because how can the mother hold, process, and re-present what she does not understand (Slade, 2009)? The baby is left alone in her suffering, and the mother, feeling rejected and like a "bad mother," is now anguished and alone as well. Her mentalizing function falters even more now under the weight of her emotional response to her baby's baffling behavior. It is not hard to see how this interaction, repeated over time, could become a dark Rorschach pattern of mutual alienation.

Mentalization is deceptively complex at this early stage. How does a mother represent her baby's emotional state such that the baby is able to differentiate the mother's reflecting of the baby from emotion belonging to the mother herself? Enlarging on Winnicott's work on the mother's mirroring function, Gergely and Watson (1996) outline how the mother "marks" the affect she displays by exaggerating her facial expression and vocalization. This signals to the baby the mother's intention to mirror the baby's emotion. Given the autistic baby's difficulty processing social information such as facial expression and her failure to establish the expected pattern of mutual gaze (Carter, Ornstein Davis, Klin, & Volkmar,

2005), how is the mother to mark the autistic baby's affect? If the baby is avoiding eye contact and feeling overwhelmed, what is she taking in?

When the interaction between baby and mother unfolds smoothly, the baby does not learn only about her own emotional state; she is soothed and implicitly begins to learn about reading the emotional states of others, an area of common difficulty for many people with autism. In this context, I began thinking about the seemingly universal appeal of Disney characters and other animated figures for adults and children with autism spectrum disorders.

Applying some of Gergely and Watson's ideas to the hyperbolic facial expressions, "motherese" vocal track, and clearly defined roles of "hero" and "villain" typical of Disney characters, we can begin to understand their attraction for children and adults with autism. Perhaps in order to see the emotional forest in the trees, this population needs even more exaggerated marking. Enter Disney characters, with their huge eyes and facial expressions writ large, accompanying sound effects, musical score, and unmistakable good and bad guys. Could the autistic fascination with Disney be a kind of remedial education in emotion sought out by people who need the mentalizing equivalent of a large-print book? Additionally, could it be that the person with autism needs this amplification at a later point in development after the brain has had a chance to mature, or in an ongoing way?

Once understood, the function or meaning of behavior or tendencies can help us begin to make sense of the autistic person's experience and how her mind works. To be a "good-enough" autism parent or therapist, we need to keep an individual's particular sensory proclivities in mind, and bring that awareness to bear on how we understand behavior and on how we correspondingly modify our response to that behavior. The wider world repeatedly reacts to the unusual behavior of autistic people with looks or voices that seem to say, "What is *wrong* with you?" Remaining mindful of sensory differences and approaching behavior as meaningful, we can respond with sensitivity and, most important, with respect, providing a small counterbalance to the larger world's intolerance.

The trees and the forest

In his 1943 landmark paper, Leo Kanner observed that autistic children possess an "inability to experience wholes without full attention to constituent parts" (pp. 45–46). To my knowledge, this is the first mention of what was later described by Uta Frith (1989) as weak central coherence – that is, the piecemeal way people with autism tend to process their environments. They over-focus on detail and as a result do not consider the big picture. Perhaps the details are perceived with such intensity that they overwhelm the whole. In her moving account of living with autism, Donna Williams (1992) describes it this way: "Anything I took in had to be deciphered. . . . Sometimes people would have to repeat a particular sentence several times for me, as I would hear it *in bits*, and the way . . . my mind had segmented their sentence into words left me with a strange and sometimes unintelligible message" (p. 69, emphasis added).

Peter Vermeulen (2012) has extended Frith's central coherence theory, demonstrating that not only do people with autism spectrum disorders over-focus on the trees at the expense of the forest, but they also do not use the forest to contextualize the trees. He uses the term "context blindness" to refer to a "deficit in the ability to use context spontaneously and subconsciously to determine meanings" (p. 318). Considering Williams' description of hearing things "in bits," it seems that for some people there is no context, or it is so over-dotted with details that it gets lost.

Context guides our interpretation of everything from gesture to facial expression to pronunciation of the written word. We process context unconsciously in fractions of a second, enabling us to solve the problem of ambiguity across our sensory channels (Vermeulen, 2012). For example, the correct pronunciation of the word "bow" differs depending on whether it is used in the context of a gift or a curtain call. Tears may indicate sorrow or joy depending on context. Could context blindness explain why children with autism are not able to generalize social skills from one situation to another? Williams explains, "the significance of what people said to me, when it sank in as more than just words, was always taken to apply *only* to that particular moment or situation" (1992, p. 69, emphasis added). Given the complexity and sheer number of factors that account for what is appropriate to do in which situation, we cannot possibly cover every contingency when we teach a child social skills. If you are not able to spontaneously factor in all of these variables, if you do not select the right ones as important and screen others out, it becomes impossible to grasp the "big picture," let alone to parse each particular social situation.

Recently, I visited my daughter at her home in a community for adults with disabilities. I was loaded down with bags and boxes coming from the car. My daughter and a friend happily greeted me, standing right in the middle of the doorway. They began talking excitedly about where we should go for lunch, not picking up on my need for them to move out of the way, hold open the door, and relieve me of a bag or two. Before I had a chance to ask for help, my daughter gasped, "Mom! Your toenail polish is chipping! Mom! Your toenail polish is chipping!" This detail seized my daughter's attention, and she was unable ignore it, even temporarily, to prioritize the more socially salient information.

This example raises the question of what role sensory sensitivities play in context blindness. If the small details of a sensory field are perceived with overpowering intensity, might they crowd out the whole? Does the chipped nail polish jump out at my daughter and claim her attention so loudly that the big picture is lost? Keeping this possibility in mind, along with its fallout of confusion, embarrassment, anxiety, and even sensory pain, we can begin to imagine what effect all of this has on a person's internal world, the ultimate context of our subjective experience. If perceptions register in bits, or certain small details eclipse others at the expense of the big picture, or sensory input is experienced so intensely as to be disorganizing, how can you build stable and coherent representations of the world, yourself, or others? Coming full circle, could this fragmented and fragmenting internal experience then play a causal role in some of autism's other characteristics? At the very least, it seems likely that sensory processing problems and their consequences contribute to perpetuating social and communication impairments and rigidities.

Transitional experience

Imitation is a normal part of language learning. For children with autism, echolalia, the echoing of speech, often persists beyond what is developmentally expected and becomes a communication device. It seems to me that children with autism also engage in a kind of "action echolalia" – that is, the rote reenactment of scripted play. Perhaps the echolalias derive in part from the way idiosyncratic sensory processing interferes with the child's ability to symbolize and communicate his experience. Parents who believe their child has something to communicate help her to do so by decoding her preoccupations and special interests. As Sapountzis so eloquently says, "a parent's readiness to locate the transitional in the seemingly obsessive, the potentially unfolding in the seemingly rigid, [these are] important acts of containment" (2015, personal communication).

In the same way that autistic children memorize scraps and chunks of dialogue from favorite TV shows, repeating these scripts later in other contexts with surprising alacrity and aptness, the repetitive playing out of a sequence of action from a TV show, for example, can serve a similar purpose. The child whose internal world is chaotic owing to sensory dysfunction may not be able to spontaneously come up with an appropriate symbolic play sequence to capture her experience (for example, playing house), but perhaps she can recognize it when she sees it and recruit it to communicate for her. This strategy may be a kind of parallel to the classic example of the autistic child's taking his parent's hand and using it as if it were his own. This seems to have been the case with journalist Ron Suskind's son Owen. Owen's development was typical before the age of three, when he "fell silent . . . cried, inconsolably. Didn't sleep. Wouldn't make eye contact" (Suskind, 2014, p. 1). Owen began to obsessively watch and imitate the part of the Disney movie *Little Mermaid* in which the mermaid trades her voice to Ursula the sea witch. Unable to generate the language to communicate the loss of his own expressive abilities, Owen recognized his dilemma in Ariel and returned over and over again to this part of the movie – a kind of borrowed symbolic function.

I will never forget a vivid example of this behavior by my own daughter. As I mentioned earlier, she has never been able to master tasks such as tying shoes or swiping a metro card. Both actions require a combination of motor planning, timing, kinesthetic awareness and muscle coordination. In her pioneering book *Sensory Integration and the Child*, Ayres (1979) describes how some children with profound disturbances in vestibular, proprioceptive, and kinesthetic processing can feel gravitationally insecure. This helps explain why the only time my daughter's face relaxed when she was a young child was when she was in a swimming pool; why, when she was a baby, unless she was asleep, the only way I could put her down was in a wind-up swing. She needed to be nursed, held, swung, or buoyed by the gravity-free embrace of water to feel regulated and secure on the planet. It is no wonder then that being a physical self in the world was, to say the least, not fun.

The first time she went to occupational therapy and swung in a hammock that she could propel by herself, she called out to me, absolutely beaming: "Mama! It's fun to have fun but you have to know how!" This phrase, lifted straight out of Dr. Seuss, exquisitely captured her delight in discovering "fun" for the first time in her own, autonomous physicality. Previously, she had not "known how." Now, with the help of the hammock, her vestibular system was getting the input it needed in order for her to feel grounded and regulated enough to have fun. I think of this kind of verbal echolalia, as well as what I call action echolalia – that is, a play sequence borrowed from another source and made into something of the child's own – as a kind of transitional experience, an in-between phenomenon that is not completely "of" the child but that also no longer belongs purely to its originator. In Winnicott's (1965c) words, it seems clear that my daughter did not just find this representation of her experience "lying around waiting to be found" (p. 181). Rather, she needed it, found it, and yet also created it. Her phrase was at one and the same time a representation of something internal and something external (Winnicott, 1971b). In the same way that the child's blanket cannot acquire the properties of a transitional object without the mother's facilitating gaze, the child's echolalic expression cannot function communicatively without the parent's recognition and appreciation of the child's creative impulse.

Summarizing thoughts

Individuals on the autism spectrum have a tremendous amount to offer this world and yet they struggle mightily. No doubt, we could look at these struggles through any number of lenses. In this chapter, I have focused on the important role I believe perceptual processing idiosyncrasies play in the autistic experience. The enormous anxiety suffered by many on the spectrum is likely occasioned by sensory dysfunction. The resulting state of inner discord affects the development of emotional life and every aspect of functioning.

Sensory sensitivities, hypo-sensitivities, and the resulting experiences of distraction, assault, and anxiety set several complications in motion: they impede automatic consideration of context and lead to particular ways of experiencing, fending off, and attending to perceptions. As a result, it would stand to reason that representations of the self, others, and the world would be similarly atypical. Internal representations shaped by autistic experience are then brought to bear on expectations and subsequent interaction in the external world, likely further distorting or limiting that same experience and how it is understood and re-internalized. This will influence the individual's ongoing self-experience, as well as her social, communicative, cognitive, and self-regulatory functions.

Many psychoanalysts working with people on the spectrum (such as Drucker, 2009; Hobson, 2011; Shapiro, 2000; Volkmar, 2000) wisely call for thoughtful caution when applying psychodynamic principles to our work with this population. The frequently enigmatic nature of people with autism can tempt us to over-reach with psychoanalytic theories or flights of fancy. For a variety of reasons, but perhaps largely because of the challenges we neuro-typicals face in making meaning of an autistic person's feelings or conduct, and because of our own counter-transference reactions to what we see as their odd behavior (Sapountzis, 2014), the field has largely resorted to a focus on skill building and behavior change.

Yet autistic adults and children are first and foremost human beings. For them, as for all of us, interacting and building relationships with others who offer under-standing and connection is fundamental to well-being. No matter where along the spectrum a person lies, I have found that keeping in mind her sensory processing differences is crucial. It takes the oddness out of her behavior and enables me to build hypotheses about the shape and texture of her inner experience. It helps me to try to understand how that inner world might influence or interfere with func-tioning in the physical and relational worlds in a more typical way.

As parents, therapists and teachers, we need to pay close attention to our own experiences when interacting with someone with autism. Do we become con-fused? Anxious? Overwhelmed? Consideration of these countertransference reac-tions may provide us the best available window into their experience.

In the same way that a deaf person's voice gives us a good approximation of what speech sounds like to him, the autistic person's manner of relating is likely an illustration of what she experiences. For example, poor modulation of speech (e.g., volume, prosody, and quantity), difficulty gauging another's personal space, or imposition onto others of compulsions and anxieties can lead those others to feel controlled, overstimulated, or besieged. That self-same feeling may be a good representation of what it feels like for someone with autism to simply *be* in the world all of the time. Recognizing that our own perceptual experiences are not necessarily comparable to those of our child highlights the challenge to our abili-ties to empathize and mentalize – something we must keep in mind if we are to truly appreciate, understand, and be effective with people with autism. It says we are thinking of them, and it makes them feel better.

References

Adler, B. (2006). No! You don't understand! In C. Ariel & R. Naseef (Eds.), *Voices from the spectrum*. London: Jessica Kingsley.

Ayres, A. J. (1979). *Sensory integration and the child*. Torrance, CA: Western Psychologi-cal Services.

Baron-Cohen, S. (1985). Does the autistic child have a "theory of mind"? *Cognition, 21*, 37–46.

Baron-Cohen, S. (1997). *Mindblindness: An essay on autism and theory of mind*. Cam-bridge, MA: MIT Press.

Carter, A., Ornstein Davis, N., Klin, A., & Volkmar, F. (2005). Social development in autism. In F. Volkmar, R. Paul, A. Klin, & D. Cohen (Eds.), *Handbook of autism and pervasive developmental disorders* (Vol. 1). Hoboken, NJ: John Wiley & Sons.

Crane, L., Goddard, L., & Pring, L. (2009). Sensory processing in adults with autism spectrum disorders. *Autism, 13,* 215–228.

Drucker, J. (2009). When, why and how: Does psychodynamic psychotherapy have a place on the spectrum? *Journal of Infant, Child, and Adolescent Psychotherapy* (special issue on autistic spectrum disorders: current psychodynamic approaches), *8,* 32–39.

Fonagy, P., Gergely, G., Jurist, E., & Target, M. (2005). *Affect regulation, mentalization, and the development of the self.* New York: Other Press.

Fonagy, P., & Target, M. (2002). Early intervention and the development of self-regulation. *Psychoanalytic Inquiry, 22,* 307–335.

Frith, U. (1989). *Autism: Explaining the enigma.* Cambridge, MA: Blackwell Publishers.

Gergely, G., & Watson, J. S. (1996). The social biofeedback theory of parental affect-mirroring: The development of emotional self-awareness and self-control in infancy. *International Journal of Psycho-Analysis, 77,* 1181–1212.

Happé, F. (1994). An advanced test of theory of mind: Understanding of story characters' thoughts and feelings by able autistic, mentally handicapped, and normal children and adults. *Journal of Autism and Developmental Disorders, 24,* 129–154.

Higashida, N. (2013). *The reason I jump: The inner voice of a thirteen-year-old boy with autism.* New York: Random House.

Hobson, R. P. (2011). On the relations between autism and psychoanalytic thought and practice. *Psychoanalytic Psychology, 25,* 229–244.

Kanner, L. (1943). Autistic disturbances of affective contact. *Nervous Child, 2,* 217–250.

Leekam, S., Nieto, C., Libby, S., Wing, L., & Gould, J. (2007). Autism and sensory sensitivities. *Journal of Autism and Developmental Disabilities, 37,* 894–910.

Sapountzis, I. (2014). Sharing alien states and experiences through dreams: Working with adolescents on the autism spectrum. *Journal of Infant, Child, and Adolescent Psychotherapy, 13,* 98–107.

Sapountzis, I. (2015). *Personal communication.*

Shapiro, T. (2000). Autism and the psychoanalyst. *Psychoanalytic Inquiry, 20,* 648–659.

Shore, S. (2003). *Beyond the wall: Personal experiences with Autism and Asperger syndrome.* Lenexa, KS: Autism Asperger Publishing Co.

Simone, R. (2010). *Aspergirls.* London: Jessica Kingsley.

Slade, A. (2009). Mentalizing the unmentalizable: Parenting children on the spectrum. *Journal of Infant, Child, and Adolescent Psychotherapy* (special issue on autistic spectrum disorders: Current psychodynamic approaches), *8,* 7–21.

Suskind, R. (2014, March 7). Reaching my autistic son through Disney. *New York Times Magazine.*

Vermeulen, P. (2012). *Autism as context blindness.* Lenexa, KS: Autism Asperger Publishing Co.

Volkmar, F. (2000). Understanding autism: Implications for psychoanalysis. *Psychoanalytic Inquiry, 20,* 660–674.

Willey, L. H. (1999). *Pretending to be normal: Living with Asperger's Syndrome.* London: Jessica Kingsley.

Williams, D. (1992). *Nobody nowhere.* New York: Random House.

Winnicott, D. W. (1965a). On the contribution of direct child observation to psycho-analysis. In *The maturational processes and the facilitating environment.* New York: International Universities Press. (Original work published 1960)

Winnicott, D. W. (1965b). Ego distortion in terms of true and false self. In *The maturational processes and the facilitating environment.* New York: International Universities Press. (Original work published 1960)

Winnicott, D. W. (1965c). Communicating and not communicating leading to a study of certain opposites. In *The maturational processes and the facilitating environment*. New York: International Universities Press. (Original work published 1963).

Winnicott, D. W. (1971a). Mirror role of mother and family in child development. In *Playing and reality*. London: Tavistock.

Winnicott, D. W. (1971b). Transitional objects and transitional phenomena. In *Playing and reality*. London: Tavistock.

5

Mastering the fear of life-threatening food allergies

Matt's story

Lizbeth A. Moses

The story of our son Matt's food allergies began when he was only 11 months old. We were having dinner at the house of old friends. Matt was chewing on a packaged hazelnut cookie. He was enjoying the cookie, but then he started to scratch and cry. Hives appeared all over his body. Fairly new to parenting and knowing nothing of food allergies, we didn't understand what was taking place. So we did the logical thing and put him in a tepid bath and tried to distract him from his discomfort by playing soothing lullabies on a tape player. We also gave him a teaspoon of Benadryl to calm down the hives.

Since his physical reaction had come on so suddenly, we made an appointment the next day with a pediatric allergist. Matt was given a series of skin tests that revealed significant food allergies. We then went to see a leading specialist at Johns Hopkins Medical Center. Our drive to Baltimore would become an annual pilgrimage. The doctor taught us the many things we would need to do to keep Matt safe – at home, in schools and restaurants, and really anywhere he might go. At that moment our family life changed dramatically. We no longer occupied the safe bubble in which we could trust that our child will be fine.

By the time Matt graduated from high school, his life-threatening food allergies had landed him in the emergency room a handful of times. In spite of constantly asking questions about food presented to him or being clear with peers and adults about the severity of his allergies, he remained vulnerable to accidents – a sushi roll glued together with hidden peanut butter, a friend's foreign housekeeper who served him a bowl of Pralines 'n Cream instead of the Cookies 'n Cream he had requested, and so on. Every event was terrifying. Still, over the years Matt learned how to live well with his disability, and he grew into a sensitive and confident young man.

As Matt was getting ready to go off to college, there was one lingering question in his mind (and ours) about whether he would be fully able to manage his food allergies on his own. His doubt centered on the fact that in all his bouts of anaphylaxis, he had never been able to inject himself with epinephrine. Not when his mouth began to tingle, not when his pulse quickened, and not when his trachea locked down and he couldn't breathe. In short, he couldn't bring himself to do what he needed to do because the needle, the injection process, and his memories of past mishaps were just too scary.

Throughout his adolescence Matt had carried around in his pants pocket a classic EpiPen. A couple of years ago a more user-friendly product called Auvi-Q came on the market. When you remove its plastic cap, a calm robotic voice talks you through four steps of injecting the medicine. But even with this less intimidating device, Matt still couldn't bring himself to use it, preferring to go to the ER to let the doctors urgently administer epinephrine via an IV drip. So the big question lingered. And lurking underneath that question was the doctor's message: "Without epinephrine, your body can shut down and you can die." Matt knew that so many times he had been lucky to get to the ER quickly enough without that self-administered shot of epinephrine. But he also knew that his luck could run out if he didn't overcome his fear.

So it was on a beautiful, cool, end-of-the-summer Midwestern Thursday night that we dropped off Matt at Macalester College in St. Paul, Minnesota. By the time we got the car unloaded, it was 11:00 p.m. and none of us had eaten dinner. So my husband David and I went down the street to a popular organic restaurant. Matt stayed behind to unpack with his roommate with the understanding that we would bring his dinner back to the dorm. We had a pleasant dinner. Our waiter was sympathetic about our emotional passage, the dropping of our youngest child at college.

At the end of our meal we ordered Matt a takeout sandwich. We did our usual checklist: No nuts, right? No peanuts, no tree nuts, no shellfish, no sesame, nothing bad even in the barbecue sauce, and no cross-contamination of allergens in the kitchen? Right, right, right? With understanding and reassurance, the waiter put in an order for a pulled-pork sandwich. We also wanted to do something nice for Matt's new roommate, who had already eaten dinner. So we decided to get him a dessert. David walked over to the bakery case and said to the waiter: "How about this 'brown-rice crispy treat'? Does it have any nuts in it?" You see, families like ours must be careful even about the foods other people eat in Matt's presence. Again, the waiter said, "No," explaining that he was very familiar with nut allergies in the Macalester student population. He insisted that we get one of the delicious bars for Matt also; so he threw two in the bag. "They're on the house," he generously proclaimed.

We dropped off the sack of food and watched Matt go off with his dorm mates. We drove to our hotel in downtown St. Paul, full of the pride and sorrow that any parent facing the emptying of their nest experiences. Before we went to bed, we received a text from Matt. "Great night, Mom and Dad," he wrote. "Everybody is so welcoming and friendly. Even though it's a little overwhelming, it's just what I was hoping for at school." With relief, we could already envision a happy farewell at Matt's eighteenth-birthday breakfast that we all had planned for the following Monday before we headed to the airport for our flight home.

The next morning Matt got a head start on his new-student orientation. He received two special guided tours related to his allergies. First, the head chef of the campus cafeteria took him to every food station in the dining hall and told him what to watch out for. Then the chef took Matt to a special station just for diners with food allergies. Next, Matt went to the student health center and got a tour of the facility by the head doctor. The doctor welcomed Matt and assured him that they would care for him well. Then, very seriously, she said, "But, Matt, you need to understand clearly our protocol if any emergency with your allergies arises." She continued: "If something happens on a weekday, then come right here immediately. But if it's after our 4:45 p.m. closing time on a weekday or any time on a weekend, you must do the following: one, give yourself the epinephrine shot; two, call 911 for an ambulance; and three, tell a friend or dorm mate what's going on so they can help you and inform other people."

When we saw Matt that night after our own parent orientation, Matt proudly told us about the two special tours. We were elated by his initiative, his competence, and his sense of security from day one of his new college life.

When we got back to our hotel, we were emotionally and physically exhausted. I promptly conked out about 11:00. David stayed up a while longer, texting Matt about how the Nationals' bullpen blew another late-inning lead. He then did something uncharacteristic: he turned the ringers on our cell phones to vibrate, thinking he was gifting me the deep sleep that was much needed under our momentous circumstances.

Sometime later David anxiously awoke in the darkness. He hoped that it would be close to dawn, knowing that he would have trouble going back to sleep in the strange hotel room. He got up, went to the bathroom, and on his way back to bed checked his phone on the desk for the time. He saw that it was only 3:40 a.m. Then he noticed four missed calls (the loud air conditioner fan must have drowned out the vibrating phones) and two text messages. All the communications were from Matt.

The first text came at 11:50 p.m., just a half hour after David and Matt had been texting baseball. It read: "In an ambulance headed to United Hospital. The bar you gave me was straight peanut butter." David screamed and I woke up immediately. He told me about the text. In our shock, we cursed in disbelief. Then David read the second text, which had arrived just 10 minutes before he had gotten up in the dark. "I'm on my way back to school," Matt wrote.

Relieved by the follow-up message but still shaken up, we collected our thoughts and pieced the story together. We figured that Matt must not have eaten the dessert bar on the Thursday-night dorm drop-off but instead ate it for a midnight snack on Friday night. And, we concluded, the bar wasn't brown because of brown rice – but because it was bound not by marshmallow as vouched by the waiter but rather by "straight" peanut butter as confirmed by Matt.

We called Matt, who was already back in bed in his dorm room. He answered in a whisper, not wanting to disturb his sleeping roommate. He said curtly, "I'm fine, and I want to go to sleep." Even in the whisper his anger was loud and his sense of betrayal palpable.

We tried but couldn't get back to sleep. So we got dressed and drove at dawn to the emergency room where the ambulance had taken Matt. Ironically, the hospital was just a few blocks from our hotel. A nurse reassured us that Matt was treated and then released. She said that a dean from school had come to take Matt back to campus at 3:30 in the morning. We were amazed by the conscientiousness of the school and grateful that Matt wasn't entirely alone in his ordeal.

We didn't want to rouse Matt from his much-needed sleep. So we didn't see him until late on that Saturday morning, encountering him in the central quad. Matt was still very angry. He repeated that he was tired but fine. He then said that he had "followed the protocol," but provided no detail. Finally, he announced: "And I can take care of myself better than you can take care of me. So I want to say our goodbye this afternoon."

As Matt insisted, we all met later that afternoon for the moved-up farewell. We drove our rental car up to the curb at his dorm so that we could bring up the supplies we had bought for him at the local Target. We also needed to fetch some of his empty luggage. Matt sensed that we wanted to go upstairs to see his unpacked room, but he said that he could carry everything himself. His defiant independence was breaking our hearts, but our empathy for what we knew he was feeling helped get us through. Finally, Matt relented a bit. He said, "OK, Mom, you can come up, but, Dad, you wait in the car." He was especially angry with David for having selected the rice-crispy treat.

David sat in the car, wondering how Thursday night's euphoria had so quickly evaporated. Neither the storybook birthday-party ending nor the choreographed parting that we had so carefully planned would occur. A while later I emerged from the lobby doors. David noticed that I had a smirk on my face, which he thought was odd given the tense circumstances and shed tears. When I got back into the car, David asked, "Why are you smiling?" Silently, I handed over the Auvi-Q that Matt had insisted I take home. "Open it," I said. David uncapped the epinephrine dispenser. The calm recorded voice said, "This device has been used and should be taken to your physician for proper disposal and a prescription refill."

Two days shy of his eighteenth birthday, Matt had conquered his fear. We had all grown up.

6

Parenting my disabled sister

Devra Adelstein

In the first moments of my little sister's life, the doctor told my mother that her new baby hadn't received adequate oxygen during the delivery. The significance of this for her development would remain unclear until she reached school age. To the best of my knowledge, my mother tried to withhold this news from my father in hopes that my sister would not be significantly impaired. Vigilant for signs of delay, my mother worried as my sister's developmental milestones lagged behind mine. By the time she was six, and failing first grade, Lori was diagnosed with educable mental retardation (EMR). This term was used to describe a moderate level of retardation: individuals with this condition reached a mental age of somewhere between eight and twelve years and could learn at about a fifth-grade level.

Parents of cognitively impaired children must balance reality, grief, and disappointment over what will never be, and determination to never give up the fight, while they raise their child to become maximally self-reliant. My parents were unclear as to my sister's potential and how to plan for her future and they assumed time was on their side.

When our parents' premature deaths catapulted me into the role of substitute parent, I had to continue the work they had only begun and support my sister's move across the threshold toward greater independence.

This chapter explores the significance of growing up in a family with a disabled child whose developmental course and path toward self-reliance was unclear. A shock to our family system, my sister's handicap challenged our coping mechanisms and held sway over our daily lives.

For my sister and me, the ordinariness of sibling rivalry was made extraordinary on an uneven playing field. The rivalry of an older sister who wasn't allowed to shine as brightly as she might have for fear of outshining, and a younger sister who could never shine brightly enough, combined to interfere with pleasure in growing up. As adults, Lori and I had to consider years of misunderstanding and our feelings for and about each other. Our developmental tasks were challenged and changed, highlighting the ways that we were more alike than different.

I can still picture myself at five, before Lori was born, climbing onto my new bicycle with block pedals to help me reach. The first time I rode without training wheels, my father walked behind me, lightly holding the bike upright while my mother cheered us on as if it was the most spectacular thing she'd ever seen. Most evenings found us on the couch reading together. My father claimed I could read at four, though I'm guessing I had memorized the countless stories and poems they'd read to me. We lived in an apartment complex surrounded by my grandparents, and other close family. Barbeques, walks to the nearby park, afternoons of sledding, or hitting golf balls on the lawn were standard fare.

This delight faded as my sister's birth drew near. I detected I was an outsider in my parent's relationship and worried their plans for a new baby meant that I wasn't good enough for them. One gloomy winter afternoon, they announced we would soon move from our comfortable apartment with family all around to a new house in an unfamiliar neighborhood. I'm told I was inconsolable. "We need room for the new baby," they said, hoping the facts would help with the feelings.

As an only child for over five years, and my mother's constant companion, I studied her moods and behavior. I noticed a shift during her pregnancy and again after my sister's birth. Everything felt different. Certain that something was wrong, I clung to my mother even more tightly. I blamed myself for her irritability and my parents' frequent arguments and concluded there must be something about me that displeased them.

While eager to be a big sister and have a playmate, I was unprepared for the intensity of my rage when the new baby captured my parents' attention and depleted their energy. They didn't understand my inability to adjust and I didn't understand their laughter when quoting my desperate protests, "I hate her. Make her go away!"

As is always true, parents' backgrounds and individual histories influence their parental role. What is most relevant for this story is my father's immigrant status. In 1920 my grandparents, their infant son in tow, fled the Russian pogroms for South America. With his father's death, my father, just sixteen years old, became the head of his family. As a young adult, he left his home in Argentina for upstate New York, where he worked for his uncle, a tailor. As an immigrant, my father felt inadequate, and struggled to present himself as a dignified, successful man. He ultimately sent for his mother and siblings before settling down to marry my mother.

My mother, an only child, was a close companion of her doting parents. My grandparents, immigrants themselves, felt my immigrant father was "not good enough" for their daughter and didn't hide their disdain for him. They shunned my father's mother, who was poor and spoke little English. Despite their wealth, my mother's parents refused to lend my father money and to support his ambition to open his own business. The tension resulted in their move from an apartment directly across the street from us, to an apartment across the country. This solution was meant to spare my mother the agony of the daily loyalty conflict between her parents and her husband. Instead, it left my mother and me bereft. It left my father guilty and even more eager to prove himself. While he ultimately opened his own successful business, the rupture between my father and my grandparents never fully healed.

Prior to my sister's birth, life for my parents held the hope of the son my father longed for, or at least two "normal" children. Instead of a highly valued male child, my parents had two daughters, one with a cognitive impairment.

Solnit and Stark (1961) describe the potential deleterious affect of an impaired child on his/her parent:

> The psychological preparation for a new child during pregnancy normally involves the wish for a perfect child and the fear of a damaged child. It is very likely that there is always some discrepancy between the mother's wishes and the actual child; to work out this discrepancy becomes one of the developmental tasks of motherhood that is involved in the establishment of a healthy mother-child relationship. However, when the discrepancy is too great, as in the birth of a defective child, or where the mother's wishes are too unrealistic, a trauma may occur.

The above perspective highlights the trauma that may occur for a mother when she gives birth to a defective child. Seldom addressed in the literature is the effect of such a child's arrival on the emotional development of other family members.

My sister's uncertain developmental potential left my parents confused and unable to plan for her future. In *Far from the Tree*, Andrew Solomon (2012) discusses the importance of clarity with regard to diagnosis. "Unmanaged or uniformed parental expectations are a poison and specific diagnosis of the disabilities any individual has are a huge help" (p. 366).

During her infancy, my sister was cute, seemed happy, and didn't require anything special of my parents. Since my mother had been cautioned that her disabilities might not be evident until school age, I suspect that she was more watchful of all aspects of Lori's development. As her milestones lagged behind mine – she talked later, walked later, rode a bike later – it became increasingly difficult to deny the reality of her delayed development.

With her more noticeable impairment, my parents were deluged with disappointment. My father initially had to face the reality that he would not father a son. In retrospect, I wonder if he felt producing a son and heir would alleviate his feelings of inadequacy and perhaps repair the hole created by the early loss of his own father. He also had to face the fact that my mother had tried to keep my sister's potential disability a secret from him. He blamed my mother for his feelings of anger and loss and she accepted the blame along with her own feelings of grief and disappointment.

My mother carried an additional burden. She had to raise a spirited, temperamental older daughter and a developmentally delayed younger daughter, both of whom challenged her already shaky self-esteem.

My own rivalry grew more perilous in the face of Lori's increasingly apparent fragility. Younger siblings ordinarily grow up into sturdy individuals in their own right, and thereby reassure older siblings that their aggressive wishes haven't wreaked havoc. I couldn't help but connect my sister's weakness and damage with my own aggressive wishes that she would disappear and leave me the better one, the winner. And worse, I had to tolerate the awareness that my sister's needs would likely always take precedence over mine.

When I breezed through first grade, finished my work before the other students, and demonstrated reading comprehension, my teacher suggested that I skip second grade. My parents were so thrilled with my early success, they failed to consider the disadvantages.

Once I'd skipped a grade, I couldn't recall my pride and success from first grade, and could only feel that as a third grader I didn't know as much as everyone else. I remember the first day of third grade, when my teacher instructed us to write a paragraph using our best cursive handwriting – and realizing that cursive, or script as it was called at that time, had been taught in second grade. I had missed it.

What I didn't realize was that my feelings as an inadequate third grader who could never measure up replicated my sister's experience. Our predicaments were similar. We both had to struggle just to be good enough.

The parental task when there is a developmentally delayed child is complicated by the parents' need to help their "normal" children process feelings about the developmentally delayed sibling, as well as to watch for developing difficulties in the "normal" siblings. It is common for parents of cognitively "normal" siblings to inhibit their success. Because I had evidenced success by skipping a grade, my parents must have felt assured that I could allow myself to succeed. They were unaware of the bind I felt; succeed, do well, but don't overshadow.

The following scene from when I was about eleven lingers in my memory. It occurred just as the extent of my sister's disability came to light.

Sitting at my desk, I stare at the blue-lined notebook paper. The desk's glass top covers dark grey fabric with burnt orange flowers. It is my grandmother's dressing table transformed into a desk for me.

Now in fifth grade, I feel pleased to have real homework. Today's assignment is: Write about what you want to be when you grow up. I try to picture myself grown-up but I can't see anything. The tiny clock on my night table signals I have to hurry if I'm going to finish in time to watch my favorite shows, The Mickey Mouse Club, Leave it to Beaver and The Life of Riley.

Hearing my mother's and sister's rising voices from the kitchen, I can't concentrate. There is always tension when my sister has spelling homework. My mother sounds impatient and I hear the rhythmic pounding of the same words I've heard before – "How many times do I have to tell you?" Lori isn't able to learn to read, or sit still and pay attention in school. Her problems no longer go unnoticed. My parents have been told that she needs to be held back or else go to a special school for children who aren't smart.

I wish my mother would stop yelling. I'm glad that at least she's not yelling at me, but I hate when she's mean to my sister. Suddenly, I do have an idea about what I will do when I grow up! I will teach children who have *learning problems. Smiling, I start to write. I only have a couple of sentences down, when I hear my mother coming up the stairs. Arriving at my room at the end of the hall, she pushes the door open, and cocks her head. "How's your homework going?"*

Pleased with my idea, I start to read. "I am not sure what I want to do when I grow up, but I think that I would like to be a teacher. I especially want to work with children who have trouble learning."

My mother looks stunned and angry, as if I've slapped her. Through clenched teeth she says, "That is our business and no one else's. And besides, I won't have you using your sister as a guinea pig." Slamming my door behind her, she stomps back down the stairs.

I feel confused and my face feels hot. Not for the first time, I wish my mother would just die. Tears fall on the writing, and begin to blur the lines. I crumple my paper and throw it in the wastebasket. Now I don't know what I will do when I grow up. I don't want to write my ideas down though. I know that.

On reflection, this incident derailed my clumsy efforts to cope with my dawning awareness of my sister's handicap. I wanted to help, to make it better. Instead, I learned that talking about my sister's difficulties was wrong and made my mother angry. If I wasn't careful, I might cause more damage. My only solution was to retreat, to "pull my punches," and hide if not stifle my accomplishments. I had skipped second grade and my sister was about to repeat first. Just the telling of this story some fifty years later reminds me of my mother's admonition – "Don't use your sister as a guinea pig!" Am I exploiting my sister's handicap, betraying a family private matter? Perhaps my shame over wanting a normal sister and over my sister's failure to live up to my expectations made me feel I didn't deserve to write about it.

Unaware of my parents' feelings about Lori being different, I was keenly aware of my own shameful feelings. She wasn't like any of my friends' younger siblings. It was only with maturity and the shift in my role, from sister to substitute parent then back to sister, that I began to wonder if I had taken on my parents' feelings of shame and disappointment. Had my parents acknowledged their own feelings and grieved the loss of perfection in themselves and both their children, we all might have benefitted.

My sister's disability was finally named when she was in first grade. However arduously my parents tried to make her normal, the move from a standard public school classroom in 1964 to a center for children with special needs made her difficulties impossible to ignore. "Where are your girls in school?" people would ask. "Well, Lori goes to the Foreman Center,'" my mother would say, sometimes adding, "It's a school for kids with perceptual handicaps." The year 1964 saw the beginning of an effort to be politically correct and improve on the term "EMR," or educable mental retardation. On the euphemism treadmill, "mental retardation" would slowly be replaced by "perceptually handicapped" or "learning challenged," and each euphemism would eventually become pejorative as well. Because my sister's diagnosis had been uncertain, my parents likely had to grieve all over again as they learned the reality that she was indeed disabled.

According to Andrew Solomon (2012, p. 367), "One of the goals with a kid with special needs is how to help them reach their potential. So it's helpful to know what their potential actually is." He suggests that once a disability is named, people can begin to deal with it. Even with the diagnosis of EMR, my sister's potential was unclear and my parents were uncertain as to how to plan for her future.

In some ways my parents' task might have been easier if their daughter were severely disabled. My sister was close enough to normal to "pass" for normal, and yet far enough from "normal" that she always felt like she must reach beyond her capacity. My parents' dilemma, like that of all parents of disabled children, was how much to do for her in an effort to push her over the threshold into adulthood and how much to stimulate her to reach her own potential: to separate and become autonomous and experience herself fully with all her strengths and weaknesses. Whichever path they chose had to be done while wanting to shield their children and themselves from the pain involved in exposing vulnerability and disability to the world. I sometimes wonder if it might be easier, kinder even, to shield a child, and disavow any incapacity. Questions about all developmental milestones – including progressing through school, extracurricular activities, religious ceremonies, dating, driving, college goals – all contribute to feelings of shame and the tendency towards secrecy. The challenge for parents is to find the balance between facing the situation with honesty and skirting the truth to spare their child's feelings.

My parents' task was enormous – facing the reality of a future, coming gradually closer, that could not be what they had hoped. The thinking of the time only highlighted the problems they faced. In 1962 Simon Olshansky wrote, "The parents of a mentally defective child have little to look forward to; they will always be burdened by the child's unrelenting demands and unabated dependency." Parents of "normal" children can raise them to be completely independent and look forward to their launch outside the home. This possibility is closed off to some degree to parents of the disabled.

As my sister grew, so did her cognitive challenges and her socially inappropriate behaviors. She would interrupt, ask unrelated questions, and walk away in the middle of a conversation. She begged to do whatever I was doing, whether having a bat mitzvah or taking the bus downtown to shop with friends or having sleepovers. Her entreaties weren't met with the usual, "It will be your turn soon." Rather, my mother would distract, avoid the subject, or when pushed, just say, "You won't be able to do that. End of story." For my sister, each step I took towards young adulthood might be permanently inaccessible to her. I wonder if my mother lacked compassion for Lori's distress because she felt so distressed herself.

What I enjoyed the most was driving. Unlike other milestones, this achievement was not at her expense. I experienced pure freedom just because I had turned sixteen. Sometimes my sister was my passenger, as I carted her to after-school activities, but this was not nearly as fun as having the car to myself. Once, I was in such a hurry to get away to my friends after dropping her off at home, I backed out of the garage with the door open, not realizing she had neglected to close it. The open car door caught on the side of the garage and tore partway off.

My graduation from high school symbolized my move across the threshold to adulthood. Lori's special school did not grant high school equivalency diplomas and provided no available path toward independence. It became unflinchingly clear that one of my parents' children would leave and one would likely stay home.

My parents' ability to balance hope with reality's demands was handicapped. There were no clear plans for Lori's future, as we had no clear knowledge about her capacity for independence. I was in college and dating my future husband, who was a medical student. During his pediatric rotation, he met a developmental specialist who we thought might be able to help. I was eager for my parents to be more vigorous in their efforts to plan for my sister, but worried they'd be angry with me for interfering in their denial.

The waiting room, a pistachio ice-cream green, confined us to one corner with wood-trimmed vinyl chairs. I sat opposite my parents waiting for the doctor. I both hoped and feared the results of his evaluation might shed additional light on the causes of her retardation – birth trauma, genetic abnormality, or an undiagnosed syndrome. And might help us know more about her potential.

Picking at my cuticles, I suddenly felt concerned. Among that list of options, maybe there was another, a secret I had harbored. Don't be ridiculous, I thought. I remember how my father always told the same story – "You were so jealous when your sister was born. You'd sneak into her room at night and punch her, bam, bam, bam and run back to your room." I never liked that story, which forced me to remember my sneaky, jealous feelings. But now, as I recalled that story, it was especially painful. I worried I might have done some real damage.

The evaluation did not expand my parents' or my understanding, though I suppose it did clear my conscience when the doctor confirmed that the most frequent cause of cognitive impairment was indeed a lack of oxygen to the baby's brain during delivery. I also had a secret worry about a genetic abnormality, as I planned to have children, and the evaluation disabused me of the worry that something of my sister's difficulty could be inherited. Despite my criticism of my parents for trying to make Lori "normal," I feared having a child with a cognitive impairment.

At the end of the meeting, the doctor shocked my parents with the suggestion that they might want to have my sister sterilized. It would surely have been better had he suggested that Lori would have her hands full trying to take care of herself, and might therefore have been overwhelmed caring for a child of her own. Because of the shock and distaste in his suggestion, neither my parents or my sister would be able to think through whether Lori might feel freed by a voluntary decision to have her tubes tied. The reality that it would be better for her not to become a mother, juxtaposed with my wish to become a mother and avoid having a child like her, increased the distance between us.

My marriage accented another milestone potentially closed to my sister. My husband David and I planned an informal outdoor wedding and we each chose only one attendant. I chose my sister, and remember feeling proud of her that day, which contrasted with my more usual shameful feelings. At sixteen, she walked carefully down the aisle ahead of me. I still don't know how she felt about my getting married, whether she longed to marry one day, or even thought about it as a possibility. We never talked directly about our feelings, wishes, or dreams.

When Lori neared graduation age, my parents faced a crossroads. In our family, college had been an unwavering destination, but Lori lacked a high school diploma. I'd graduated from the NYU School of Social Work and in one of the school newsletters, my parents learned of a two-year program wherein young adults with "learning disabilities" could become childcare workers. My parents found this the perfect solution. It was essentially a college program that my sister might be able to attend without a high school diploma. The problem was, my sister did not technically have a "learning disability" – which for NYU's purposes meant a normal IQ with a difficulty such as dyslexia, or difficulty processing numbers. My sister's IQ sat resolute, below 70, in the EMR range.

Lori was accepted provisionally into NYU's program. The acceptance letter stated, "While she does not technically fit the criteria of learning disabled as laid out by the directors of our program, we would be glad to accept her and watch carefully to see if she progresses through the program's milestones." At that time, I worked as a school social worker at a local social service agency in Cleveland, where we had moved for David's medical residency.

Five months before Lori was to begin her program, on a wintry March afternoon, my phone rang. I answered it in the bedroom of our Cleveland apartment. It was a long distance call from Mexico City where my parents were vacationing. My father's voice sounded brave. "Your mother had a seizure this afternoon. The hotel doctor just left. They think the altitude caused it. We're going on to Acapulco tomorrow for a few days' rest. We wanted you to know."

I imagine that most people, after receiving such a call, would have immediately called a sibling. My sister was at home with my grandmother, and they weren't to know about my mother's seizure. My father felt it would upset them too much. This was not the first secret I kept.

Perched on the edge of my bed, I studied the Merck manual. In those pre-Google days, few options existed. I discovered that the differential diagnosis for grand mal seizures did not include altitude. Several months later, while at home, my mother experienced a second seizure. The preliminary diagnosis suggested a TIA or small stroke caused both seizures. A CAT scan, several days later, indicated a brain tumor and the doctor scheduled my mother for exploratory brain surgery. I drove 200 miles to be with my father, grandmother, and sister during my mother's surgery. After several hours, the surgeon emerged through double doors. He came toward us and removed his surgical cap letting it dangle from his hand. We leaned in to hear his quiet words. "We found a tumor, but it is the kind that is so advanced and wrapped around different structures in the brain that we had to leave it alone. It's called a glioblastoma and unfortunately, most people don't live beyond eighteen months from diagnosis."

I've tried unsuccessfully to remember the blur of spring and summer events that followed. As best I can recall, we tried to steady ourselves against the storm of my mother's deteriorating function. In the fall, I accompanied my parents and my sister to New York City to help my sister start her NYU program. We toured the dorm and classroom with other families. This time, my sister's difficulties needed no explanation, though I noticed she seemed more developmentally delayed than the other students. My mother's tumor had progressed. She perseverated, and her right-sided weakness required a constant companion. Now her needs took precedence over my sister's. My mother lived almost eighteen months after her diagnosis and died expectedly yet shockingly on an October morning. I was so wrapped up in my own grief and dismay, at 26, it didn't immediately occur to me that my sister was only 21.

While our family confronted my mother's diagnosis, my father had ignored his worsening abdominal pain, as if my mother's illness was a protection against more trouble. In the summer before the end of my mother's life, he was diagnosed with colon cancer. As with my mother's diagnosis, initially things looked hopeful. But repeat studies of the scans suggested a dismal prognosis.

Following my mother's death, my father had periods of health and was able to look after my sister. They traveled together, even attending the winter Olympics in Sarajevo. Lori had finished the program at NYU but, deeply affected by the loss of our mother, made little progress towards independence. She recalls my father as moody and difficult. I still lived out of town and continued to work while monitoring things from afar.

With the growing awareness that my father didn't have long to live, I suggested we investigate living arrangements for Lori. My father could barely tolerate my ideas but agreed to look at group homes. When we finished touring the first one, he curled his lip, and turned to face me. "This won't do," he said. "I don't like the neighborhood and she's higher functioning than the other people in those places." I wasn't sure he was right, but as often happened when faced with my parents' denial, I sank into a pool of despair. I hated my own cynical thought that we'd have to wait until he died to do right by my sister.

My father was secretive about the fact that he'd prepared for Lori financially, setting up a trust, big enough to last her throughout her life. "You think you know everything," he charged, unwilling to share any details. "Your sister will be all set. She'll never have to worry about anything." My father almost always insisted that we have the best, but finding a proper institutional setting was beyond the scope of his understanding. While he was stubborn with regard to options for my sister, and continued to be disappointed that she wasn't "normal," this didn't say the smallest bit about the depth of his caring for her. And, while he acknowledged that there would be money, he refused to give me the details that I'd need to prepare myself to become her guardian. As I reflect on this, I realize I was faced with the same dilemma as my mother: how to deal with Lori and plan for her future, while allowing for my father's denial. As my father's condition deteriorated and he needed frequent hospitalizations, he relented and allowed Lori to move into an apartment with another young woman.

My father was not ready to die. He had started dating soon after my mother's death. Having grown his typewriter business into a computer store, he was about to be awarded the Apple computer dealership in upstate New York. Perhaps most important to him was the anticipation of the birth of my first child, his first grandchild, a boy. When Jonathan was two months old, we drove the four hours to introduce my father and my sister to him, as my father was too ill to travel. He was also too weak to stand up, but reached out, tears streaming down his face, to take his infant grandson. The picture in my mind, is of my son, with fading forceps marks on either side of his head, and my father with red triangles on either side of his head, targeting the radiation he was getting for brain metastases.

My father died a week later, approximately six years after we'd lost my mother. At the time of his death, shortly after Labor Day in 1984, Lori was living in an apartment with a young woman, also cognitively impaired. The girls had trouble getting along, and we needed to find a different arrangement. My sister, now 27, had picked up the same communicable opinions that my parents had, that there'd be no assisted living or group home for her.

As I write this story, I realize how little I knew about my sister before my parents' deaths. For the first forty or more years after her birth, I carefully guarded the description of my sister, and because that was so hard to do, I'd barely spoken of her. A college friend once told me, "I don't think I knew you had a sister until we were sophomores." I remember my reaction – What kind of sister pretends her little sister doesn't exist?

For years after my parents died, I resented them and Lori for dumping the responsibility for her life onto me. I took care of financial tasks but had as little to do with her as I could, farming out much of the work to a case manager. I didn't like the person I was but had two small children, and didn't really make room in my life for Lori. If only they had allowed her to settle into a group home, or helped her to accept herself, handicap and all, my life would be so much easier. When I discussed it with friends, I'd receive supportive responses. "Your parents really saddled you with a lot," they'd say. Or, "Who could blame you for feeling resentful?" But deep down I felt terrible and wished I could be a better sister. The hated case manager once suggested I "try to be a loving compassionate sister." While I knew she was right, I couldn't tolerate her saying it. Within time, after firing her, and finding a more understanding case manager, I was able to take the original advice.

My sister and I each handled our grief over the loss of our parents in different ways. I didn't want to dwell on it, or even talk about it. She was full of emotion, crying easily at the mention, especially, of our mother. "I miss Mommy," she'd wail as if she had just learned of the death. Her reaction irritated me, as I was trying to push away my own constant sadness. I wished so much that my mother could be present to help me become a new mother. As I became more aware of the depth of my own sadness and grief, I became more patient with my sister. But until then, her need to express feelings verbally and my wish to silence her was another turn of the tables. Instead of my mother silencing me, I was silencing Lori.

One morning while writing this chapter, I called Lori, reluctant to say that I was writing a book chapter on the two of us, but eager for information. Telling a partial truth, not wanting her to know I was writing about her, I said, "The anniversary of dad's death was on September sixth and I was thinking about how things were when he died. Remind me where you were living." With a questioning tone, as if wondering why the heck I was really asking her these questions now, she started to talk. It was always as if there were right or wrong answers to my questions. She and I both assumed I knew best. I remember being bossy and acting like a "know-it-all," perhaps to cover over all I didn't know. Lately as my wish to know and understand is more genuine, she seems less dubious about my motivation.

If I squint, I imagine I can see the small apartment where she first lived with a schoolmate whose parents were attempting to get their daughter launched. A day program leader who was teaching daily living skills had suggested the two girls share an apartment. "I think she knew that dad was dying," Lori said, "and she thought I should be living on my own before he died." I am relieved to remember that other people had been looking out for my sister. Before my parents died, I felt little gratitude, only anger at them for leaving me with the responsibility of figuring out how my sister would become an adult. I try to remind myself that my burden was intense. My husband and I had just become actual parents – our son was two months old when my father died. The inconvenient truth of becoming my sister's substitute parent, while mothering an infant and grieving my father, was indeed daunting.

While alive, my parents functioned as an outboard motor, a kind of external energy source for my sister, whereby they carried her above and beyond her developmental capacity. Whereas she had always had to push herself ahead by relying on them, now she was devastated by their loss and unprepared to depend on herself. While my parents were alive, I felt that I had to succeed, yet hold myself back, so as not to wound my sister's already damaged self-esteem. With their loss, I now had to push myself beyond my developmental capacity in order to help her. Suddenly, I was in the same boat as my sister – my tasks surpassed my developmental capacity. I became the surrogate parent of an adult child, after just having had my first baby. My task was to go from a place in which I had to hold myself back to a place where I had to push myself forward. My parents' deaths had leveled the playing field.

While I felt somewhat prepared to become a parent to an infant, I was completely ill equipped to parent a 21-year-old developmentally delayed adult. I had collected internal criticisms of my parent's ways of parenting my sister, and me for that matter. But I had no idea what it had really been like for them to parent my sister. My parents and I hadn't had enough time together as adults for me to ask about their feelings and experiences of raising Lori.

It had been easier for me to sit in judgment of my parents than it was for me to become a substitute parent and to guide my sister through her early adulthood toward a satisfying life of her own. This task required fortitude and I felt like a resentful coward. I was uncomfortable stepping into my parents' shoes and too guilty and responsible not to. My father was right – it helped immensely that my sister didn't have to worry about money. However fortunate it was that he had left money for her, the trust raised new issues. As trustee, I had power over how the money was spent. I could decide what she could and couldn't have and this power wasn't good for our already lopsided relationship. Whenever I called her to ask a question, she assumed I was criticizing her and heard everything I said through the lens of my mother's yelling. It was as if I was the impatient mother now. It reminded me of my mother trying to help my sister with the homework that was too difficult for her, or yelling at me for bringing the secret of my sister's handicap out into the open.

Soon after I became a substitute parent, it became clear that I needed help with helping my sister. While we considered having her move to be near me, I dreaded this option and fortunately she did too. She was happy living in the town where she grew up, and wanted to stay. We were directed to a social worker who specialized in helping handicapped adults. She was critical of my sister and of me, often telling me how to talk to my sister. I assumed I couldn't talk to Lori about her, but this led both of us to feel more isolated. One day on the phone, Lori started complaining about how Margaret talked to her. "She thinks I'm a baby," she said, "and that I don't know anything." "I don't really like her either," I said. "Why don't we see if we can find someone else to help?" Lori and I both found relief when we could agree about important issues.

In her mid-twenties, Lori met a young man. This relationship helped with her loneliness and ongoing grief. I wondered how my parents would have felt about him. Though he was cognitively impaired, his strengths and weaknesses were different from my sister's. He was more socially comfortable than Lori. Whereas she couldn't carry on a conversation, asking others about themselves and talking about subjects of mutual interest, he could. I wondered if, ironically, my parents would have felt he wasn't good enough for her. Matt's last name sounded like a derogatory Yiddish word, and I could picture my father joking about this, critically, but perhaps over time, affectionately.

When Lori and Matt decided to get married, I became the surrogate mother of the bride. We shopped for her dress, found a venue that my parents would have approved of, and planned the menu. I was to be her only attendant, as she had been mine. Whereas we had often squabbled when we talked, she now seemed relieved to have my help and to allow my experience to guide us and not make her feel the lesser of us two. I felt some pleasure in our relationship for the very first time, the opportunity to work together fading the differences between us. Her vulnerability was endearing, not embarrassing.

One weekend, my family drove in to help my sister plan her wedding. My immediate family had grown to four. Jonathan had been joined by a little sister, Emily, now eighteen months old. While Lori and I were out doing wedding errands on Saturday afternoon, we ran into one of her "high school" teachers. It took a few minutes for them to recognize each other. This teacher was utterly pleased to see my sister and regaled us with tales of her memories of Lori. She spoke so proudly of Lori and I enjoyed it the way a parent might.

The complexity of Lori and Matt's wedding day brought together all the feelings of pride, sadness, lost opportunity, and newfound strengths. I was disappointed that my son had refused to be the ring bearer, but needed to respect his wish to stay out of the limelight. I think he felt unprepared to walk down the aisle at a wedding, perhaps feeling too young and small. My parents would have been unbearably proud of this little boy, smiling in his blue blazer and kelly green tie, and his vivacious younger sister. Emily, a toddler now, cried at the back of the sanctuary, as she watched the ceremony begin. My mother-in-law held her and tried to comfort her. Having to put my sister first, I couldn't pay enough attention to my daughter. I preceded Lori down the aisle as her matron of honor, unprepared for all our parents' friends' faces. My tears flowed freely as I proceeded toward the *chuppah*. When David walked Lori down the aisle, everyone in the congregation seemed to connect with us – touched, pleased, saddened, and missing our parents.

A year or so after the wedding, in a phone conversation, my sister brought up the issue of becoming a mother. She had always loved children, and wondered whether she and Matt might be ready to have a baby. I panicked, wondering what I might say to talk her out of it. I couldn't imagine how she could take care of a baby who would likely be of normal intelligence when she could barely take care of herself. Whenever I visited, she looked unkempt, with spots on her clothing and hair not brushed. Neither my sister nor Matt could take care of their apartment. It was overrun with items they didn't need. Boxes of food covered the kitchen counter, laundry spilled out of the hamper. I continued to listen as she talked about wanting a baby and as she told me that since Matt was Methodist and she was Jewish, they might have two children and raise one Methodist and one Jewish. It was at this point that I could no longer keep quiet. While I don't remember exactly what I said it was probably something like, "That's a terrible idea!" Trying to collect myself, I talked about the difficult work of parenting, and wondered if there might be a way she could be involved with helping young children without actually becoming a mother. "I like that idea," she said. Relieved, I realized that although she might long to be a mother, she might also understand that this was an unrealistic plan.

Lori was able to get a job, as an aide in the synagogue preschool, but couldn't sustain it. In short, she behaved too much like a child herself to be of help to the teachers. Ashamed of her failure, she refused to try other jobs. Ultimately, she enrolled in an adult day program where she, as one of the higher functioning members, took care of other adults who needed assistance. This has continued to be a source of good feeling for her.

One recent Saturday afternoon, my sister called outside of our regularly scheduled calls. Now in her fifties, she had just attended a large group bar and bat mitzvah for handicapped adults who had never been expected to accomplish this rite of passage.

"I want to do it too," she said. I could hear her smile through the phone.

"You should definitely go for it," I said.

When she approached our family's temple, the Rabbi suggested a group ceremony might be unnecessary. She would be able to have one of her very own. In May 2014, at the age of 57, my sister became a bat mitzvah. After months of preparation that involved weekly study of her Torah portion, and all the incidentals such as printed invitations, plans for a celebratory reception and dinner, she felt ready. Again, our working together on mutually enjoyable preparations galvanized our relationship. Did she like the combination of navy and yellow on the invitations, or did she prefer spring green? Who did she want to invite and where should we have celebratory dinner? On the afternoon of her rehearsal, I stood behind her and watched as she pointed, not to the English transliteration but to the Hebrew words she had memorized and was speaking. She was trembling with anxiety and perhaps a lack of recognition of this newfound part of herself.

The next morning at the service during the part of the ritual where a bat mitzvah walks through the congregation, carrying the Torah, there were several points when it looked like Lori might lose her grip. I remembered my own bat mitzvah, the pleasure in my accomplishment, yet always on the precipice of faltering. I leaned over to help her regain her hold on the thirty-pound Torah. We both smiled with the realization of the universality of our worry.

I spoke during the part of the service where the parents often speak. I talked of Lori's persistence, her bravery, and told her I loved her, something I don't think I'd ever known or said out loud. She told everyone that I was her best friend and that we had worked out many of our difficulties.

At the end of the service, the president of the temple, who speaks at each bar and bat mitzvah throughout the year, stood up on the bimah and faced my sister. I don't remember his exact words, but they went something like this: "If there is anyone in this congregation today who isn't inspired by what they've just witnessed you accomplish here this morning, Lori, I don't know what it would take to inspire them." Indeed he spoke for all of us.

References

Olshansky, S. (1962). Chronic sorrow: A response to having a mentally defective child. *Social Casework, 43*, 190–194.

Solnit, A., & Stark, M. (1961). Mourning and the birth of a defective child. *Psychoanalytic Study of the Child, 16*, 163–538.

Solomon, A. (2012). *Far from the tree*. New York: Scribner.

7

Parenting through enactments of loss

Karen Earle

It is evening. My 4-year-old Molly's bedtime. I lay beside her. The bedroom is unfamiliar, a room in a house we are renting in a small city in decline in the industrial Midwest. We have moved there for my husband to accept an academic position at a local college. I am reading to my daughter. *Make Way for Duckings*. The book cover is green, the story about springtime and summer in Boston, the Public Gardens all a-flower. It reminds me of home and just how far away from home I am.

Soon the wife of one of my husband's fellow professors will come to care for our daughter while my husband and I attend the first in a series of childbirth classes at the local hospital. I don't know this woman, but she has reached out to help us. We have only lived in this small city, in this rented house, for a little over two weeks and I have accepted her help with gratitude and apprehension.

It is snowing. As I wonder if the childbirth class will be cancelled because of the snow, I feel a warm liquid leave my body. I stand quickly, not wanting to wet the bed. I try to smile at my daughter and say, "Molly, time for Mommy to go now." I kiss her good-bye. The warm liquid grows cold, puddles at my feet. I know that my water has broken weeks earlier than anticipated.

On the drive to the hospital our ancient Buick careens over the unplowed road. The snow falls fast and then faster. I laugh, not thinking of the dangers ahead, saying, "Well, this will make a great story some day!" In denial? Perhaps. Unaware of the consequences of the moment? Certainly unaware of how that moment and the days to follow would reach back into the past, forcing on it meaning where there had been none and forward into the future, for decades to come, shaping and reshaping my image of me as "mother," my understanding of my relationship with my own mother, my relationship with my daughters and they with me. One collusion, one collision, one enactment at a time.

My second daughter, Josie, arrived that evening, premature, breech, by C-section. The storm had grown into a blizzard. Without a neonatal intensive care unit, the hospital sent our new baby in a specially outfitted emergency ambulance because a lack of visibility prevented the helicopter from flying. Not allowed to go with her, I was numb that night and for the days that followed, too numb to imagine her or to imagine the loss of her. It continued to snow.

Days later, Josie returned to the local hospital. She was four pounds, a tiny lump of a human being. I had worried while I was pregnant about whether I could love any child as much as I loved Molly, my first. But Josie didn't give me time to wonder. As I held her in my arms, she turned toward me, latched onto my breast, and began to nurse with an intensity that inhabits her to this day. She latched onto me as if to say, "Where have you been?!" Her life-demanding ferocity stood in stark contrast to the deadening chill of the "lake effect" winds that blew down on us that winter, burying us in a record amount of snow. Her insistent need captured my attention and I surrendered, spending much of that winter holding her, monitoring her breathing by holding the palm of my hand against her back, nursing her.

This memory: I am standing by a window, Josie close in my arms. I watch as Molly and her father wander the snow-covered yard through a grove of evergreens, branches heavy with snow. To my eyes, Molly and her father seem far away, drifting like the snow. More than the window glass separated us. At that moment and for a long time after, it seemed to me as if a transparent but impenetrable wall magnified the emotional distance between us. For a long time, they seemed like ghosts wandering beyond my reach.

Spring arrived. Josie was gaining weight, off the infant monitor that recorded her breathing, out of danger. That's when the emotional blizzard broke loose. As a new hire, my husband taught classes scheduled at the worst hours – early mornings and in the evening. Consequently, most days I was alone with my daughters for long stretches. One night as I was putting Josie into her crib, Molly came in and asked, "Can we give her back?" I said, "No, sweetie, we can't." She screamed, "Then throw her away! In the trash!" In a flash, imagining infants discarded in subway trash barrels, I said, "No." Then mustering all her 4-year-old rage, Molly threw herself on the ground kicking and screaming. When I asked her to come lay beside me, she stamped her way out of the room. I did not follow.

In that moment, I felt as if Molly and I had suffered a grave rupture. I blamed myself for the rupture, blamed myself for having chosen to give birth to another child, felt as if the rupture between Molly and me had no repair. Not until Molly's late adolescence, when she began the process of separation as she launched into her adult life, did I begin to understand the complicated nature of the rupture, my complicity, and finally the way toward repair. Only then, after long years of our collusion that all was well between us, did we have the courage to collide, enacting generationally unresolved feelings of loss. Again and again. Until we got it right.

Like Josie, I am a younger sister. My one and only living sibling is 3 years older than I am. I was born a twin, and my twin sister died three days after our birth. At the time of my twin sister's death, my father was on "one final bender" with friends. I imagine my mother mourning the loss of my twin sister alone. I "imagine" because – although I do know that I had a twin named Kathleen who died three days after our birth – I know little else, never asked questions, never felt I had permission to ask about the situation of my birth or anything else that had to do with my mother.

I suspect my mother had mourned alone before. Her own mother – an Irish immigrant who may have had her own unspoken history of loss – died when my mother was 13 years old. My mother refused to speak about her mother other than to say, "she was always sick." More losses and silence followed. My parents became engaged before my father went into the army. My mother said he returned "a changed man," marked by his World War II service in the Pacific campaign, then as part of the Occupying Forces in Japan. When he returned, my parents married. The father I knew was intermittently loving, distant, angry. Suffering as he did from what would now be classified as post-traumatic stress disorder, he was ill equipped to provide my mother with solace. I can only imagine the effect of my sister's death on my parents. Or rather, I can only piece it together from what followed.

As a part of post-war America's aggressively optimistic grand illusion – war-over-and-all-is-well – that allowed for the baby boom and the economic prosperity of the 1950s, my family moved forward and achieved by burying their many traumas and losses in history's vast potter's field of memory. Such burial is normal and necessary when one cannot integrate discordant pieces of experience. Our survival demands that we maintain a fluid and complete sense of self without succumbing to conflicting self-narratives (Van der Kolk, 2014). According to Wallin, when experiences of trauma and loss are dissonant with, perhaps even threatening to, a present reality, these discordant pieces of experiences:

> tend to be dissociated and undeveloped rather than repressed. Rather than being defensively "forgotten" they are instead relegated to the very edge of awareness. There they remain as unwanted or disowned parts of the self until, in the context of a new state of mind determined by a different set of circumstances, what was previously peripheral now becomes all too central.
>
> (2007, p. 172)

This necessary dissociation allowed us – my family and so many other families in America and around the world following World War II – to continue. In my family's case, dissociation allowed for a family narrative of upward mobility and well-being but silenced a sadder inheritance of multiple unresolved and unresolvable losses, an inheritance from my mother to me, until what had been peripheral became central.

My premature birth and my difficulties throughout childhood challenged my family's ambitiously hopeful narrative. Unlike my older sister, who excelled at school, I had trouble learning to read, paying attention, behaving properly enough to win affirmation from the Catholic nuns who were my teachers. My parents ignored the psychologist's diagnosis of my dyslexia in favor of their preferred diagnosis of recalcitrance. My mother's treatment of me during my childhood was harsh and dismissive. We fought often. I felt "less-than" when compared with my successful older sister and cousins. My mother and I fought most furiously during my adolescence when I went out with friends. Why stay home? I felt that there was little reward for me there. When I was home, if my mother and I weren't fighting, we seldom spoke to one another. An angry silence held the space between us. So her rages when I went out confused me. Most confusing of all, when I moved into an apartment in the city while attending college, my mother shut the door behind me with amazing speed.

My mother's mother died when my mother was 13 years old. According to family legend, my mother responded to the loss by taking over the care of the household. Whatever the complex of feelings my mother felt around the time of her mother's death, I strongly suspect they were retriggered by the death of my twin. She may have needed to distance herself from me in order to avoid overwhelming feelings of anger and loss, and perhaps also her misplaced sense of guilt in causing those deaths. I believe she displaced her disowned feelings onto me: like her, I was the one who survived, therefore guilty for the death of the other. She held me liable – for the death of my sister, for my academic failure, for my stubbornness. I now suspect my comings and goings during my adolescence stirred in my mother long dissociated feelings of loss, perhaps even an angry sense of having been abandoned. When I left home to attend college and later to marry, she treated me as if I were now the one dead to her.

My earliest memory is of my mother walking away. I remember I was screaming, shaking the bars of my crib. She was dressed in a black party dress, the bodice covered in rhinestones. Her face was round, pale, and impassive, the one spot of color her bee-stung red lips pursed into a frown. I remember my mother's face as a moon face – distant, hanging in a dark sky, unsmiling, moon shadows moving from impassive to angry and back again. Nothing more. A face to look at but not into.

In *Play and Reality* Winnicott (1971) uses "mirror" as physical actuality and metaphor. He writes, "The precursor of the mirror is the mother's face" (p. 111). He emphasizes the mother's role in accurately reflecting the infant's mood and links the accuracy of her reflection to later emotional and behavioral health, including an individual's ability to be creative and/or to be independent. He warns, "If a mother's face is unresponsive, then the mirror is a thing to be looked at but not to be looked into" (p. 113). Although Winnicott does not go into particulars, they seem implied – mirror as precise representation, distortion, or void; reflections that vary, shaped by the quality of the glass or shifts in the surrounding light; reflections shimmering with nuance or rippling – buffeted by the winds of anxiety, a funhouse hall of distorted images, a clouded glass. Or, perhaps, a clear surface, once in full view, then turned away, leaving blankness where once there had been reflection. "The precursor of the mirror *is* the mother's face." But neither mirror nor face is static or still at all or for long, watcher and watched always moving through space and time, always shape-shifting with the multiple realities people hold and reflect – the realities they capture, edit, and avoid. I had hoped to be a better mirror for my daughters than my mother had been for me.

When Molly, my first, was born, I imagined the gift of a granddaughter might bring my mother and me together, but it didn't. Mostly, my mother raged about my inadequacies as a mother. By then, I understood her rage as projection – a comment more on her feelings regarding her parenting than mine – but I was powerless to change our dynamic. A smoker since she was 13 years old (the age she was when her mother died), my mother died of cancer when Molly was 3 years old.

Despite my mother's criticism of me, I believed myself to be a good mother, perhaps even exceptional. I was attentive to my daughter's every need, quick to mediate every sorrow, every pain, quick to respond to every gesture, eager to talk to her, play with her. I was enraptured – yes, that is the word, "enraptured" – by Molly. She was my idealized other, the child of my husband's and my hopeful beginnings, born into the sunshine of the southwest, into an Austin, Texas, with its brashly uplifting 1980s soundtrack – a mixture of progressive country and punk – providing the background music to our new lives. Molly was born when the future seemed to belong to us and to our new infant, as we made a new beginning together, far from the cold winds and fog of our Atlantic seacoast past.

I remember not long after Molly's birth, sitting with her, my legs up and at an angle, my thighs supporting her back. Face to face, I watched her every gesture – the soft curl of her lips, her hazel-green eyes following the light, her rosy cheeks glowing, the small trace of milk pooled in the corner of her mouth – losing track of time, never wanting to turn away. And for a very long time I didn't.

When she was around 3 years old, Molly did a series of pictures, in gentle watercolor hues on large sheets of white paper. She did them while she was away from me with a babysitter. She filled each large sheet with one round face, alert eyes intently looking forward. Small eyebrows raised as if in wonder. A thin line of a mouth, less smiling than attentive. For a long time I wondered why she drew the same face again and again. I have come to understand those pictures were of me looking at her and, perhaps more significantly, her internalization of me, suggesting the depth of our connection, suggesting the way in which I had been her mirror and she had been mine. This most recent understanding makes the rupture between us when she was 4 years old even more painful, the rupture that occurred when, after a long period of gazing steadily, I turned away.

In subtle and not-so subtle ways, Josie's birth maps onto mine. Like Josie, I was born prematurely during a blizzard and, like Josie, I spent time in a neonatal intensive care unit. Like Josie, I have a learning disability. I identified strongly with these shared problematic similarities, perhaps over-identified, neglecting many differences. Despite these similarities, or perhaps because of them, beginning when Josie was born prematurely into an actual and emotional blizzard, I was determined that my relationship with her would be different from the distant and rejecting one I had had with my own mother. At the same time, Josie's premature birth triggered fears instilled in me by my mother, fears that I might lose Josie because of my inadequacy as a mother, fears that infants died because of me, fears I dissociated, burying them deep beneath anxious hyperfocus. I also identified with Josie's physical need, projecting my own unanswered needs, perhaps dormant since my infancy or early childhood. I realized retrospectively that I needed to dissociate my fear of inadequacy because it so deeply threatened my ability to function adequately as a mother, because it so profoundly threatened my core sense of myself as able and loving.

So I worried about Josie, intently focusing my gaze. Josie, however, did not remain a passive conduit for my fear. She vigorously determined the contours of our relationship, voicing her needs loudly from the start, holding my attention when she was a toddler and young child, her playful bursts of creative energy and delight alternating with furious battles of will. She defied me often and we fought with great emotional intensity. I grew to identify with not just her prematurity and disability but with her creative spirit and her willfulness. Over time, my fears regarding my ability to keep her alive, to sustain her, which had triggered my own deeply disowned vulnerability, dissipated. Like me, she had a learning difference. But unlike me, she had a mother and a father who acknowledged her need, advocated for her, believed in her ability, delighted in her as a central part of our family.

Although she struggled socially and academically during middle school and high school, when it was time, Josie bravely chose a college at a distance. When her father and I left her at the door of her college dormitory, she said good-bye and without a tear walked away. At the end of orientation week, she called and said that she was happier than she had ever been. That very week she found friends who continue to be her friends to this day. She excelled academically and socially. Second semester, she met a fellow student who became the love of her life. They married several years after graduation. Josie is now a married professional with a demanding job. She and I remain close. Despite her struggles as a child and an adolescent, despite her learning difference, when she was ready, Josie launched with startling ease.

Molly's launching, also a surprise, offers a study in contrasts. Molly and Josie were very different children and adolescents and remain very different young adults. While Josie was intermittently playful and volatile, Molly was more even-tempered, an "easy" child – well behaved, serious, hardworking, intelligent. The infant of the hopeful and sunny Southwest continued to be my idealized other. She excelled academically in all the ways that I valued, in all the ways that I had wished for myself. Somewhat shy, Molly intermittently struggled socially, but she was able to make and keep close friends. She presented herself to her father and me and to her teachers as mature, capable, independent, ambitious. She chose to attend an academically challenging college and excelled there as well.

But while Josie's launching from home to college was dry-eyed and rapid, Molly's launching was tearful and played out over years. When her father and I left her off that first day of college, she cried harder than I had ever seen her cry. I tried to comfort her, but she pushed me away. These tearful good-byes continued throughout her college years. In retrospect, I realize that Molly's many difficult good-byes were an expression of unresolved feelings of loss. These many difficult good-byes triggered my own unresolved feelings of loss. In time, these unresolved feelings grew into enactments that locked Molly and me together and pushed us apart both emotionally and geographically.

Enactments – the acting out of unsymbolized emotional material (Jacobs, 1986) – occur when one individual's vulnerabilities intersect with another's. For Molly and for me, our vulnerabilities intersected at the point of maternal abandonment. Often, enactments lead to relational inflexibility and a narrowing in freedom of thought (Wallin, 2007). That was certainly the case for us. Eventually, the spell of these enactments was broken, but only when both Molly and I were both ready.

After Josie went to college, after she was securely launched, Molly and I began to fight with a ferocity that we had not had before. Often we seemed to shout past each other rather than talking to one another, like two enraged creatures unable to understand the other's language. Most often, these arguments happened at points of transition – back from college at the end of a semester, leaving for winter study abroad, preparing for a trip with friends. The quality and timing of these arguments, and my response to them, were different from what I had experienced in my relationship with either of my daughters up to that point. When Josie and I battled frequently during her childhood and adolescence, I felt up to the task of setting boundaries and making amends. When Molly and Josie fought as children, adolescents, and young adults, I felt overwhelmed and powerless, blamed myself when they didn't get along. Caught between their competing demands, I felt vulnerable and powerless. During Molly's childhood and early adolescence, Molly and Josie often fought furiously, but Molly and I seldom fought. When she began the process of launching, however, Molly and I became locked in painful emotional battles – angrily spinning away from each other, then anxiously colliding at full speed together. These emotional comings and goings paralleled and were intensified by Molly's coming and goings through the world.

Hard work, scholastic ability, and determination gained Molly early and frequent access to the world – at age 11 and 14, trips to Mexico with a youth group; at 15, on a summer-long scholarship as an exchange student in Germany; at 16, volunteering in Tennessee with Habitat for Humanity; in college during winter term, also on scholarship, with a study group to Morocco; after college, trips to France, Italy, Turkey, Kenya, Zanzibar, and Mexico to visit friends but often traveling alone. When she traveled alone, I worried about her safety. When I voiced my concern, she'd shut me down, criticize me for being timid. When I confronted her, she pushed me further away. I grew timid. When she pushed me away, I felt a door close between us – like the door that had shut so quickly and so completely between my mother and me, like the door Molly slammed shut when she stormed out of that room when I refused to throw away her baby sister, like the door I shut when I chose not to pursue Molly in that moment.

After college, she planned to move to New York City, to find her way in the world. I summoned up my courage – anticipating pushback from her – and suggested she take the summer off, work at the shore, slow down a little. To my amazement she agreed. Her father and I visited her there. Walking along the water, she revealed for the first time how she had struggled with depression through high school, but particularly during college, a struggle that she kept mostly to herself, a struggle I seemed to have been mostly blind to. We offered help. Still she struggled. After she moved to New York, she and I spoke by phone, often daily. Despite these frequent conversations, she seemed to resist almost all my offers of material help or comfort. Despite her frequent calls to me, she seemed compelled to prove that she could make it in the world without my help. I came to realize that when she asked my opinion, it was most often in order to tell me I was wrong.

Change came when I stopped seeing these communications as a way of blaming me for not having been a good enough mother. I came to understand that Molly's developmentally appropriate pulling away triggered in me the feelings of abandonment and loss I had never been able to acknowledge. I tried to monitor my anxious reaction to Molly's behavior. Rather than respond to her pulling away as a rejection of me, I tried to affirm her need for autonomy. Rather than voice my concern, I tried to affirm her need for geographic and emotional space. Gradually, she began to talk about her own negative thoughts and feelings, about her fears, her thwarted ambitions. Rather than hear her words as a condemnation of me, I acknowledged to her and to myself the pain of limitation and the universality and inevitability of loss.

But enactments are two-sided. I suspect that Molly needed my anxious attention for a time in order to finally break away. The literature emphasizes that enactment occurs when the vulnerabilities of two individuals collide. This suggests a certain randomness that belies my experience. I believe that – at least based on this example of my daughter and me – we find one another when the time is right. Molly and I colluded for a long time, imagining that all was perfect in our family and between us, colluded until we were strong enough in ourselves and confident enough in one another, free enough to focus on one another, and perhaps, humble enough to allow our vulnerabilities to be revealed. Josie's launching had opened the space for Molly and me to play out our enactment of loss.

I have come to believe that during all those years from Josie's birth until Molly left for college, Molly "relegated to the very edge of awareness" (Wallin, 2007, p. 172) her feelings of her loss of me. These feelings paralleled my own dissociated feelings of loss regarding my mother, feelings of loss in my sense of myself as a perfect mother able to keep all harm from my children, and my feelings of loss in my relationship with Molly before Josie was even born. These dissociations were necessary in order not to threaten Molly's and my relational bonds. For me to acknowledge, and perhaps more significantly to feel, that loss would have forced me to identify with my own rejecting mother in ways I would have found threatening. To own these feelings would have demanded that I come to terms with my own unwanted and disowned parts, long since pushed to the very edge my awareness. These dissociated feelings waited to emerge until Molly no longer had to fight with Josie for my attention.

In *Standing in the Spaces: The Multiplicity of Self and the Psychoanalytic Relationship*, Philip Bromberg (1998) defines emotional health as "the ability to stand in the spaces between realities without losing any of them – the capacity to feel like oneself while being many. . . . to make room at any given moment for the subjective reality that is not readily containable by the self [that is experienced] as 'me' at that moment" (p. 274). These dissociated feelings – these disparate internalized realities, these discordant narratives – waited until Molly and I were, at last, able to stand in the spaces alone and together, in a fuller acceptance of the losses we had suffered alone and together, to look at and see one another again. And to begin again.

My difficult beginnings with a difficult mother unable to reconcile with her difficult past offered me only "an impenetrable surface." When I looked into that mirror – that is, when I turned to my mother for comfort or even for information – she grimaced and/or turned away. I was determined to do better – that is, to be a more attentive mother – so when Molly was born I did give her my full attention for 4 years until her sister was born. Another mother might have had the resources to shift her gaze – back and forth – from one child to another. I understand, retrospectively, that with the birth of my premature daughter my vulnerability had been triggered. I was overwhelmed by anxiety, fearful that if I unfixed my gaze I would cause her death. Her birth triggered my guilt at the death of my twin sister. But to acknowledge those feelings, that self, would have rendered me too vulnerable to care for either of my daughters. My one recourse was to rigidly fix my gaze until I was certain of Josie's survival.

With Molly, my idealized other, early on – from the time of her birth until her sister was born – I was enraptured by what seemed like perfection, and I never turned away. However, as a young first-time mother, I may not have had the emotional resources to fully acknowledge her needs, because to fully acknowledge her needs – some that may not have been answerable – might have suggested to me that I was inadequate as a mother. With Josie's launching complete, Molly expressed her anger at me for failing to fully attend to her, for not seeing clearly enough, for not understanding the depth and breadth of her need, for letting her fall out of my direct line of sight, for turning away. But during our years of conflict while Molly was in college and after, I grew better able to recognize my daughter's needs as needs, rather than failures on my part. Concurrently, my daughter left and returned again and again, left and returned enacting her loss of me, until I was able to understand, until this time we got it right.

I could have taken the 4-year-old Molly's words "Throw her away" to mean "I don't like the new baby to get all the attention" or to mean "I need you to pay less attention to the new baby and more attention to me" – the former focused on Molly's feelings of competition for attention with her sister, the latter focused on her need for my continued attention. At that time, though, I wasn't able to acknowledge Molly's anger, to accept her rage, to metabolize it, because to acknowledge her rage I would have needed to accept my own vulnerability, to understand her need as something other than an indictment of me as her mother, to tolerate imperfection in both my daughter and especially in myself.

More specifically, the selves I was not able to acknowledge to myself because of my own vulnerability – shaped by my relationship with my mother – in turn shaped my relationship with each of my daughters and made it difficult for me to "stand in the spaces" with them, difficult for me to be fully visible to each of my daughters, difficult for me to reflect each of them accurately. In turn, my inability to fully "stand in the spaces" with each of them, to mirror each of them clearly, flattened my relationship with each of my daughters for a time and in ways that I will always regret. Now I am able to stand in those spaces, more at ease with the often-conflicting multiplicity of vulnerable selves I have been and am, particularly in my role as a mother. Now I am also more able to stand in the spaces with the often-conflicting multiplicity of selves that make up each of my daughters. As Daniel Stern observes, "The forces that would have us stay the same and those that would have us change interweave. . . . [They] reflect a dynamic tension between the old and the new, security and risk, the 'repeated relationship' and the 'needed relationship'" (Stern as cited in Wallin, 2007, p. 279). The slow process of change began only when I was able to see and to say what had been missing, what was needed.

After Josie was settled in college, successfully negotiating the world beyond home, Molly began to express her feelings more directly, enacting, I believe, in her comings and goings our yet-to-be completed emotional work, replaying that "throw-her-away" moment again and again, until we got it right. Retrospectively, I imagine us during those years of her launching as two mythical creatures fiercely locking horns, filling the emotional forest with the sounds of battle, until, exhausted, we fall silent. The forest fills with a mournful thrumming mixed with the sounds of loss that echo and, finally released, begin to fade away.

Molly, Josie, and I sit in a yard, under a grove of tall trees, glad for the deep shade they offer in the midst of hot summer. We are talking about babies, what they like and what they need. Molly is holding her newborn gently in her arms, her attention fluid, wandering back and forth between Josie and me and her baby. He is her first child, my first grandchild. His fingers stretch and curl as if to gently test the space around him. Molly says, "I remember when Josie was born. I remember how incredibly stressed out you and Dad were." I say, "Really!?" I'm genuinely surprised. She has never mentioned her memories of that time, now 30 years ago. She was so young then, too young to understand what we were going through as a family, and I had thought too young to notice the stress we were under. I was young too and naïve, so much of me invisible to myself and to her. There was space, but we couldn't stand in it. Not then. And I think about Josie's birth, which was like mine. Both younger siblings, we were born into families already in process. Her birth, like mine, a small pebble tossed into the pond, rippled a once sure surface, altering the reflections, spreading fences of light. Moving slowly, careful to hold her infant just so, Molly gently hands her newborn to Josie, offering her a turn to hold him close. He fusses softly, then settles. We're all born into families, into generations of families already in process, the once sure surface always moving, breaking, settling, over and over, again and again.

I think, it's all about looking and loss. We gaze into a mirror. When we look away, the image vanishes to be replaced by another. All about looking and loss, again and again, and finding a way to inhabit the spaces between.

References

Bromberg, P. M. (1998). Standing in the spaces: The multiplicity of self and the psycho-analytic relationship. In *Standing in the spaces: Essays on clinical process, trauma, and dissociation* (Chapter 17, pp. 267–290). Hillsdale, NJ: The Analytic Press.

Jacobs, T. J. (1986). On countertransference enactments. *Journal of the American Psycho-analytic Association, 34,* 289–307.

van der Kolk, B. A. (2014). *The body keeps the score: Brain, mind, and body in the healing of trauma.* New York: Viking.

Wallin, D. J. (2007). *Attachment in psychotherapy.* New York: Guilford Press.

Winnicott, D. W. (1971). *Play and reality.* New York: Basic Books.

Part III

Unbound

New definitions of gender

As technology and the digital world have expanded, many borders that had seemed impenetrable have become more fluid. Many of us have greater access to a broader array of people across greater distances, more avenues for communication across diverse platforms, and a greater sense of openness to change and acceptance of difference – and definitions of gender have begun to open up as well. Old norms are being questioned. Today's adolescents and young adults are commonly more familiar with and accepting of diversity – sexual, racial, ethnic, religious, and cultural.

In particular, we have begun to learn more about the psychological, medical, and social needs of transgender youth and have become better equipped to understand and respond in ways that support the optimal health and development of these youth. Even the American Psychiatric Association has begun to broaden its view, offering a deeper understanding of gender fluidity by replacing the term "gender identity disorder" with "gender dysphoria," highlighting that being transgender is not in itself a disorder. Rather, if treatment is indicated, the clinician is oriented toward addressing the underlying distress associated with having a body that is not consistent with the gender an individual feels he or she is. Often, as an individual undergoes gender transition, the dysphoria and other mood-related difficulties begin to resolve. Trans teens and young adults may thrive when they transition in adolescence. Now, medical and technological advances and greater psychological understanding have made gender transition more possible and more accessible for trans youth.

Parents and families often go through their own transition as they come to understand and work through their trans child's gender transition. Mary Collins and Irene Smith Landsman reflect on the strange, modern grief that the parent of a trans child may encounter today. Both Collins and Landsman describe the process of relinquishing the child they thought they had while simultaneously learning to marvel at the emerging young adult who had been present, yet concealed, all along. Collins reflects on the geography of modern grief that she faced as a mother losing her daughter, while loving her trans son. She explores grief and the adaptive function it serves as individuals grow accustomed to loss and change that are beyond their control. Landsman refers to the sense of "disenfranchised grief" to explain how, in spite of a parent's willingness to understand and come to terms with her child's transition, she may lack social support for her own sense of loss. And she cannot turn to the child for help or further explanation for fear of compromising the bond of parental support. Thus, the parent may struggle to create a coherent narrative of her experience.

Ultimately, both Landsman and Collins sensitively describe how a parent's grief at "losing" the child they thought they had in no way impairs their gradual full acceptance of the child's transgender status. Rather, they show how working through grief is an important psychological transformative process in the parent's own development that facilitates personal growth and deeper engagement with their young adult.

Noah S. Glassman's chapter offers a view of modern parenting from the vantage point of a gay parent raising children in today's culture. While society in general is in some ways more accepting than in the past, in other ways Glassman shows how gay parents and their families continue to experience the impact of both historical and modern-day homophobia, which may be cloaked but is often still present. Glassman describes how a parent's legacy of growing up gay becomes interwoven in that parent's experience of and fantasies about raising his own children. He highlights how families can ultimately succeed in building a strong, positive identity around an acceptance of and pleasure in individual variance.

8

Personal essay

Mapping modern grief

Mary Collins

"I am transgender," my teenaged daughter, J., says, her green eyes squinting with anxiety.

"Trans?" I ask. "What's that?"

I am still thinking about mundane things, like the dirty dishes on the counter. We sit at my favorite place in the house, the round kitchen table by a window with lacy curtains, where I drink tea and read my newspaper every morning.

"*Trans*, Mom. I am a man trapped in a woman's body."

The summer day's simmering breath coming through the screen suddenly feels like a panting animal.

"What?"

My first fully modern loss.

It does not feel the same as when my father died when I was 14.

It does not feel the same as when the love of my life left me when I was in my twenties.

In that moment at the kitchen table, I experienced a loss only made possible by our current culture, which allows – even empowers – a teenager to take steroids and have "top surgery" (trans speak for a double mastectomy), all before age 20, so his gender can match his person.

When J. legally changed her name to Donald and insisted we use male pronouns to refer to him, I resisted for a short time, but eventually gave up on "she," "her," and the entire idea that I have a daughter at all.

But when I said I thought Donald was moving too fast with his physical transition, the counselors, school advisors, and medical professionals told me I must face the inevitable.

When I said I was sad about the unique obstacles my child will have to deal with in the larger world as an adult, they told me to tamp down my homophobia and trans bias. Seek counseling to overcome your prejudices, they advised.

I am not ashamed or biased, I told them.

I am grieving the loss of my daughter, and that does not mean I do not love my trans son.

Modern loss. Modern grief.

None of them grasped any of it, so I share a story with one of the school advisors.

When the school had a mother-daughter tea for Mother's Day, Donald and I did not go, and instead skipped over to a nondescript Dunkin' Donuts in a strip mall. As we finished our iced coffees, both milky-white with extra cream, I noticed two guys with heavily tattooed arms sitting two tables away listening as we chatted about Cher's trans son, Chaz, who had been in the news a lot.

The men's shoulders seemed tight, their lips closed.

I eyed the pickup truck outside.

I stared at the ice cubes in my cheap plastic cup.

I told Donald we needed to leave.

He thought it was because I'd finished my drink.

In that moment I did not feel shame, I tell the advisor, just fear.

I take no issue with any individual's right to affirm and assert his or her identity.

But I know that outside the super-accommodating world of my child's liberal school, 40 percent of Americans disapprove of homosexuality. Imagine how they must perceive someone who is transgender? Even within the LGBT community, the T falls at the end of the continuum.

In that moment, I explain to the advisor, I understood my daughter would never return. Her *person* remains, but my trans son faces a day-to-day life I never imagined for my child. As I drove Donald back to school, my fear transformed into something else, something that now follows me through my days, something I can only describe as grief.

I know from reading books and articles about parents with children who do not fall within "normal" parameters, in particular Andrew Solomon's book *Far from the Tree: Parents, Children, and the Search for Identity*, that millions of families struggle with this unusual form of grieving. Two tall parents might have a dwarf; a scholar might have an autistic boy who does not speak. Counselors focus on "acceptance" of the situation rather than processing the grief first, which, unfortunately, falls right in line with the American Psychiatric Association's recent decision to identify depression associated with deep grief as mental illness, not a natural reaction that an individual should be encouraged to feel and move through without guilt or shame. Leave it to American culture to take a fundamental human emotion and classify it as a condition.

I reflected on how I handled my father's death to help me cope with my situation with my trans son, but that only brought back memories of how poorly American culture handles even this most timeless of losses.

All I remember of the moment when I first heard my father had died were the white walls of my small bedroom, my mother by my bedside shaking from the stress of what she had to tell me, the sense of dislocation I felt when she spoke the news. I remember wrapping the cotton bedspread around my shoulders and leaning into the softness and warmth. I don't remember leaving the room or going downstairs or how I told my friends. I now associate white, not black, with death, and have purple, lilac, deep blue, yellow, and other colors on the walls in my house, but not white.

The general world treated my loss as sad, unfortunate, but nothing so out of the ordinary that I wasn't expected to return to school, to sports teams, to my student work job at my high school within the week. We had a church service, a burial; I missed a few days of classes and that was it.

Only now, as an adult researching grief and loss, have I discovered that just 4 percent of children in the United States under age fifteen lose a parent. When I asked my sister to guess the percentage (and she's a health-care professional), she said about 25 percent. In places and time periods in which such losses were more commonplace, the larger society was better equipped to recognize grief and loss as an ongoing experience – not something with concrete stages that you go through in lockstep, but something you carry with you, often always.

In American culture we do not celebrate a Day of the Dead as they do in Mexico; we don't have secular altars in public spaces to honor those who have passed, as in many Eastern cultures. Here grief is more of an individual responsibility, a framework that encourages isolation and often morphs into debilitating depression. The fact that modern American life continues to add ever more complex types of loss just exacerbates the problem.

My emotional journey with Donald seems to more closely mirror more nebulous losses, such as moving away from someone I will never see again. The average American moves twelve times in his or her lifetime, and one in five children eventually move far away from their families, a geographic mortality rate, for want of a better term, that's startling when you consider that for most of human history, the majority of people rarely traveled more than fifty miles from where they grew up.

Similarly, a single woman like me can have dozens of romantic relationships over a lifetime; that's a tremendous freedom but one that comes with a price: you become intimate with a much larger pool of people, but you also experience the loss of that intimacy anew each time the relationship doesn't work out.

I call that "good-bye grief."

When Donald came home after the top surgery, he felt freed of the physical binders he had used to compress his breasts for years. He could wear a light T-shirt with nothing on underneath on a hot July day. His shoulders sprang back when he walked now, instead of being slouched. He held his head differently, more confidently, and looked outward instead of downward. He felt more at home in his own body.

I looked at his now slim torso and saw a fawn before me – all legs, reddish-brown coat, and so vulnerable I wanted to hire a bodyguard for him.

Donald's radical adjustment has made it easier for me to remember to use male pronouns when referring to him; I only slip up when I am out of Donald's presence and around strangers who ask about my family. At one point, while Donald was still in college, a contractor building a porch for me wanted to know if I had children. Without thinking, I said, yes, I have a daughter who is a sophomore in college.

Two weeks later Donald came home, and as we pulled into the driveway the contractor stuck his head in my car to say hello.

"Oh," he remarked later, "so you have two kids."

Oh.

I had no vocabulary to explain the complexity of my situation in such quick passing conversations.

Instead, despite taking great pride in being an honest and direct person, I say little and am left with what I wryly call my own grief geography, territory that no one else can navigate or fully know. Of course our ancient ancestors had their own grief maps as well, terra incognita to us now. Which leaves me with the timeless question: Why did we evolve to grieve? It leaves us despondent, lethargic, and plagued by headaches and stomachaches; none of these things are sexy or enhance our ability to interact with others. The trauma is so great that stress hormones can literally cause the heart to enlarge temporarily. Research in evolutionary biology proves that even though we don't want to experience this emotion, we can't be fully mature without it.

At a physical level, our faces cannot fake either happiness or sadness. When a person forms a sincere smile, they engage the muscles around the eyes that lead to crow's feet. You cannot fake that motion in the face.

There is also a sincere grief muscle, the corrugator muscle, which pulls together the eyebrows and wrinkles the forehead.

At a deep biological level we evolved to know for *certain* if someone is truly happy or sad.

At a deep biological level our entire body systems are programmed to handle losses, to allow emotions to vent and wax and wane as we recover. Indeed, most emotions only last seconds and rarely last more than hours.

I must acknowledge that at a fundamental level I actually gained some benefits from losing a parent young. I turned inward, rethought assumptions, felt less entitled, developed more empathy, paid closer attention to other people with sorrow, and emerged with a new identity, one infinitely more layered than the self-absorbed athlete I had been.

And as a teenager, I had listened to my father. I took his advice. And when he was gone, I had his words, and I did not challenge them.

"Be sure to love your work. Be good citizens and enjoy what life can offer. It can be a lot of fun if you let it," he advised in a handwritten letter in pale blue ink that now hangs in my study. "Remember me and the good times that we had and don't dwell on the sorrowful aspects of life."

I turned down law school and became a writer and a professor of creative writing, in part, because he empowered me with these words and with his early death.

Love your work. Be a good citizen.

I have never admitted that I benefitted in any way from experiencing such a deep loss at such a young age., because I've somehow felt it inappropriate to express such conflicted feelings. In America, you're either grieving the loss of someone or you're "over" it.

I either love my trans son or I don't.

How do we do a better job of breaking free of such rigid thinking so we can accept a much wider range of griefs (yes, I am making that word up) as we face an ever evolving range of losses in modern life?

Step one: Get over the shame.

When I first started working on this essay, I felt so self-conscious writing about grief and loss for an American audience that I labeled the story file "G-Stories" so anyone walking in and out of my office area would not pepper me with questions about what I was writing. I feared they would think I was sad (I was not) or depressed (I was not), otherwise how else could I explain spending my precious hours on such a topic?

At least one of my distant relatives lacked such inhibitions.

While clearing out an estate for an aunt on my father's side, my family came across some handwritten letters in a cloth bag hidden behind a picture frame. The time line at the top of one of the first pages read: *Clonmel, Ireland, November 12th 1871*. My great-grandmother's father was sending news from the home country to his daughters in America. He wrote of churchyard sales, the death of his son, and his longing and sadness because he knew he'd never again see the children who had sailed across the Atlantic. Now that the son who stayed in Ireland was gone, "we are left lonesome," John Sheedy wrote. "We have neither son nor daughter to call on when we have need of them. The grave and America left us a lone couple in Our Old Days."

His grief, hidden behind a frame for decades, came fully into my heart as I read his careful penmanship. At first, all I could think of was the Catholic knack for laying on the guilt, but then I also saw that by simply writing, by putting his true feelings to paper and sending it across the ocean for his daughters to feel, he'd let go of shame about his situation.

I am sad. I am lonely. I am full of grief because you are gone and your brother has died.

Clearly his daughters shared their father's pain, and perhaps even felt motivated by it to do the best they could in America, so that all the loss would result in true gains: good jobs, a good education, and a better world for their own children and grandchildren.

I cannot say these things for certain, but they did save the letters.

Now, John Sheedy's great-great-great granddaughter has become a grandson. The girl I set sail into the world came back across the water a different gender. Like John I know my daughter will never return. Like John, I have put my various griefs in a bag and hid them behind a proverbial frame.

But the geography of my grief was terra incognita in his time.

Despite the counselor's advice, I pull it out now, like a map, with this essay, for all to see.

Further reading

- John Archer, *The Nature of Grief: The Evolution and Psychology of Reactions to Loss* (New York: Routledge, 1999). On separation anxiety and the evolution of grief.
- George Bonanno, *The Other Side of Sadness: What the New Science of Bereavement Tells Us about Life after Loss* (New York: Basic Books, 2009). On how humans are hardwired to grieve, and on the positive side of grief.

- Mikaela Cowley, "Heartbreak Can Take a Physical Toll," Tribune Newspapers, March 6, 2013. On data the heart sometimes enlarges when one is grieving or under great duress.
- "Calculating Migration Expectancy Using ACS Data," US Census Bureau, 2015, www.census.gov/hhes/migration/about/cal-mig-exp.html. For data on how often the average American moves in his or her lifetime (11.7) times.
- National Survey of Families and Households, Intergenerational Proximity; National Center for Family and Marriage Research. For data showing that one family in five has a child who moves far from home.
- Paul Ekman, *Emotions Revealed: Recognizing Faces and Feelings to Improve Communication and Emotional Life* (New York: Times Books, 2003). On the use of facial muscles to show grief and happiness.
- Ted Gup, "Diagnosis: Human," *New York Times*, April 3, 2013; Benedict Carey, "A Tense Compromise on Defining Disorders," *New York Times*, December 11, 2012; Stephen Adams, "Grief Should Not Be Treated Like Depression," *Daily Telegraph* (London), February 17, 2012. On grief defined as a mental disorder.
- Janice L. Krupnick et al., "Bereavement During Childhood and Adolescence," in *Bereavement Reactions, Consequences and Care*, ed. Marian Osterweis and Frederic Solomon (Washington, DC: National Academies Press, 1984). On data that only 4 percent of children under age fifteen lose a parent.
- *Lancet*, "Living with Grief," editorial, *Lancet* 379, no. 9816 (February 18, 2012): 589.
- John Ratey and Eric Hagerman, *Spark: The Revolutionary New Science of Exercise and the Brain* (New York: Little, Brown, 2008). On movement and improving depression.
- Jessica Samakow, "Gender Conformity Study Says Kids Outside of Norm Are at Increased Risk of Abuse," *Huffington Post*, February 12, 2012. About a 2012 study in *Pediatrics* on data showing that 10 percent of children under age eleven identify outside gender "norms."

9

Transparenting

Journey without a map

Irene Smith Landsman

Ages and Stages didn't prepare me for this. Dr. Spock had nothing to say, and Parent Effectiveness hadn't caught up.

How did I know? How did I find out? As a thoughtful psychotherapist tries to do, I finally "heard it in the material." A patient talks about her greedy landlord, how much she'd like a raise, whether she should charge for feeding a neighbor's cat; I finally ask how she's feeling about the fact that I've raised my fee. Someone else recalls feeling abandoned at day care, suddenly wonders if he really needs to keep coming to see me, is having trouble sleeping; I might explore his reactions to my vacation.

I was not quick to pick up E's signals, for the same reason that a therapist is sometimes unable to understand the patient's associations – I wasn't ready to acknowledge what all the stories and signs pointed to. For the better part of a year, E's Facebook page had frequently highlighted articles and links having to do with transgender people, issues, politics, rights and needs. Well, I thought, there's that trans friend. I've met her. I mean him. E is open, aware, sensitive to others, progressive. I admire all that.

I'd adjusted 10 years earlier to E's announcement that she thought she was bisexual, that she had a girlfriend. In college there was a boyfriend, and by graduation a serious relationship with another woman. We adjusted, thrived, embraced the new reality, and grew. We visited often, got involved in the Marriage Equality movement, celebrated when it came to our state. I was excited about wedding plans.

At Christmas, E wanted to come home for an extended visit; her partner would be with her own family for the holiday. I sensed that she had something she wanted to tell me, and as had happened before, she seemed to need me to give her an opening. When I finally realized that the only thing keeping me from asking the question was that I didn't want the answer, I had to move forward.

"I can't help noticing how involved you are in transgender issues," I began, "and how concerned you are about trans people, your friends and others."

Maybe she held her breath.

"And I guess I'm wondering how this all applies to your own life?"

That's all it took.

Relief, almost excitement. "I'm so glad you're asking." she said. "I have been thinking about this for a long time, and I need to tell you and Dad that I'm questioning my gender identity."

I didn't want to hear that. I realized how much I'd suppressed my suspicions, bargaining in an irrational way, thinking "at least we don't have to deal with *that*; it would be so hard."

We like to think we're good, modern parents. We're open, accepting, wanting to learn. And of course in this case we listened and tried hard to be supportive and tried even harder not to be hurtful. I'm occasionally asked if being a therapist makes me a better mother, and I usually respond that I think perhaps my job has given me a longer list of things not to say. "How could you do this to me?" is something I'd never say, but might be in fact what I felt. "You're not trans," E's now-ex partner had already said; I kept the thought to myself. I secretly doubted this was even "real," based entirely on the fact that I knew so little about being trans and didn't really know any trans people. My fervent wish, morphed into a belief or at least hypothesis, is that E didn't really have to transition at all. I thought E must be unhappy, anxious, maybe depressed, and that commitment to therapy and Zoloft would be a better way to feel better. I wished there were some other way toward self-fulfillment that wouldn't entail upending so much about E's life. And mine. I particularly resisted the thought of the body I'd given birth to being modified radically, and when I did speak that thought, "I hope there will be a way through this that doesn't entail surgery," I saw in E's eyes the extent of that empathic failure.

I didn't quite realize until E's next visit how much I'd been hoping this would go away.

It wasn't going to go away.

This is as much as I knew: Someone who is transgender feels themselves to have, or be, a gender that is not the same as what was assigned to them at birth. To the extent they are able to identify as, present themselves as, and/or physically transition toward the other sex they feel more coherent, more whole, more secure. Not surprisingly, they are happier when they can live the identity that they feel is most essentially their own.

Transgender identification is not a new phenomenon, but a way of being that has likely always been part of the human condition. What is new is *visibility*. The rise of the Internet may have made it possible for the first time for trans individuals to discover that they are not anomalous freaks but part of a significant minority of society. The civil rights and women's and gay rights movements paved the way for trans people to live openly as they are and to claim their civil rights. The sense that society is faced with a new phenomenon is an illusion, but the challenge of dealing honestly, fairly, and openly with these issues is real.

Some 1.4 million people in the U.S. identify as transgender. That's only about six-tenths of a percent of the population, but the estimated incidence increases with each subsequent survey, and it is virtually certain that the actual number is higher (Flores et al., 2016).

The public coming-out was on E's 27th birthday. Non-binary, gender-queer, pronouns *they, them,* and *their*. Even at that early stage, with all aspects of life much in flux, E seemed happier, more centered and at peace than ever, as well as profoundly relieved. I began a confusing and painful transition of my own, facing a significant change that, like all real change, entailed a degree of loss.

While grief is most commonly thought of as attending bereavement – the death of someone close to us – it is clear that we respond to many other life changes with similar emotions. "Grief is the conflicting feelings caused by the end of or change in a familiar pattern of behavior," (James & Friedman, 2009, p. 3). The "necessary losses" (Viorst, 1986) experienced throughout life include giving up infantile illusions of symbiosis and omnipotence, confronting the realities of marriage following the bliss of first love, and stepping to the front of the line when parents die.

Parenting itself brings a series of changes and endings as a child progresses from infancy to toddlerhood, childhood, adolescence, and adulthood. The term "empty nest" usually refers to the departure of a teenaged child for college and is recognized as a common challenge. Some parents (and I count myself one) have a conscious sense of loss at even earlier transitions, tearing up while packing away baby clothes, weeping at the graduations from kindergarten, middle school, and high school, feeling bereft on the drive away from summer camp. It isn't that we don't want the new version of a beloved child but that we are still attached to the one just past.

The gender-identity transition of a child presents a new confrontation with changed reality, bigger than sending a child off to college, maybe more momentous than seeing them get married. One of the complications is that, for almost all parents, the child is going through something we have never experienced. It disrupts the feeling (the fantasy, really) of being able to understand our children through our own experiences.

For the same-sex parent, fantasies of similarity or even identity are seriously disrupted. While my husband and I both found this life change demanding, my own reaction seemed to be deeper than his. Mothers and fathers often respond differently to challenges posed by their children, and the same-sex parent may be in a uniquely difficult position when a child transitions.

"Little girls operate from the gender premise 'I am female like you, and thus we are bonded through sameness' . . ." (Goldner, 2011b, p. 161). That sameness-bond seems to capture something about how I experienced the relationship between E and myself. Perhaps E's necessary individuation and self-discovery, entailing disavowal of such a significant "sameness," felt like a potential rupture of the attachment bond, not just a difficult transition, but a traumatic loss.

Loss recapitulates loss, and any similar experience revives the memories and feelings that attended prior losses. One's own divorce stirs up painful memories of parents' split decades earlier, the death of a pet revives the sorrow felt at an earlier bereavement. For someone whose early life contained too much disruption and relocation, even a wanted move to a new house may bring seemingly unaccountable depression. To heal from a new loss or disappointment one often has "to revisit those that came before. They are all part of your experience." (Boss, 1999, p. 50).

In my case, almost every separation from my daughter had revived a primal loss. My own mother left the family when I was an adolescent – she moved to California, leaving me with my father on the East Coast, and we had little relationship for years. E's move to the Pacific Northwest after college had already revealed my unconscious fear that when a mother and daughter are separated by an entire continent, the distance might cause a permanent and irreconcilable rupture, "the essential female tragedy" of mother-daughter loss (Rich, 1986, p. 237).

It seems obvious that the early stages of many parents' reactions to realizing a child is transgender may include grief – in all of its well-known manifestations, and not necessarily in order (Kübler-Ross, 1969). Denial, anger, bargaining, depression, acceptance are states of mind that parents may experience repeatedly. It isn't possible to find new things to be interested in and to love if we aren't able to experience the feelings that attend loss of a whole set of assumptions, patterns of relating, and expectations.

Grief *as a phase* of adjustment does not preclude full acceptance of a child's transgender status. In fact, the longer-term experience may entail personal growth, as parents come to understand transgender phenomena better, meet more transgender people, even become involved in projects to further the rights and social acceptance of variously gendered people.

I would argue, however, that to the extent this grief is not recognized, it is problematic and may be unnecessarily prolonged. The concept of *disenfranchised grief* (Doka, 1989) refers to grief that is not socially recognized. A child's gender transition may constitute an *ambiguous loss* (Boss, 1999), an experience that, in contrast to more familiar events such as the death of a spouse, may not be regarded by others or even by the person affected as entailing grief. Examples include the decline of a loved one into dementia, the death of someone with whom a relationship is not known or not sanctioned, loss of a familiar home and neighborhood, miscarriage and stillbirth.

Loss itself is integral to human experience and is not in itself an insurmountable problem. But unrecognized, unsupported, *unattended* loss (Levine, 2005) is a complication that makes a necessary life adjustment more difficult than otherwise. "Just as ambiguity complicates loss, it complicates the mourning process. People can't start grieving because the situation is indeterminate. It feels like a loss but it is not *really* one" (Boss, 1999, p. 11).

A related difficulty in coming to terms with a loved one's gender transition involves an early stage of adjustment to loss or trauma that is not always recognized. "Forming an account" (Parkes, 1983; Landsman, 2002) when something untoward occurs, entails coming to understand in most basic terms *what* has happened and *how* it happened. An adequate account of an accident, a death or any life-changing experience is needed to restore a sense of coherent narrative, basic cognitive mastery, and the illusion of control that makes life manageable. *The other driver was speeding. The young man had a hidden heart defect. The 401K was wiped out in the stock market crash.* Before we grapple with "why?" and "what now?" we have to get a grip on what has occurred.

This suggests that an early task of coming to terms with the gender transition of a child is to form some kind of understanding of what has occurred. For some families the coming out may not be a surprise, but the emergence of something that had been considered a possibility for some time. For others it may be completely unexpected, and the first questions may indeed be, "How did this happen? And where did this come from?"

A parent newly grappling with the ambiguous loss of a child's gender transition will not immediately find answers from the public position and statements of the transgender community itself. "Given the stakes," writes psychoanalyst Virginia Goldner (2011a, p. 154), "the trans community has taken the social recognition of gender variant persons to be its defining project." This is as should be, as the stakes are indeed very high. Despite the popularity of figures such as Laverne Cox and Caitlin Jenner, transgender people experience widespread discrimination and are more likely to be unemployed or underemployed. Trans individuals are still at shockingly higher risk of depression, anxiety, and suicide when not supported in their gender identity, and of homicide when they are "out" in situations of transphobia and violence (Grant et al., 2011).

Inescapably, though, the basic meaning-making task of forming an account may be frustrated early for a parent confronting a child's transition. Advice to parents emphasizes what it's *not* about – not something in parenting, nor being bullied, nor exposure to other gender-variant people. One finds in the professional discourse about transgender phenomena a similar reticence when it comes to theorizing about causation. The trans psychotherapist and writer Griffin Hansbury (2011) is deliberately a-etiological, holding this position as an analytic thinker in no small part because early analytic speculations constituted a wounding as well as mistaken constellation of trans-phobic theories that pathologized gender variance. Two decades ago another analyst made a similar point in writing about homosexuality, saying his work with gay patients is "guided by the question, '*How* homosexuality?' . . . as opposed to what I consider to be the ill-conceived etiological project of '*Why* homosexuality?'" (Corbett, 1997, p. 499).

We are living in a time when for transgender people the struggle for societal acceptance is paramount, when thinking people want to undo the harms of the past and mitigate the threats of the present.

It is understandable that, within the trans world, questions of "why" are viewed with suspicion, and not surprising that, by extension, being a good "ally" means avoiding any speculation about causality. What is unavoidable, however, is that the essential processes of forming an account and working through loss are compromised by what can feel like a gag order. This prescribed restriction of thinking makes this life change harder to process, and to the extent the adjustment entails mourning, it will be a "complicated bereavement" (Rando, 1993).

I didn't know nearly enough about transgender people, their needs and challenges. I didn't know any transgender people, period (now I know to say, "that I knew of") and my initial searches for information and support came up against the current political reality. Most of the information I found for cisgender people (those who identify with the gender assigned at birth, or consistent with external sexual characteristics) was energetic instruction on how to be a good ally and avoid unintended micro-aggressions. The preferred term is *transgender, not* transsexual. Transgender, *not* transgendered. *Don't* refer to sex change. *Don't* confuse sexual orientation with gender identity. *Avoid* gender stereotypes. Sexual orientation is not the same as gender identity. Don't assume. Don't ask. Listen.

I didn't and don't have any objection to all that. But I needed something else, something like, "How are *you* doing with all this?" or even, "This is going to be very hard at first." Some acknowledgement that for a parent the child's transition is a transition of one's own, to a new interpersonal reality that might take more than a little getting used to. Of course to get that kind of support I'd have had to be able to talk about it, and for a while I couldn't seem to. E was out of the closet, but now I was in a closet of my own.

When I was widowed suddenly in my mid-thirties, I didn't go to a support group for a year. It didn't take quite as long for E's father and me to find P-FLAG's Trans-families group, but in both cases the reluctance was really about not wanting to be *in* the group I knew I now belonged to. When I did begin to speak up, I was pretty touchy. I didn't want to hear from one friend how shocking, even terrible, this sounded. But I didn't want another friend's cheerful certainty that there would soon come a time when I'd no longer remember E as a girl, or think of myself as having a daughter. It reminded me of my younger struggling self, infuriated by those who assured me I'd marry again, but desperate to find some hope for the future. In both cases, timing was the problem. I didn't want to think my life was ruined, but I needed more time to adjust than the world seemed able to allow.

Early bereavement had been the catalyst that led to changing careers, becoming a psychologist and then something of an expert on trauma and loss. As that was more thoroughly assimilated and I began to confront the even more damaging effects of my mother's departure decades earlier, I came to psychoanalysis and eventually to memoir. In contrast to the years spent coming to terms with those life events, my efforts to engage with the transgender world and embrace a more complicated family scene have been relatively minor. I haven't become a transgender expert, but I do go to the support group, help organize a local Transgender Day of Remembrance, and have written this chapter. It's not so much, really. I'm still someone who needs to learn in order to feel a sense of mastery, but there wasn't so much to this in the end. In fact it did, as it should, enrich my life and expand my ability to deal with ambiguity and complexity.

I remember with great fondness the little girl I had, the child who gave me the chance to mother a daughter well and completely, a recompense for the fraught and prematurely ended mother-daughter experience I'd had myself. I cherished her little-girlness, and found meaning in constructing for a girl child what I had not had, a life protected and celebrated by both parents.

It turns out I didn't and don't need E to go on being a girl, don't need us to be the same in all ways, don't need to see myself reflected in E's life. I get to behold a person essentially familiar and precious, who does things I don't and can't do, who exists in the world in ways I admire. E is making a map while moving forward with life, and that's a map I can follow.

References

Boss, P. (1999). *Ambiguous loss: Learning to live with unresolved grief.* Cambridge, MA: Harvard University Press.

Corbett, K. (1997). Speaking queer: A reply to Richard C. Friedman. *Gender and Psychoanalysis, 2,* 495–514.

Doka, K. (1989). *Disenfranchised grief: Recognizing hidden sorrow.* Lexington, MA: Lexington Books.

Flores, A., Herman, J., Gates, G., & Brown, T. (2016.) *How many adults identify as transgender in the United States?* Los Angeles, CA: Williams Institute, UCLA School of Law.

Goldner, V. (2011a). Trans: Gender in free fall. *Psychoanalytic Dialogues, 21*(2), 159–171.

Goldner, V. (2011b). Transgender subjectivities: Introduction to papers by Goldner, Suchet, Saketopoulou, Handsbury, Salamon & Corbett, and Harris. *Psychoanalytic Dialogues, 21*(2), 153–159.

Grant, J. M., Mottet, L. A., Tanis, J., Harrison, J., Herman, J. L., & Keisling, M. (2011). *Injustice at every turn: A report of the National Transgender Discrimination Survey.* Washington, DC: National Gay and Lesbian Task Force and National Center for Transgender Equality.

Hansbury, G. (2011). King Kong and Goldilocks: Imagining transmasculinities through the trans-trans dyad. *Psychoanalytic Dialogues, 21,* 210–220.

James, J. W., & Friedman, R. (2009). *The grief recovery handbook* (20th anniversary expanded ed.). New York: Harper Collins.

Kübler-Ross, E. (1969). *On death and dying.* New York: Scribner.

Landsman, I. S. (2002). Crises of meaning in trauma and loss. In J. Kauffman (Ed.), *Loss of the assumptive world: A theory of traumatic loss* (pp. 13–30). New York: Brunner-Routledge.

Levine, S. (2005). *Unattended sorrow: Recovering from loss and reviving the heart.* Emmaus, PA: Rodale Press.

Parkes, C. M., & Weiss, R. S. (1983). *Recovery from bereavement.* New York: Basic Books.

Rando, T. A. (1993) *Treatment of complicated mourning.* Champaign, IL: Research Press.

Rich, A. (1986). *Of woman born: Motherhood as experience and institution.* New York: W. W. Norton.

Viorst, J. (1986). *Necessary losses: The loves, illusions, dependencies, and impossible expectations that all of us have to give up in order to grow.* New York: Simon and Schuster.

10

Gay fatherhood and the homosexual imaginary

Reparative fantasies, parenting across the gender divide, and good-enough narratives

Noah S. Glassman

For someone like me – a gay man old enough to have witnessed the ravages of AIDS, young enough to be a parent with another man – these are dizzying times of change. Not only is gay marriage legal at the federal level, but now same-sex couples can finally adopt in all 50 states because a federal judge recently struck down Mississippi's ban on gay-parent adoption (e.g., Reilly, 2016). Mississippi, with its 16-year-old prohibition, was the last holdout among several other states with similar bans, such as Alabama, Florida, Michigan, and Nebraska. And yet, while so much is changing, much remains the same. In North Carolina legislators and the governor passed a law, in record time, preventing municipalities from creating antidiscrimination policies for lesbian, gay, bisexual, and transgender (LGBT) individuals. Voters in Houston dealt a similar blow to gay and transgender rights a few months earlier, and legislators in Kansas, Minnesota, South Carolina, and Tennessee are considering comparable measures. Presidential candidates, like Senator Ted Cruz, meet with pastors like Kevin Swanson, who call for "the punishment of homosexuals by death." As the author Katherine Stewart (2015) noted in a recent *New York Times* op-ed, "When presidential candidates court support among the audience of a pastor who openly discusses the extermination of millions of their fellow citizens, why is this not major news?" Stewart proposes that because same-sex marriage now seems to have much public agreement, "pundits would have us believe that the culture war is over." And yet, anti-LGBT legislation will not die. In 2015, the same year the Supreme Court legalized gay marriage, 115 anti-LGBT bills appeared at state and local levels around the country. In 2016, so far, there have been 160. Moreover, many health professionals make a direct connection between anti-LGBT legislation and the rates of depression and anxiety seen among LGBT individuals (Broverman, 2016).

This is the backdrop to gay parenting in the 21st century: a mix of new possibilities and old, familiar hatred. We live in a climate where our entitlement to love, parent, and even live is seemingly "legitimized" one moment and vehemently fought the next. To put it differently, this is also a culture in which what it means to be gay is in flux. Steve Botticelli, a psychoanalyst (and my husband), has coined the term the "homosexual imaginary" to refer to:

> the universe of ideas about and representations of homosexuality that circulate in the culture. These include culturally prevalent homophobic images, representations and formulations that nevertheless do not wholly constitute the imaginary, and which . . . may or may not overlap with the lived . . . experience of gay [people]. They form a powerful ideality that shapes experience both within and between individuals of any and all sexualities. As new ideas, images, etc. about homosexuality come into being, as they have in recent years, it is in the nature of this unconscious cultural formation that . . . these become agglomerated onto already existing structures, rather than supplanting them.
>
> (2015, pp. 275–276)

The homosexual imaginary reflects the capacity for change in societal attitudes about homosexuality – as we are witnessing in the present cultural moment – as well as the persistence of conscious and unconscious representations of homophobia, and in this way goes beyond colloquial notions of stereotyping. Psychoanalysis has certainly contributed to the homosexual imaginary in its history of pathologizing homosexuality and unconventional gender (for reviews, see Drescher, 1998; Isay, 1989; Lewes, 1988) – a history that analysts of more recent generations have tried to address. While the idea that gay men can be parents has evolved to be far from shocking today, as reflected in popular culture (e.g., on TV, *Modern Family* or *The New Normal*), homophobic anxieties still permeate the society. Abigail Garner, a writer and adult child of a gay man, notes that she often fields questions from concerned heterosexuals, such as "Is it true that gay parents molest their children? Did your father try to make you gay?" (2005, p. 3). Similarly, new gay parents often want her to speak to questions such as "Will it be easier for children growing up with LGBT parents now compared to when [she] was a child?" – with the anxious hope that their children will not be subject to discrimination because society is changing.

Potent confrontations with various aspects of the homosexual imaginary occur often during the coming-out process, which is not a one-time event but rather is revisited throughout a gay person's life. Some gay people may feel that they are as "out" as possible in their pre-parenting lives but then find that having children can produce many more occasions for outing (Johnson & O'Connor, 2002). Gay parents and their children may have to explain their family repeatedly to new teachers, other school personnel, doctors, religious groups, and the parents of children's friends (Garner, 2005). These can be complicated, pregnant interactions in which it is unknown what one will encounter within the other or within oneself – homophobic or otherwise. (For example, will a child's preschool teacher prevent the display of a drawing of a family with two dads out of concern that it will be "upsetting" to other children? How does a gay father feel about Mother's Day?).

At these moments, the homosexual imaginary intersects with what it means to be a father or a mother in our society, or what it means to be maternal or paternal. This intersection is the crossroads of gender and the structuring of hierarchical power, as what is gay and what is feminine can both be devalued and demeaned in our culture.

Drawing upon my experiences as a gay parent, as well as those of my patients, I delineate here certain aspects of gay fatherhood subjectivities as shaped by the homosexual imaginary and gendered categories. I use these experiences to speculate, as well, about the nature of kinship in the psyches of gay men and the children they raise. With families formed through adoption, or with egg donors and gestational surrogates, gay parents and their children create novel origin stories that veer from the traditional and that raise questions about what constitutes "good-enough" narratives about family and belonging in today's world.

In discussing gay parenthood, my focus is on gay men in particular. Lesbian, bisexual, and transgender parents may have some overlapping experiences, and much that is different – not least because of differences in living within a patriarchal hierarchical power structure. Nor do I address specifically some of the most potent forms of "othering" when they happen to accompany being gay, such as race or religious minority status, which are also subject to power hierarchies (see Saketopoulou, 2011, for thoughtful work with such intersections). The writer Ta-Nehisi Coates (2015), in talking about race and power, incisively spells out that "race is the child of racism, not the father. . . . And the process of naming 'the people' has never been a matter of genealogy and physiognomy so much as one of *hierarchy*" (p. 7; italics added). In coming to terms with his own capacity for homophobia and its origins in societal power structures, he elaborates, "Hate gives identity. The nigger, the fag, the bitch illuminate the border, illuminate what we ostensibly are not, illuminate the Dream of being white, of being a Man. We name the hated strangers and are thus confirmed in the tribe" (p. 60). Othering can be a way for any of us to attempt some foothold in the hierarchy, a purchase created by standing on the backs of those who are "worse than we are." Coates acknowledges the desire for place and entitlement in American culture.

Reparative wishes meet interpellation and gender shame

Power hierarchies structure the homosexual imaginary and the experiences of growing up gay as well as living as gay parents. Perhaps especially for gay men of a certain generation, fantasies of parenthood may contain reparative wishes of empowerment born of the injuries of feeling "other" throughout their lives (Glassman & Botticelli, 2014). While *any* prospective parent's desire for a child may be permeated by redemptive wishes[1] (e.g., "I'm going to do it better than my parents did"), for some gay men, childhood and young adult experiences of being stigmatized and marginalized may shape powerful longings to feel and be seen as "normal." There may be fantasies that one's family of origin will finally become more accepting of one's homosexuality and one's partner if there is a child in the picture (Johnson & O'Connor, 2002). The hope might be that the child will provide an avenue for a sense of belonging and recognition within the family and the world at large.

On the other hand, being gay parents out in the world can be fraught with feelings of alienation and a sense of being under a microscope, watched closely by the heteronormative surround. Gay parents in public with their families can feel looked upon as representing *all* gay parents and their competence and entitlement to raise children, while heterosexual parents represent only themselves (Garner, 2005), without the burden of proving the fitness of their group. Years ago Steve and I were on a plane with our son when he was an infant. We were trying, unsuccessfully, to get him to take a bottle as the plane cabin was being pressurized; we hoped the swallowing would ease any discomfort in his ears. He started to cry, *loudly*. An airline attendant told us she could not believe so much sound came from such a little person, as she repeatedly (and, it felt, somewhat aggressively) made suggestions for what might help. We were mortified at being those gay men with the crying baby, the gay men who couldn't soothe their child. Our mortification was certainly inflected by the homosexual imaginary's representations of gay men as "unnatural" parents, even pedophiles, dangerous to children, having no business raising them. The grip of these aspects of the homosexual imaginary does not recede as children get older. Several gay parents in my practice have described the fear of being seen as predators by other parents when their children have play dates in their homes, and some gay fathers have had parents outright refuse to allow their children to come over.

These are moments when gay fathers can feel caught in the headlights of being named, defined, isolated by the culture at large. Borrowing from philosophy and Marxist theory, Guralnik and Simeon (2010) used Althusser (2000 [1969]) to introduce psychoanalysis to the concept of *interpellation*, referring to the ways that the authority of social institutions can "hail" us into social existence:

> Althusser's famous example is of how we feel when hailed by a policeman. "*Hey you!*" toward which we turn guiltily, "*What did I do?*" We immediately morph into *self-as-criminal*, thereby revealing where the force of the State and our identity as individuals meet.
>
> (p. 407)

Gay fathers can similarly be "hailed into being" by the homosexual imaginary, having their subjectivities co-opted in everyday moments. Interpellation, unlike projective identification, carries the force and impact of society's delimiting structures.

A related phenomenon has also been described by social psychologists in research on *stereotype threat*, which is the growing sense that what one does or how one is being perceived in a given moment could confirm negative stereotypes about one's group (Steele & Aronson, 1995). For years, this body of research has looked at types of stereotype threat among black Americans and has broadened its scope to other areas, such as gender-relevant stereotype threat and, more recently, stereotype-threat processes in gay men. If stereotype threat is evoked, one's behavior/performance is affected, presumably due to anxiety – conscious or otherwise. In one study, researchers had heterosexual men and gay men interact with children in a nursery school during free-play time (Bosson, Haymovitz, & Pinel, 2004). Just before these interactions, half of the men (straight and gay) filled out demographic questionnaires in which they were asked to indicate their sexual orientation; that is, half of the gay men were reminded of their stigmatized group membership. The researchers found that these "primed" gay men exhibited greater nonverbal anxiety during their interactions with the children and demonstrated less competence in their ability to communicate with the children and provide childcare, compared with gay men who had not been reminded of their sexual orientation and to straight men in either the primed or not-primed conditions. Interestingly, while the primed gay men did not *self-report* more anxiety on questionnaires, they *exhibited* more fidgeting, lip chewing, nervous smiling, stiff posture, and eye aversion. Presumably, these men were "caught in the headlights" of notions of gay people as harmful to children, hailed as, at minimum, incompetent, if not interpellated as outright pederasts.

The persistence of these aspects of the homosexual imaginary are noteworthy given the proliferation of research demonstrating that developmental outcomes for children of gay parents are just as "good" as those of straight parents (for a review, see Goldberg, 2010). Historically, there have been several reasons for gay parents to have a somewhat defensive stance on how well their children are doing and to support this kind of research: for example, in situations when a husband and wife divorced after one member of the couple came out as gay, child-outcome research was necessary to ensure that the courts would not deny the gay parent custody or parental rights. Gay parents had to show that they would not adversely affect a child's development (e.g., Garner, 2005). This needed to be demonstrated as well to adoption agencies that refused to work with gay clients. Only relatively recently, with some legal protections in place, has there been the psychic space to consider differences between the children of same-sex parents and other children (e.g., Stacey & Biblarz, 2001; see also Glassman, 2015). For instance, some children of gay parents have a more flexible approach to expressions of gendered behavior (Fulcher, Sutfin, & Patterson, 2008; Golombok et al., 2014) and are more likely to consider same-sex attractions for themselves (Goldberg, 2010), although ultimately they do not identify as gay or bisexual in higher numbers (Bailey, Bobrow, Wolfe, & Mikach, 1995). Garner (2005) quotes the 28-year-old son of a gay father: "[I] can drop my masculinity sometimes. . . . I can be more effeminate and openly affectionate with other men and not have to feel insecure or weird about it" (p. 32). (I will return later to speculate further about potential differences for the children of same-sex parents.)

Gender, however, can be a site of traumatic injury for some gay men, especially for those who transgressed as boys in their gender expression or who experienced themselves internally as gender inadequate (Corbett, 1993, 1996; Drescher, 1998) – an aspect of self often damaged through having grown up in a homophobic society that conflates gender with sexual orientation and has little tolerance for gender expansiveness or creativity (Corbett, 2016; Ehrensaft, 2016). Gendered injuries can shape fantasies around parenthood for some gay men, conjuring possibilities for further injury and/or repair as their children begin to perform gender. For instance, raising seeming "boy" boys (as opposed to the more "girly" boys some gay fathers may have felt themselves to be, or the "girly" men they feel they are as adults) can evoke echoes of childhood gender shame. Once, when Steve was playing soccer with our son, Steve complained of injuring himself. Our son, at this time a "boy" boy 10-year-old who was well versed in cultural (peer) mandates regarding masculinity, told him to "man through it" – a loaded injunction for some gay men to hear, and perhaps loaded for some children of gay dads to say. Gay fathers can be left to parse out what is a homophobic expression or challenge, what is a mimicking of language bandied about on the soccer field, and what is a child's effort to find his or her place in the gendered culture at large. What would it feel like (and mean) for our son to say to one (or both) of us, "That's so *gay!*" – a common enough indictment in today's middle and high schools?

Revisiting sites of past injury, however, can also open new routes for feelings of inclusion and reclamation. As our son became interested in baseball and Little League, I was taken aback by my intensely anxious reaction to participating with other dads; my childhood experiences with team sports were largely humiliating and an occasion for being singled out as "fag" and "Nellie" (Glassman & Botticelli, 2014). Experiencing the game through my son's enthusiasm, however, also gave me a different relationship to sporting events, putting me in greater touch with my own capacity for enjoying these stereotypically masculine events, while still claiming my particular gendered history and identity as a gay man. Several patients have also been surprised by their own athletic prowess as they have moved into competitive sports with their children. Previously, they had not had the opportunity to explore these latent talents because childhood gender transgressions, and the ridicule and bullying that ensued, closed off possibilities for safe-feeling, expansive play involving their bodies.

Parenting across the gender divide

Gender also infuses the gay parenting experience, as it educes questions about what is paternal or maternal – for gay men as well as for psychoanalysis – with the specter of the oedipal also reverberating through the homosexual imaginary. Psychoanalysis has evolved to conceptualize gender as potentially more fluid (e.g., Harris, 2005), incorporating notions of multiple self states to include gender multiplicity within any given person (e.g., Davies, 2015; Diamond, 2009), and multiplicity in expressions of masculinity and femininity across individuals and cultures. Person (2009) asserts, "Gender is a term that must be understood to incorporate the variety of masculinities and femininities that in fact exist" (p. 17). Until recently, however, psychoanalytic theorizing about parental functions has been intertwined with traditional notions of masculinity and femininity and parental genitals, so that "anatomy [becomes] parental destiny" (Samuels, 1996). In these essentialist lines of thought, early childcare is assumed to be a largely female activity, with motherhood conflated with nurturing, soothing, symbiosis, the "natural," and the preoedipal. Fatherhood, by contrast, has been associated with activity, the outside world, heightening tension through more lively play, authority, and a necessary separating third presence who eventually inserts himself into the mother-child dyad, ushering in oedipal dynamics (Davies & Eagle, 2013; Freeman, 2008; Hughes, 2015; Samuels, 1996; see also Atlas, 2016). Traditional thinking about the nuclear-family requirements of the oedipus complex, in part, created the necessity for such separate, gendered functions (Glassman, 2015). Of course, these are limiting constructs that eclipse various possibilities, such as the mother who "lays down the law" or the father who is intimately involved and nurturing with his infant.

Nontraditional family structures, like same-sex couples with their children, challenge the cultural imaginary's nuclear family constellation and its psychoanalytic underpinnings. Gay men caring for infants can face a double bind around doing "women's work" or primary caregiving in a patriarchal society that overvalues and privileges the masculine while idealizing the maternal as natural (Badinger, 1981) – when maternal functions are provided by a woman. These men may not be performing masculinity well enough (or may feel they are not) while also not being good-enough "mothers" by virtue of not being biological women. Of course, heterosexual men who are primary caregivers may also contend with the shadow of the homosexual imaginary in this way, and they may even come to this bind with a history of feeling gender inadequate (as some gay men do), but they have not necessarily had the history of knowing that one's same-sex desire is an unnatural "otherness" widely reviled. That is, the straight father on primary baby duty is at *risk* of being perceived as moving dangerously close to the emasculated-gay-man aspect of the homosexual imaginary; the gay father providing infant care *knows* he is already there.

Contemporary theorizing has attempted to de-link parenting functions and the sex of the parent. Freeman (2008), in discussing more traditional psychoanalytic notions of fatherhood, observes:

> in achieving masculine autonomy through rejecting the feminine, patriarchal males are denied access to the psychological vocabulary of love and emotional connectedness that defines the maternal sphere. This denial inherently constrains the expression of involved forms of fatherhood in adult life, a forbidden intimacy.
>
> (p. 126)

Samuels (1996) in a similar but more acerbic vein has noted:

> Our culture has employed a fear and loathing of homosexuality as a weapon
> to keep men tied into the role of provider in the family, the one who must
> therefore remain emotionally distant. The pay-off for men has been access to
> economic and political power. The cost has been in terms of paternal warmth.
>
> (p. 108)

These cultural mandates serve no one – neither men nor women, straight or gay –
except those who wish to maintain traditional patriarchal power structures in
society. As a counterpoint, research on fatherhood, and on parenting in general,
suggests that there is little evidence that the gender of the parent, or the parent's gender performance (or the parent's sexual orientation, as noted above) has
a particularly important influence on the development of children. Rather, it is the
quality of parenting and the parent-child relationship that is most important (e.g.,
Golombok, 2015; Pruett, 1998).

Space has opened up to consider the preoedipal father and the nature of his
relationship with the infant, as well as the infant's capacity for multiple significant
attachments and for early triadic relations (rather than exclusive symbiosis; e.g.,
Fivaz-Depeursinge, Lavanchy-Scaiola, & Favez, 2010). Moreover, the capacity
for providing multiple parenting functions may be present in one caregiver (Samuels, 1996). Winnicott (1987), for instance, pointed out that a mother may become
less empathically attuned, more frustrating, and more "stretching" (i.e., "paternal") in her way of interacting with her baby as she senses the infant's increasing
integration and independence. Research on parental modes of play with children
bear out the varying capacities that both mothers and fathers have for more active,
physical play (stereotypically paternal), as well as quieter, more reflective and
protective play (e.g., Raphael-Leff, 1991).

In addition, we now know that *both* women and men go through biological changes as they anticipate parenthood and become parents. Evidence has
emerged, for example, that fatherhood leads to decreases in levels of testosterone
and estradiol; the more time spent caring for children, the greater the decrease
(Gettler, McDade, Feranil, & Kuzawa, 2011; see also, Edelstein et al., 2015). If
a father – lowered testosterone and all – is being nurturing, sensitive, and caring
with a baby, is this being maternal or paternal? And can we answer this question –
in the process, categorizing behavior and interpellating an individual within the
nuclear-family imaginary – without foreclosing other possibilities that might better reflect the lived experiences of contemporary families?

It is not only heteronormative culture that can be too quick to answer this type
of question. Some gay fathers, coming under the sway of cultural norms about
what constitutes a family, may react too quickly and defensively as well. For
example, made anxious and defiant by the cultural gaze of not being a biological
mother, while providing primary infant care, a gay father might feel, "*I'm* the

mama papa" (Glassman, 2013) – an assertion of supplying the needed "mothering." Alternatively, some gay fathers – perhaps especially those with daughters – may feel pressured to involve adult female figures in the child's daily life, therefore providing what is "lacking." What may get foreclosed in the anxieties underlying such scenarios might include holding open a space to consider and talk about the experience of *difference* (What is it like for a daughter of gay men to be the only girl in the family? What is it like to be in a same-sex-parent family that is unlike those around you?). This space is a type of *family reverie* (Ehrensaft, 2008; see also Corbett, 2001), which could encompass, too, imaginings about birth "others" not present in everyday life (e.g., birth mothers / fathers in adoption; egg donors / surrogates in assisted reproductive technology births). Family reverie helps to convey what is thinkable and permissible in the construction of the family narrative. Such reverie can occur in the context of a family that is not "deficient" or "other," but that is good enough and complete. Perhaps talking about difference is complex for gay men who have always felt different in their developmental histories – in their desires, sometimes in their gender expression, too – and to open space for considering the experience of difference with their children re-evokes old vulnerabilities that no parent wants to revisit on his child.

Motherless children in the cultural imaginary

The adoption literature historically has been saturated with the "primal wound" narrative (Verrier, 1993) in which the child suffers irreversible abandonment trauma and loss because of maternal separation, no matter what age the child began to live with the adopted family. This "canonical narrative" (Hughes, 2015) continues to reverberate in contemporary analytic writing in descriptions of the "rupture in the biological ecosystem shared between birthmother and infant" (De Peyer, 2013, p. 151, as cited in Hughes, 2015). More broadly, the *cultural* imaginary has been taken with the notion of the motherless child, as reflected in the stories of Oedipus, Moses, Oliver Twist, Peter Pan (Brinich, 1993; Hughes, 2015), and any number of child-oriented movies in recent years ("Despicable Me," etc.). This cultural narrative is relevant not only to children adopted by gay men, but also to children who may share common genes with one of their gay fathers (having been conceived with egg donors and surrogates), who are also separated from the women who conceived and birthed them. Gay-father families disrupt the cultural discourse around the essential nature of blood ties and, in particular, the importance of growing up with the woman who birthed you; they violate "biological ecosystems" in a way that the child – and society – cannot recover from easily.

Elizabeth Hughes (2015) elucidates the cultural dominance of these kinds of narratives and the way they interpellate the subjectivities of adopted children. Based on her compelling qualitative research, Hughes concludes that, for the adopted child constructing a good-enough narrative of the self, what may be most important is not reunion with the biological mother (thought by some to be a necessary journey). Rather, Hughes posits that it is "making connections with an internal mother" (p. 156). She elaborates:

> Opening up a space for adoptees to explore their conscious and unconscious fantasies through stories about the parents they could have had and the life they might have lived, the focus shifts from the external figure of the biological mother as a site of resolution to the adoptive subject's internal world.
>
> (p. 156)

This is part of the psychic work – and play – of the family reverie, and can help the child, as well as gay fathers, to locate themselves in the cultural discourse, and to define their subjectivities themselves.

Gay sex and parenting: men losing their grip on gender

Potential gender transgression is but one kind of difference that shapes experience for some gay men in their development and in their adulthood – perhaps the most memorable kind, given the relentless overt cultural shaming involved (Blum & Pfetzing, 1997). Of course, many gay men, as boys, feel different as well in their erotic fantasies and in their affectional longings. These aspects of their experience are, at best, not mirrored or responded to, and at worst, felt as terrible, forbidden, and unthinkable – usually within the family as well as within society. As Blum and Pfetzing (1997) note:

> A sense of "feeling different" is difficult enough, but when one intuitively senses that it might be related to some of the most taboo, frightening, despised images in our culture, as well as in one's own family, then this is surely too emotionally overstimulating as well as cognitively disorganizing for the young proto-gay child.
>
> (p. 433)

In theorizing possible connections within the cultural imaginary between types of sexuality and the intergenerational transmission of trauma, Steve Botticelli (2015) proposes that homosexuality and trauma share a "quality of unrepresentability (homosexuality as the 'love that dare not speak its name'; trauma as that which cannot be symbolized by the mind)" (p. 276) – and both are not spoken about with children. Moreover, "Within the homosexual imaginary, gay men are considered to have lost their grip on gender by virtue of their willingness, if not enthusiasm, to be penetrated" (Botticelli, 2015, p. 285) – one of the ways sexual orientation and gender can be interimplicated. That is, for men, bodily penetration (and psychic penetration) can pose a traumatic gender-based threat, especially if it raises the specter of being unable *to* penetrate (Elise, 2001). Within this type of cultural discourse, gay sex violates gender, its pleasures are perverse, and it can be unspeakable – adding to anxious homophobic sanctions against those who practice it.

Navigating the sexual margins has always been complicated for gay men; having children in the mix can make it more so, given the ways that having children can make gay men feel more on display within the cultural mainstream. Consequently, some gay-father couples feel quite self-conscious about even "G-rated" displays of affection between them when in front of their children – even within the confines of their own home, away from the stigmatizing gaze of the public. And, of course, messages about gay sex are conveyed to our children through multiple channels. One gay father told me that after his kids had a few sex education classes at school, his children informed him that he and their other father "couldn't have *real* sex" because their sex was not procreative.

Some gay fathers, after years of experiencing homophobic attacks, may be especially sensitized to any indication of seemingly homophobic expressions by their children. For instance, a gay father of a latency-age daughter overheard her and a friend giggling with disgust over the thought of two boys kissing ("Eww!"). He became angry and chagrined that his daughter could be so discriminatory, wondering what had he done wrong. Later, however, he discovered that he had overheard only part of a longer conversation about how "gross" *any* kissing was, no matter *who* was doing it in whatever combination, whether it be a boy and girl, or two girls, or two boys. The exchange seemed more about grappling with *sexuality*, in an age-appropriate way, than deriding *homosexuality* per se.[2]

Kinship, recognition, and the good-enough narrative

Long embedded in psychoanalytic theorizing is the truism that being human involves making meaning through storytelling, constructing narratives as a way of constructing the self and one's place in the world. We tell stories to ourselves, and we tell stories to our children, often about origins and beginnings (e.g., birth stories, family stories), as a way of locating ourselves and our children. These stories are often employed to help children make sense of kinship relations (e.g., Levi-Strauss, 1969), with nontraditional families creating new forms of such connections (e.g., Ehrensaft, 2008). In previous work I have highlighted how a certain type of kinship knowledge or connectedness may be denied, obscured, or rendered unthinkable for gay individuals in their development (Glassman & Botticelli, 2014). Gay people grow up usually feeling (secretly) unlike anyone else in their immediate family, and unlike anyone in their extended family, and we often do not have access to knowledge of, for example, the lesbian aunt or the gay uncle (although this may be changing for newer generations of proto-gay children). These relatives have often been closeted, or their existence eliminated from family trees, cutting off possibilities for a sense of "alikeness" or belonging. Moreover:

> Unlike being black or Jewish, the gay man as child is both typically alone with his "differentness," as well as often unclear, confused, conflicted, horrified by "it." Unlike the black child whose parents are typically also black or the Jewish child with Jewish parents and relatives, the proto-gay child typically not only does not have gay parents, but doesn't even know what "gay" is except as a very nebulous and very negative thing.
>
> (Blum & Pfetzing, 1997, p. 431)

Nor do gay people get role models for what gay parenting looks like. There are no stories told to proto-gay children to help them locate themselves in society, much less locate themselves in family structures across the generations – other than stories about homosexuality as unthinkable, a violation of the Natural and the Moral.

I wonder about gaps in thinking, challenges to coherent narrative construction about the self, lacunae in the stream of consciousness that constitutes the sense of ongoing being in the world, and the impact of being socially unintelligible. If recognition, in its intersubjective definition (Benjamin, 1998), is "that response from the other which makes meaningful the feelings, intentions, and actions of the self. . . [allowing] the self to realize its agency and authorship in a tangible way" (p. 12), it can be in short supply for the proto-gay boy and his unthinkable sense of difference.

Guralnik and Simeon (2010) introduced interpellation – being "hailed" and defined by social structures – as "a relative of recognition," perhaps its dark cousin.

> *The space between recognition and interpellation* is where one's sense of personhood is repeatedly carved out; it is where the psychological need for recognition in order to *become*, and the social force of interpellation that allows one to be – meet, or collide.
>
> (p. 408)

I wonder about such "collisions" – between the need for recognition and interpellation by the homosexual imaginary – as they recur throughout the life of the gay boy/man/father, and the consequences for building a "good-enough" narrative about the self and being in the world. I am defining a good-enough narrative as "a flexible, mutable, living structure, capable of acknowledging gaps" in one's efforts to understand one's origins and relation to the cultural context (Glassman, 2013, pp. 117–118). The good-enough narrative may not be a single entity, but rather may employ multiple narratives, shifting depending on the momentary needs of the subject (think, for instance, of the kaleidoscope metaphor Jody Davies [2015] uses for the relational unconscious, with its shifting self states and internalized self/other configurations). I am interested here not in deficit or lack in the construction of the good-enough narrative, but rather in creative use of it in maintaining a refusal to subjugate the self entirely to the dictates of social discourse; a refusal to foreclose a space for the non-normative, allowing for new forms of the good-enough narrative to emerge.

Creating good-enough narratives involves individual as well as family reverie for gay men and their children. We have some things in common, perhaps, with our children of adoption and our children of assisted reproductive technology, as we all have gaps in our kinship knowledge and experiences of self-as-different (Glassman & Botticelli, 2014). As families navigating the cultural mainstream, we can encounter moments of illegibility to those around us – that is, moments when recognition and interpellation collide. During a museum outing with our son, age 3, in a New Jersey suburb, a museum staff member – a woman, perhaps in her seventies – said to our son, "Out with Dad and uncle, eh?" We told her that our son had two dads, to which she replied, "So he's out with Dad and grandpa!" Maybe she didn't hear us, but we were left wondering about the "category crisis" we created for her – while Steve and I, both in our early 40s at the time, also grappled with our mutual narcissistic horror in trying to figure out which one of us was the grandpa. Even in the age of *Modern Family* and gay marriage, being recognized as gay parents seemed not to be an option in this suburban context. To be unintelligible to society is in some ways to be rendered unthinkable, caught momentarily in a gray zone of potential unreality.

Life on the margins

Having lived on the margins of social discourse, gay people have long been creative about relationships and what constitutes family. Romantic and sexual relationships did not have to be monogamous. Family was not based on blood relations or marriage. Instead, family was whomever one chose to be close to – especially given that one's family of origin might have thrown one out for being gay. Gay people have also had to be creative in having children, in constructing both personal and family narratives, and in extending the usual confines of the traditional family. In my clinical and personal experience, many gay fathers have strived to integrate birth others (in open adoptions, as well as with egg donors and surrogates) into the lives of their children (see also Golombok, 2015). This has been done not necessarily out of anxiety about what was "missing" in a family, but rather out of openness to being outside of the mainstream of the cultural imaginary. This "queering" of the family (Oswald, Blume, & Marks, 2005), born despite (or because of) being "unthinkable," also opens new avenues of thought and can create opportunities for resisting forms of interpellation that close off new ways of being in the world. As the daughter of one nontraditional family put it:

> It's kind of like I shouldn't exist. And if society is telling me I shouldn't exist, then what *can* I believe? I think for me, a big thing I have learned from all of

this is the ability and necessity to be a social critic – to automatically question society.

(Garner, 2005, p. 34)

Notes

1 Qualitative research indicates that the stated *motivations* for parenthood are no different for gay men than for heterosexuals – that is, enjoying children, feeling that raising
   them is a part of life, and valuing family relationships (Goldberg, Downing, & Moyer,
   2012).
2 Just as psychoanalysis has been challenged by gender theorizing and same-sex parents to
   reconsider maternal and paternal functions, gay sex confronts heteronormative assumptions within psychoanalysis about the development of unconscious fantasy in children.
   Gay parenting confronts us with the possibility of same-sex primal scene fantasies in the
   children of gay couples (e.g., Aron, 1995). The implications of such fantasies are beyond
   the scope of this chapter.

References

Althusser, L. (2000). Ideology and state apparatus. In S. Zizek (Ed.), *Mapping ideology*
    (pp. 100–140). New York: Verso. (Original work published 1969)
Aron, L. (1995). The internalized primal scene. *Psychoanalytic Dialogues*, *5*, 195–237.
Atlas, G. (2016). *The enigma of desire: Sex, longing, and belonging in psychoanalysis*.
    New York: Routledge.
Badinger, E. (1981). *The myth of motherhood: An historical view of the maternal instinct*.
    London: Souvenir.
Bailey, J. M., Bobrow, D., Wolfe, M., & Mikach, S. (1995). Sexual orientation of adult sons
    of gay fathers. *Developmental Psychology*, *31*, 124–129.
Benjamin, J. (1998). *Shadow of the other: Intersubjectivity and gender in psychoanalysis*.
    New York: Routledge.
Blum, A., & Pfetzing, V. (1997). Assaults to the self: The trauma of growing up gay. *Gen-
    der & Psychoanalysis*, *2*, 427–442.
Bosson, J. K., Haymovitz, E. L., & Pinel, E. C. (2004). When saying and doing diverge:
    The effects of stereotype threat on self-reported versus non-verbal anxiety. *Journal of
    Experimental Social Psychology*, *40*, 247–255.
Botticelli, S. (2015). Has sexuality anything to do with war trauma? Intergenerational
    transmission and the homosexual imaginary. *Psychoanalytic Perspectives*, *12*, 275–288.
Brinich, P. (1993). Adoption from the inside out: A psychoanalytic perspective. In D. M.
    Brodzinsky & M. Schechter (Eds.), *The psychology of adoption*. New York: Clarendon
    Press.
Broverman, N. (2016, March 18). How our intolerant society contributes to LGBT mental
    disorders. *The Advocate*.
Coates, T. (2015). *Between the world and me*. New York: Random House.
Corbett, K. (1993). The mystery of homosexuality. *Psychoanalytic Psychology*, *10*,
    345–357.
Corbett, K. (1996). Homosexual boyhood: Notes on girlyboys. *Gender and Psychoanaly-
    sis*, *1*, 429–461.
Corbett, K. (2001). Nontraditional family romance. *Psychoanalytic Quarterly*, *70*, 599–624.

Corbett, K. (2016). *A murder over a girl: Justice, gender, junior high*. New York: Henry Holt.

Davies, J. M. (2015). From oedipal complex to oedipal complexity: Reconfiguring (pardon the expression) the negative Oedipus complex and the disowned erotics of disowned sexualities. *Psychoanalytic Dialogues*, *25*, 265–283.

Davies, N., & Eagle, G. (2013). Conceptualizing the paternal function: Maleness, masculinity, or thirdness? *Contemporary Psychoanalysis*, *49*, 559–585.

De Peyer, J. (2013). Sequestered selves: Discussion of adoption roundtable. *Psychoanalytic Perspectives*, *10*, 149–168.

Diamond, M. J. (2009). Masculinity and its discontents: Making room for the "mother" inside the male – an essential achievement for healthy male gender identity. In B. Reis & R. Grossmark (Eds.), *Heterosexual masculinities: Contemporary perspectives from psychoanalytic gender theory*. New York: Routledge.

Drescher, J. (1998). *Psychoanalytic therapy and the gay man*. Hillsdale, NJ: Analytic Press.

Edelstein, R. S., Wardecker, B. M., Chopik, W. J., Moors, A. C., Shipman, E. L., & Lin, N. J. (2015). Prenatal hormones in first-time expectant parents: Longitudinal changes and within-couple correlations. *American Journal of Human Biology*, *27*, 317–325.

Ehrensaft, D. (2008). When baby makes three or four or more: Attachment, individuation, and identity in assisted-conception families. *Psychoanalytic Study of the Child*, *63*, 3–23.

Ehrensaft, D. (2016). *The gender creative child: Pathways for nurturing and supporting children who live outside gender boxes*. New York: The Experiment.

Elise, D. (2001). Unlawful entry: Male fears of psychic penetration. *Psychoanalytic Dialogues*, *11*, 499–531.

Fivaz-Depeursinge, E., Lavanchy-Scaiola, C., & Favez, N. (2010). The young infant's triangular communication in the family: Access to threesome intersubjectivity? *Psychoanalytic Dialogues*, *20*(2), 125–140.

Freeman, T. (2008). Psychoanalytic concepts of fatherhood: Patriarchal paradoxes and the presence of an absent authority. *Studies in Gender and Sexuality*, *9*, 113–139.

Fulcher, M., Sutfin, E. L., & Patterson, C. J. (2008). Individual differences in gender development: Associations with parental sexual orientation, attitudes, and division of labor. *Sex Roles*, *58*, 330–341.

Garner, A. (2005). *Families like mine: Children of gay parents tell it like it is*. New York: Harper.

Gettler, L. T., McDade, T. W., Feranil, A. B., & Kuzawa, C. W. (2011). Longitudinal evidence that fatherhood decreases testosterone in human males. *Proceedings of the National Academy of Sciences*, *108*, 16194–16199.

Glassman, N., & Botticelli, S. (2014). Perspectives on gay fatherhood: Emotional legacies and clinical reverberations. In S. Kuchuck (Ed.), *Clinical implications of the psychoanalyst's life experience: When the personal becomes professional*. New York: Routledge.

Glassman, N. S. (2013). Narrative, family romance fantasy, and the adoption triad. *Psychoanalytic Perspectives*, *10*, 116–119.

Glassman, N. S. (2015). "The baby with the creampuffs": Further complications in oedipal complexities, Commentary on paper by Jody Messler Davies. *Psychoanalytic Dialogues*, *25*, 295–305.

Goldberg, A. E. (2010). *Lesbian and gay parents and their children: Research on the family life cycle*. Washington, DC: American Psychological Association.

Goldberg, A. E., Downing, J. B., & Moyer, A. M. (2012). Why parenthood, and why now? Gay men's motivations for pursuing parenthood. *Family Relations*, *61*, 157–174.

Golombok, S. (2015). *Modern families: Parents and children in new family forms*. Cambridge, UK: Cambridge University Press.

Golombok, S., Mellish, L., Jennings, S., Casey, P., Tasker, F., & Lamb, M. E. (2014). Adoptive gay father families: Parent-child relationships and children's psychological adjustment. *Child Development, 85*, 456–468.

Guralnik, O., & Simeon, D. (2010). Depersonalization: Standing in the spaces between recognition and interpellation. *Psychoanalytic Dialogues, 20*, 400–416.

Harris, A. (2005). *Gender as soft assembly*. Hillsdale, NJ: Analytic Press.

Hughes, E. (2015). "There's no such thing as a whole story": The psychosocial implications of adopted women's experiences of finding their biological fathers in adulthood. *Studies in Gender and Sexuality, 16*, 151–169.

Isay, R. A. (1989). *Being homosexual: Gay men and their development*. New York: Random House.

Johnson, S., & O'Connor, E. (2002). *The gay baby boom: The psychology of gay parenthood*. New York: New York University Press.

Levi-Strauss, C. (1969). *The elementary structures of kinship* (2nd ed.). Boston, MA: Beacon Press.

Lewes, K. (1988). *The psychoanalytic theory of male homosexuality*. New York: Pocket Books.

Oswald, R., Blume, L., & Marks, S. (2005). Decentering heteronormativity: A model for family studies. In V. Bengston, A. Acock, K. Allen, D. Klein, & P. Dilworth-Anderson (Eds.), *Sourcebook of family theory and research* (pp. 143–165). Thousand Oaks, CA: Sage.

Person, E. S. (2009). Masculinities, plural. In B. Reis & R. Grossmark (Eds.), *Heterosexual masculinities: Contemporary perspectives from psychoanalytic gender theory*. New York: Routledge.

Pruett, K. (1998). Research perspectives: Roles of the father. *Pediatrics, 102*, 1253–1261.

Raphael-Leff, J. (1991). *Psychological processes of childbearing*. London: Chapman and Hall.

Reilly, M. (2016, March 31). Same-sex couples can now adopt children in all 50 states. *The Huffington Post*.

Saketopoulou, A. (2011). Minding the gap: Intersections between gender, race, and class in work with gender variant children. *Psychoanalytic Dialogues, 21*, 192–209.

Samuels, A. (1996). The good-enough father of whatever sex. In C. Clulow (Ed.), *Partners becoming parents: The Tavistock marital studies institute*. Northvale, NJ: Aronson.

Stacey, J., & Biblarz, T. J. (2001). (How) does the sexual orientation of parents matter? *American Sociological Review, 66*, 159–183.

Steele, C. M., & Aronson, J. (1995). Stereotype threat and the intellectual test performance of African Americans. *Journal of Personality and Social Psychology, 69*, 797–811.

Stewart, K. (2015, November 16). Ted Cruz and the anti-gay pastor. *The New York Times*.

Verrier, N. N. (1993). *The primal wound: Understanding the adopted child*. Baltimore, MD: Gateway Press.

Winnicott, D. W. (1987). *The child, the family, and the outside world*. Reading, MA: Addison-Wesley.

Part IV

Social topics

In this section, our authors tackle a number of psychosocial issues, both present-day and long-standing, that confront today's families, looking at them through a contemporary lens and delving into how these circumstances may affect an adolescent or young adult. They examine how parents can support their child while at the same time attending to the press of external demands.

Hemda Arad considers the experience of transcontinental parenting from a different angle, exploring the interweaving themes of losing and finding yourself in other cultures. She traces the mysterious intermingling of heritage that occurs when raising children in a culture different from one's native land. Arad describes how children of immigrants may feel a sense of belonging to a time and a place in which they never lived but which beckons to them still. The sense of straddling two cultures may permeate their experience growing up in a world that may remain alien to their parents, yet is infused with the sensations and memories of their parents' homeland. She also describes this intergenerational dynamic as it plays out in the consulting room, when patients may experience the analyst's otherness through the lens of a shared or divergent culture.

Elizabeth Trawick's moving chapter explores a different intergenerational dynamic, one in which the trauma that she experienced as a child of an alcoholic mother re-emerges as the mother herself of an alcohol-dependent adult son. She explores how, as a parent, her mind pushed away her early recognition of her son's genetic predisposition to alcoholism. Struggling to remain present and steady as a parent, she was overwhelmed by her own painful childhood memories. For her, the pathway through her grief and anguish presented itself serendipitously one night, when she and her son, unable to breach the tremendous physical and emotional distance between them with words, began to read aloud to one another from a beloved childhood series. As this became a ritual between them, it also became a lifeline for both the author and her son.

Finally, Billie A. Pivnick explores the developmental pathways of adopted children and families. In describing her own experience of being the adoptive mother of two chosen and beloved sons, she describes her family's evolution in the context of the deepest meaning of "to adopt" – that is, to accept and embrace. She shows us how the adoption experience forms an essential part of individual and familial identity. For many children adopted early in their lives, there can be an experience of loss that has no words because it refers to the absence of something not yet remembered, or rather something that a child experiences as a kind of hole – one, as Pivnick eloquently points out, that can be made "whole" in the context of the loving family bond newly formed, and gradually deepened through both verbal and nonverbal "adopting conversations" within the family.

11

Raising children cross-culturally

Hemda Arad

"I will never have a moment like the moment before."
—— Hanoch Levin (2011)[1]

This chapter explores the topic of raising children cross-culturally and how psychoanalytic thought and practice contribute to the understanding of this phenomenon. As an immigrant, I lived in both Israeli and American culture and was exposed to nuances of each culture's language, music, literature, cuisine, and norms. Matters are complicated, as my family of origin consists of immigrants from Europe who fled Nazi Germany to start a new life in British-mandated Palestine, and then Israel, living in a language that was a mix of Hebrew and German. Now, in the United States, I was raising my children with a mix of Hebrew and English, creating traditions that were taken for granted back home, yet had to be intentionally created in the United States. Raising children who are completely American, yet who feel themselves to be completely Israeli, lends itself to a crystallization of cultural sensibilities. This cross-cultural affinity requires a finely tuned interpretive effort by the parents to help each offspring develop a personal meaning for their being American-Israeli – or, as they prefer to identify themselves now, Israeli-American. In this process, struggle and creativity surprise the parent. In this I see a parallel with the analytic realm, as part of my practice is dedicated to working with persons who emigrated to the United States from various parts of the world, including Israel and the Middle East.

I will comment on how being a foreigner both enhances and limits the psychoanalyst's efforts to understand patients who are several generations American. This includes sensitivity to cross-generational ways of being with subtle cross-cultural influences on the person's mind.

This chapter will also reflect on the unusual phenomenon in which patients from the Middle East find themselves at home with a psychoanalyst who does not necessarily speak their language, and is even considered to be from the land of their enemy. It will also explore how transference and countertransference play out in the analytic situation, especially at a time when war has erupted in the region between the patient's and the analyst's countries of origin. It will also describe how these issues of cultural closeness and political animosity are approached, finding parallels to the patient's and therapist's relational history.

The material that follows includes impressions of an immigrant mother raised by immigrant parents, my work with patients over the years, and informal conversations with immigrant mothers and fathers who are raising children cross-culturally in the United States and other places around the world.

Implicit belonging

I did not know how Jewish I was until I immigrated to the United States from Israel. I remember the first Shabbat, when traffic did not stop, stores did not shut down early Friday afternoon, neighbors did not walk all clad in white to the synagogue or greet each other with "*Shabbat Shalom*," when no fragrance of chicken soup or home baking scented the stairwell of the apartment building. Later in the evening, I noticed the absence of the familiar Shabbat chanting in neighbors' apartments. Very few around me spoke my language, or sang the same songs, and the radio did not play Hebrew songs at four in the afternoon every day. But it was not just the language that I missed. With the small number of Hebrew speakers around me, I could not have the kind of intellectual discourses that I had back home. When you move away, you find that things you thought were ubiquitous are not. Although I am as secular as they come, if I wanted to feel at home, I needed to actively create an environment that felt Israeli – and yes, Jewish. Much of what I fought against throughout my earlier life in Israel, particularly the religious coercion in every aspect of daily life there, was now also mine. Mine to defy, mine to critique, but part of me nonetheless. I am not easily deceived, but here I had to admit that I was Jewish, not just Israeli. It was then that I was surprised when a new person I met idealized Israel and its people. It sounded so foreign. I felt an immediate distance and the conversation died quickly. Total admiration of the place and people of Israel left me lonely. When you have a lived experience in which things are less than ideal, such idealization leaves you bereft.

Passing down trauma

For a while following my immigration I could understand why my grandmother, who fled Nazi Germany in the 1930s, refused to learn the Hebrew language. There was something that my grandparents wanted to preserve from that place that had purged them. They spoke German at home, read books in that language, had their rituals in their secret clubs, and could not restrain their dismay at their children and grandchildren talking back and minding themselves more than they minded the adults' rules. As a child, I saw the flow of generational deterioration in the Germanic rule, and their astonishment at this change, which my refugee grandparents and their cohort had a hand in creating by immigrating to Israel.

Hogman (1998) focuses on the resolution of trauma over generations, stressing the second generation's adjustment to their parents' suffering. It takes generations to work through experiences that on paper seem to be only a distant memory. My grandmother would invariably call after my teen cousin to take his "battledress" jacket when he left the house, regardless of the temperature outside. In Germany, you wouldn't leave the house without its protection. Although she left Germany in a hurry, for decades she used the terms from her old country, though the words themselves contained the fear of being attacked. Now owning a battledress jacket felt to her, and by extension to us, her grandchildren, like a protective cape against the imagined dangerous world awaiting us when we left her sight.

Oftentimes the magnitude of the Holocaust makes second-generation suffering seem inconsequential in comparison. That can be manifested in the form of a child trying to protect the parent, who in their mind suffered enough and may not be able to sustain the blow of learning about their child's emotional suffering due to trauma. At other times, when the child presents the parent with mishaps, the parent may convey to the child that her suffering is nothing in comparison to what the parent had to go through in their own childhood. Because the cloud of the Holocaust always hovers overhead, the offspring as well as their survivor parents have a hard time seeing that there is little use in adhering to such a comparison for traumatic events. It takes much work for the traumatized child to recognize that their suffering is not reduceable because of their parent's suffering.

Translating others – a consequence of growing up across cultures

My father, a child hidden during the Holocaust who came from a family with rather strict sets of rules about how strangers referred to each other, was flabbergasted one day when he went to my junior high school's administration to collect my study books. The administrator asked him jokingly, in a very typical Israeli informal manner, why it was that his daughter did not come herself: "Is she sick or something?" My father took this comment literally and felt hurt at what he perceived to be a very rude comment. "Why would she assume that my daughter is sick?" To him, these words had the power to render me sick. He brought his differences with the administrator home, and, as often happened, I translated the attitude he met and helped him minimize the damage to his soul and mine. I was simultaneously embarrassed for him for being so foreign, and upset that as much as he wanted to help he could not learn his new country's ways of being.

Children who grow up cross-culturally must develop the capacity to translate others, all the while having to live fully in both cultures. At the Institute for Learning and Brain Sciences (I-LABS), founded by Patricia Kuhl and Andrew Meltzoff, developmental researchers have found that children who are bilingual are exceptionally creative in comparison to children who are raised in households in which only one language is spoken (Ramírez, Ramírez, Clarke, Taulu, & Kuhl, 2016). Bilingualism does not lead to general intelligence, but there is increasing evidence that bilingual children (and adults) have improved executive function skills (Ramírez et al., 2016). We often think of these skills as "cognitive flexibility," because they allow a person to switch between tasks easily, maintain more information in working memory, and update their information about the environment to generate new and creative solutions (S. R. Lytle, personal communication, October 20, 2016).

Bilingual children understand that there are at least two ways to describe an object or a situation, and therefore there must be more than one solution to any given problem. At a university program where I was teaching methods to advance the learning capacity of youth to succeed at the college level, I asked a group of teachers from a rural region to slow their minds down and describe the natural way they can tell whether it was safe for them to cross a busy road. Typically, people would mention something about a traffic light, looking left and right and left again. However, this group was stymied by the problem. I asked them to think about their procedural memory, to recognize the subconscious action as an example of deconstructing their natural learning process. Then came an answer that I did not anticipate. One teacher said, "I follow the donkey." I was the only one in the room that had difficulty keeping a straight face. To everyone else this solution was familiar, and made all the sense in the world. They momentarily became my teachers, showing me that when you are part of the dominant culture, you think that your way of understanding the world is the only way. Yet there are other worlds in which you must be fluent in both ways of thinking if you want to make it. It is easy to dismiss the other's way of thinking, but it can certainly enrich one's life to listen.

We can speculate that most children who grow up bilingually also grow up across cultures. Language learning requires social interaction. Children who are raised cross-culturally may not have the benefit of the full cultural complexity of the country of origin, and may miss some cultural markers. For example, I found that when we visited Israel with our young children they invariably returned to the United States with a much more fluent Hebrew, but also with a richer cultural expression because of their interaction with our family and friends and their nuanced cultural distinctions.

Relocating, loss, and mourning

Relocating to a different country is a complex endeavor and its outcome may be predicated upon any number of factors, which can affect the parent and the child's experience. Tummala-Narra (2004) writes that, for those who have emigrated to another country, mourning occurs when conditions in the host country are unexpected. There are different ways of dealing with the sense of loss and mourning, and they depend on the circumstances that led to the relocation, among other significant factors. This influences the many ways different immigrants cope with the task of creating the old culture anew in the host country. Was it a war that forced the relocation, was there violence or some family event that caused the move, did they have children before they came or did they come alone, was the move initiated to seek better life conditions? Each of these factors in turn lead

to various levels of emotional coping and relational solutions. In his consideration of the psychological causes at play in determining the engagement with the
immigrant experience, Akhtar (1999) names the motivation of the move as an
important aspect of the relocation experience.

When my father's affluent family arrived in Israel after the Second World War,
they were relocated to a tent camp (within eighteen months the population of
Israel doubled from 650,000 to 1.3 million people [Kaplan, 2015]). My grandmother stubbornly walked around the refugee camp with her nice city clothes.
While mourning the loss and the radical change from her previous life, she created a mini farm to feed the family, but also to deal with the wasteland around her
and engage in something that she had loved in her old country, as if the war and
the forced immigration never happened. Like many other immigrants, she was
promised that she would be brought to the land of milk and honey, and she was
adamant about creating it if it was not provided by the state. A couple of years
later, when the family was moved to a tiny apartment, my grandmother recreated
the mansion of her childhood in those five hundred square feet within the immigrants' block, and took over a parcel of the neighborhood's rocky land, turning
it into a fruit and nut garden with a small vineyard, ignoring the fact that things
were not all splendid. Her sons continued with activities that were appreciated
in Europe, but at the time were rejected in the Israel they immigrated to. These
practices, such as playing classical music, had to be the family's secret pleasures –
my father still keeps this musical tradition, although he paid a high emotional
price to maintain it throughout his life, given the mocking of his old-world preferences. For him, being raised by a mother who did not accept the fact that she
lived in a place significantly different from where she came, clashed with his need
to immerse himself in the new land. He stayed forever a foreigner in both lands,
feeling different in any environment. On the other hand, occasionally, my grandmother recounted the fear and horror of being persecuted, with gory details that
were frightening to me as a little girl. Years later, when I asked my father about his
uncle being beaten nearly to death, my father was astonished that I'd learned this
story from my grandmother. Sitting alone with her as she dissociated into her horrific experiences was gut-wrenching, and I never knew if she would be restored
to her sensible self to care for me. I reckoned that telling my parents about these
bouts caused them to never leave me alone with her, but this meant there was a
loss in not hearing more stories about a land I never visited but about which I had
profound curiosity.

Cross-cultural bridges

Salima, an Egyptian woman who immigrated with her parents to the United States
as a child, described a different kind of cultural bridge she created for her daughter. Growing up as a single daughter in a traditional family, she never questioned
her father's demands when it came to dating. With her own daughter Aya, now
sixteen, Salima often feels the urge to request tighter curfew rules, like those she

experienced. She is torn between her anxieties about the potential truth in her parents' insistence on the traditional norms governing women's appropriate acts and her identification with her daughter's chance to choose her own lifestyle with greater freedom than she ever experienced growing up in the United States in a family of immigrants from Egypt. She continues to envy her close cousin, who respectfully ignored their family's cultural expectations, with minimal repercussions. Yet Salima suffers from bouts of anxiety about allowing Aya to date, fearing that in so doing she is lending a hand to the destruction of Aya's future. She oscillates between preoccupation with her responsibility and concern about the lack of control that came with choosing to allow Aya to be a typical American teen. For Salima, the task of holding in her mind both her own past traditional experiences and her daughter's future is a work in progress.

When the therapist works cross-culturally

Being a psychoanalyst in a foreign land creates unusual bonds. Over the years, I have had the privilege of working with people of various cultures and religions, among them persons who grew up in the Middle East in Muslim families, and others who were either immigrants or children of immigrants. A Jordanian-Palestinian patient I will call Amina, whose family was displaced in 1948, and who was first-generation Arab-American, found her way to my office precisely because I was from the region in which she grew up. She reported that her prior work with an American therapist left her feeling lonely and not understood, because that therapist, although compassionate and attentive, could not be brought up to speed on the meaning of growing up in the Middle East, in particular the centrality of the family and extended family in every aspect of a person's life. In addition, this patient felt that if the therapist had not experienced life in another culture or known first-hand what it means to have a strikingly different appearance and a pronounced foreign accent, she could never understand the level of constant humiliation piled on the relatively simple task of speaking with coworkers, or the harsher realities of feeling rejected by men of her own culture, as well as men in the host culture. This patient and her struggle to fit in led her to me, not without reservations, since I was the product of a country that had been her people's enemy for many decades. She explained that I was from a close cultural background, as she knew Israelis cared and were involved deeply with their families in a way very different than in the United States. She said, "You will never tell me to ignore my mother. You understand that this is not possible in the Middle East." With time, it became a bit clearer that there was some overlap between our religions' attitude toward the family bonds, just as between the Palestinian and Israeli attitudes toward the family. I was also aware that we both changed somewhat in our respective cultural expectations about the family, and that may have drawn her toward working with me, since there was the expectation that I would be able to understand her anxiety about forever losing her ability to live in the original culture and her inability to establish herself and feel at home in much of the host culture's meaningful and intimate levels of engagement.

Listening to the radio on my way to work one day, I heard the news that fights had erupted again in the West Bank between Palestinians and the Israeli army. I suddenly stopped breathing for an instant. Thinking of my patient, I grew anxious about our meeting. What would it mean for her, for me, and for us? I was worried that somehow Amina would blame me for the overpowering onslaught of the Israeli air force. I was not only guilty by association. I had spent my military service in the air force, though I love to say that it was at the time after the Israeli-Egyptian peace treaty, and fortunately I had no hand in fighting. Yet I felt guilty. I can only describe the walk between my office and the waiting room as marching into uncharted territory, and the way back, in which Amina followed me, as preparation for drowning. I noticed a knot in my throat as I sat down and looked at her. I felt awkward, as if I was the mother who could not protect her child from an abuser. Amina sat down and began to talk as if there was no "camel" in the room, though she felt to me to be more distant than usual. I felt stymied and more formal, and she responded in kind, which increased my discomfort. I noticed that I became defensive, even without being openly blamed. Amina talked about her friend who wanted her to pretend nothing had happened between them after a recent fallout. I asked if it was just like us, given the political situation between our countries. She immediately denied that, and said she knew I wasn't in favor of the status quo of the conflict, and that I lived in the United States and had nothing to do with the current dangerous encounter over the border. Then she began to tell me how horrible my country was to respond to the Palestinian uprising against the occupation of her country. "I know it is not you, but it is stupid," she said. After being quiet for a while she added, "For all I know, your brother may be fighting there against my people. He could kill my family members." I had to bite my tongue to not defend myself with the shield of my brother's refusal to serve beyond the border, and consequently serve time in military jail before returning to complete his military service. I had to recognize too that neither my personal story nor my political views mattered. Amina needed to tell me that I was limited in how much I could help her to make it in the new world. I was just like her mother, who offered her nicer clothes to help her find a decent American boy to marry. Was I minimizing who she was, an invisible woman no longer able to go back to Bethlehem, and unable to find her deserved place in the United States? We had to sit quietly with my exposed powerlessness, and with hers. Though we continued to work together, the realization that Amina needed a mother that she could not find in her own mother or in me stayed with us for a while longer. The limitation of a promised land of the mind consequently helped Amina out of her depression. She sighed herself into greater command of her life, waiting less for others, in whom she put her trust, to rescue her from the abyss of living in two cultures she only partially recognized as her own. We found a new language in turning a multiculturalism that she had segregated in her mind and in her life into cross-culturalism in which she was less invisible to herself and therefore to others.

My work with Amina reminded me how as a child I felt split between my German and Romanian grandparents, each with their own set of culturally sterile environments that rejected the other's essential beliefs. When I was young, it all seemed confusing, and it took a mental transition to shift to the other language, behavior, and truth regarding how life should be lived. I remember the loss and mourning I felt with each transition, and the anxiety I felt on the rare occasion when the two sides of the family came together in our home.

Akhtar (1995) suggests that moving at a young age to a different culture can be described as a "second individuation." While the term was coined by Blos (1967), however, especially for those migrating at later stages in life, for Akhtar this "is more a matter of adult adaptation than of a replicated childhood scenario, though the two cannot be entirely separated. The term third individuation should therefore be seen as denoting an adult life reorganization of identity" (Akhtar, 1995, p. 1053).

We can think about immigration as a second individuation process from the original culture, which allows the discovery of new, previously unknown experiences. As Akhtar (1995) writes, "This coexistence of culture shock and mourning causes a serious shake-up of the individual's identity" (p. 1052). Every day, parents raised in a different culture and children raised cross-culturally experience minor trauma. In addition, they have the burden of knowing about the difference and feeling ambivalent about the impossibility of changing much of it.

As in the example of the best method of crossing the street I mentioned earlier, the people who wish to succeed in Israeli academic and professional life must learn the many different ways in which the receiving culture converses about issues, while the receiving culture must recognize differences without dismissing them. The dilemma for parents, educators, employers, and psychoanalysts is how to find a way to maintain open-mindedness regarding the person who is dealing with the demands and advantages of different cultures. The result of this "confusion of tongues" can be devastating if there is no mental flexibility to support expanding the notion of truth to include sensibilities derived from both cultures.

Parenting strategies

Nesteruk and Marks (2011) suggest, following Berry (2007), a four-pronged framework describing acculturation strategies. The strategies include assimilation, separation, marginalization, and integration. "The type of acculturation strategy that immigrant parents adopt will influence their childrearing decisions and parenting strategies in a host country" (Nesteruk & Marks, 2011, p. 811).

To give a personal example, one evening in late autumn I was riding on the long road near the Lebanese border in Israel in my ancient bright-turquoise VW Golf, returning from a lecture I had given at a kibbutz the previous night. On the side of the road I spotted a woman of about sixty wearing a head scarf and a long dress. I slowed my car down and brought it to a full stop by her side. I reached over to roll down the passenger side's manual window. "Where to?" I asked. At that time, my friends and I had initiated a campaign for women to give rides to other women, to help decrease the instances of sexual assault while hitchhiking. In my mind, I profiled this woman as a hard-working house cleaner. She told me where she was headed. It should have rung a bell. Perhaps it did, and I ignored it. I said I would take her there, though it was about fifteen minutes out of my way. She protested, and I agreed to drop her off at the junction so she could catch another ride home. We went on for a few minutes. I said the day was hot, and that she must be tired. In a thick North African accent, she said that indeed she had a long and hard day. She had visited her brother's family. After a moment she said, "You are Hemda, right?" Surprised, I said yes, and immediately it clicked. I said, "You are Tamar's mom!" I was struck by a mixture of pleasure and shame. Pleasure for stopping in the middle of nowhere to help my boarding school roommate's mother after a long day and to bring her home. Shame that I profiled her as a poor old woman who cleaned houses, from the height of my privileged position as a dead-beat car owner, already a professional in my early career, fulfilling the promise to leave no woman behind. How did I not recognize the woman who hosted me in her home for a whole weekend less than a decade ago? Worse, I did not remember her name. Of course, I insisted on bringing her back to her home, and she relented when I promised to come in and have tea with her. Tamar, my friend, was away at university, but the moment I entered their small house, I recalled my admiration of this mother. With a knowledge of only the most basic Hebrew, she had had the foresight to watch over her children and insist on the importance of their education. She first entrusted her young children to her brother, who was a teacher, and then sent them away to a boarding school to give them a chance to float above their modest beginning, caused by being new immigrants from a very different culture and discriminated against for that reason.

Both of Tamar's parents were from North Africa, the mother having emigrated from Morocco and the father from Tunisia. In their home, I learned that they had had distinct traditions that until that visit I had not fully appreciated. One simple example came to my mind in a recent conversation with my son, who is spending a year with a host family in Morocco. "Mom," he said, "in Morocco they only make couscous on Friday." I suddenly recalled that even though Tamar's mother was from Morocco, she prepared couscous on other days as well to accommodate her husband's culture, not without reservation. A tiny difference, but one that required an adjustment in Tamar's family. I came to recognize then that what I had previously lumped into one region of origin exposed my ignorance, and taught me to ask more often than just assuming, a skill I am still honing. I then understood that Tamar and her siblings faced the seemingly insurmountable task of relating to her family's traditional religiously observant lifestyle and the primarily secular, nontraditional coeducational boarding-school life. What did it take for Tamar's parents to allow their gifted daughter to move away from a protective home as a young teen? I only understood this later in life, when I became a mother to children who I raised in a culture quite distinct from the culture in which I had been brought up. I also knew that her brother, who left home for a boarding school, promised his parents that Tamar would be well cared for in the boarding school.

Parenting my children cross-culturally

Unconscious parenting experiences may only reveal themselves many years into a child's life. I noticed that moving to a country with no compulsory military service was on my mind before conceiving a child, a girl or a boy. Growing up in a culture that lived by its sword whether defensively or proactively took a toll on me, as it did on so many others. Just picture, at age five, living in trenches dug for "safety" and in later conflicts in bomb shelters, worrying about your father and other men in your life that disappeared for weeks on end during wartime, seeing the devastating effect of battles' physical and mental toll on those injured and on families. Hearing mothers wailing by the graves of their fallen sons as you represent your junior high school at the funerals. Holding a wreath with a black satin sash over fresh graves. Hosting a friend whose brother was just killed in the war, losing your classmate in high school to friendly fire in another war, watching broken families, broken lives, realizing in later years the hurt that was caused in my name to Palestinians. In light of this, I felt a need to extricate myself from my homeland. I thus subjected my children to an experience similar to what my parents and I had had to face, being raised cross-culturally by immigrants. Yet without my conscious awareness, I also chose something different for my yet-to-be-born children: a life without the consequences of never-ending military trauma. I remember the first war in which I did not participate. Seeing a picture of my brother in a sealed room with a gas mask over his face during an attack from Iraq, and hearing my mother refusing to shelter herself during the attack that hit an apartment building near her, made it difficult to accept the dark humor that developed in Israel around this time. It raised the question, "whom can I parent from afar?" It increased my guilt over not being there to personally make sure my family and friends were protected. My first child was born shortly after that war ended. Experiences like these informed my decisions on where and how I should raise my children.

I thought raising my children with clear awareness of the price of war on all sides involved would serve as an antidote to choosing to solve conflicts by exacting blood. Developing compassion for the other with whom you disagree could help reduce a continued participation in such escalating situations. I had the fantasy that by removing myself from the actual fire, I would be saving my children from the scalding environment. Instead, they all chose to be in the fire in one way or another, striving for change within the framework of revenge. In hindsight, I realized that I made a choice to raise my children with an emphasis on the more ubiquitous cross-generational cultural affiliation, as opposed to simply a national affinity. To give one example, I chose to underscore the importance of music when my children were young. Beyond the spoken language, I introduced them to the importance of the language of music to express themselves emotionally. That was not a national but a cultural affiliation that transcends generations and the life in a specific country, keeping a cultural thread that connects my children with myself, with my father and our ancestors, no matter where they live. When my second child was born, I remember wanting to keep the close attachment with my oldest child, so I chose to introduce her to music practice, over which we could bond daily. This creation of cultural ambiance connected multigenerational appreciation for the meaning of musicality that transcended several continents within less than a century. Perhaps this experience is another manifestation of unwittingly translating the world to the cross-culturally raised child. Although adding intensive musical exposure may have seemed like an expansion of experience, it also had a limiting effect on alternative influences that were available in the new host culture, such as participating in team sports from an early age and recognizing televised narratives. Instead, my children were raised in a household that had no television, that favored conversations and collective book reading as a pastime, and that encouraged speaking at home in a different language, one that none of their friends spoke. Conceivably, it was an unconscious effort to highlight the importance of dreaming in childhood, as living in both cultures constantly keeps one in a state of dreaming. While one culture is in the forefront, the other is hibernating in the background, ready to be booted into awareness at any moment with its detection of discrepancy and integration of various cultural influences.

Perception of the self cross-culturally

Often when we think about immigrants, we profile them based on our limited personal familiarity and impressions from the mass media. Children of immigrants are not spared from seeing themselves and their parents as different, and often as "the ones who do not belong." This adds to greater embarrassment, seclusion of the family, requests from the child for the parents to not show up in public places with them. This self-consciousness is not the terrain of children of immigrants alone, but seems to be exacerbated by that fact. In turn, these responses increase the segregation and the misperception fostered by lack of familiarity. Many children and youth experience greater pressure to succeed, to compensate for their parents' sacrifice, by obtaining higher education and a "good profession." In more traditional cultures, there is an extra burden on young girls and adolescents to acquire success through traditional expectations, which include staying close to home rather than venturing away, behaving in modest ways, and getting married and raising a family as a career contingency. These patterns may often conflict with the new cultural expectation, and tension is raised when the young female wishes to follow the footsteps of her friends or even her own brothers. For instance, in the case of Tamar, I learned that it was only when her brothers, who had ventured away from home to pursue better education and thus gained a new perspective on females in this educational system, vouched for their younger sister's educational aspiration and promised to keep an eye on her, did the parents relent.

First generation vs. second generation perception of trauma and belonging

Longing, pining, and expectations are at the base of parenting children cross-culturally. The parent who wishes to stay connected through language, culinary traditions, and deep-seated habits that belong to a territory the parents and children no longer live in is the center for a host of attempts to both maintain the ways of the lost motherland, and to provide a better life to the children who are raised in the new land, who may speak the language of the parents but must simultaneously adapt to the new land with all its cultural differences.

I noticed a conflict of this kind in a mother who was born in North America shortly after her parents emigrated from Croatia. In her family as a child and adolescent, Sophia felt the constant burden of her parents' struggle to make it in the new country. There was no doubt in their minds that they would raise Sophia as a Croatian child, just in a foreign land. At home, the only language spoken was Croatian, the music they listened to originated in Croatia, and their social circle came from the same region. This both helps and hinders successful immersion (Tummala-Narra, 2004). When Sophia entered kindergarten, she remembers the shock she felt. No one spoke her language. She did not speak English or understand the social cues proffered by her classmates. She looked different, seemed painfully shy, and could not communicate with teachers and peers. Over the next several years, Sophia taught herself English. She came home, started watching television, and learned the language and the norms of Disney popular culture. With time, she adopted some of the more acceptable ways of being in her new culture, though she felt that it somehow lacked the immediacy of a lived experience.

In reflecting on her early educational experience, Sophia reckoned that she was floating by, never feeling an integral part of her adoptive culture, constantly struggling to negotiate her home life with that of the school. When I met Sophia one day, she had a big smile on her face. Her daughter had graduated high school the previous week. She told me about the moment she saw an enormous Croatian flag flying in the bleachers. It was her son. She was so proud that he chose to celebrate his sister's graduation with a reminder of the culture they belong to. Even though he was a second-generation American born, he knew first and foremost he was from a proud Croatian family. It made Sophia happy that it mattered to him. She was surprised and proud of his gesture. Then, a dark cloud covered her face. She said that she did not get the opportunities she was offering her children. She wanted them to remember and respect their heritage, yet made a point of introducing them to the language and immersion her family of origin did not know to offer her. She also remembered her childhood home, with its struggles and parental discord, and a deeper, more sinister sense of prevalent abuse by her father that felt overwhelming to the child that she was – yet another way of feeling foreign in the new country.

Sophia had fallen into a depression that took a toll on her health. She did not go to college, though she developed a career through an alternative path. She married a Croatian man who shares her traditional and religious beliefs. He is, though, someone with whom she can also share raising their family in a more open, inclusive way, without losing sight of the language and culture of their immigrant parents. It is a constant struggle to watch the American culture seep through their young offsprings' choices, yet the memory of Sophia's regret over her too-close upbringing and the losses she had to endure until she left home are a beacon and a cautionary tale as she chooses her cultural battles. She is relieved to see that her children are well adapted, yet irreducibly Croatian.

As Tummala-Narra (2004) writes in "Mothering in a Foreign Land," this vignette demonstrates a creative solution to the mother's experience of envy toward her own children's experience of successful immersion. The differences we see in Sophia's story are between first- and second-generation immigrants. Her son, as a second-generation Croatian, can relate mainly to the cultural and pleasant aspects of his heritage, though with some anxiety-driven parental encouragement to make it. Sophia, as a first-generation Croatian, carries the pain of her parents' struggles in the new land, encumbered and exasperated by the presence of trauma.

Language and therapy

Among many elements of the analytic work, there are two aspects to elaborate. One concerns the analyst who grew up in a cross-cultural family, and who is new to the American culture in which most patients are rooted. The other has to do with the emotional distance that is offered to patients who are analyzed in a different language than their own. The feeling is similar to dialing down an *internal scream* that in the original language and environment used to activate anxiety and dissociation, as the triggers are not as pronounced in the host language and surroundings.

Language is an important organizer of experience and its related thoughts and feelings. It is used to express, but it also hinders traumatic experiences (Amati-Mehler, Argentieri, & Canestri, 1993). I accidently found, however, that a benefit of being analyzed in a foreign language is the creation of distance from the subject of trauma. Think of an experience in the cultural environment into which you are born as a sonorous bath in which you are immersed. Every part of that environment is registered in a particular form that includes sounds, words, volume of speech, familiar pleasant or unpleasant touch, personal space, facial expressions, smells, and particular relational ways of being together – how many people are too few or too many; who are the people you can joke with safely; what are the means of discipline, and many more. These are learned from birth, and become more established and more sophisticated and ingrained in the person's reciprocal relationships throughout the lifespan. When there is trauma in a child's life, many triggers in the environment fire neurons down the traumatic neuropathway with all the senses involved. When that person moves away into a new environment, there is a reduction in some environmental triggers, though not all. When a patient is analyzed in the new host culture's language there is potentially a chance to describe traumatic events with some distance and with a lower risk of dissociation, as the story does not contain all the elements of the trauma. In my clinical work, I have found this to benefit patients who cannot otherwise talk about the unspeakable.

In that case, one result of changing the environment, including the language in which the trauma occurred, may be that the *inner scream* that is reproduced internally by triggers similar to the original trauma can be somewhat muffled through the use of a different language performed in a different environment. We can further speculate that if a parent changes the language they speak with their son or daughter, a similar benefit may apply.

In contrast, patients often lament the loss of their language in the clinical setting, saying that they cannot sufficiently express how they feel or what transpired when they cannot use their mother tongue. I find that when I offer to refer a patient's friend or family member to another therapist they insist on my helping them find a native speaker first, above other important qualities, despite their near-perfect command of the English language. This is especially true for patients who are parents and who hope to receive help for their marital and parental relational struggles. It is as if they will only let themselves trust a therapist who lived through similar cultural experiences.

On the other hand, if the patient is quite removed from his or her emotions, I may ask him or her to speak in their mother tongue, even if I do not speak that language. The benefit is twofold. Speaking the language of the emotional events, the patient can engage emotionally, and knowing that I do not understand what is said makes the embarrassment and humiliation more tolerable. Typically, following this kind of interaction, more can be said about the experience of the past and of the moment in the common language so that we can look at it together. It also gives the therapist an opportunity to observe the patient's nonverbal communication in a deconstructed form, and lets her ask questions about what she noticed that are not muddled by attention to words. Think of it as the use of the couch in which the psychoanalyst's facial expressions are hidden, although not all of the analyst's nonverbal communication goes unnoticed by the patient, who is left with some important expression of where the psychoanalyst resides emotionally in relation to the patient.

Another aspect of cultural difference has to do with the analyst's accent and their special use of the English language. I found that there is a mystique attached to my accent that adds to the transference, as my slight German accent at times causes patients to assume that I am somehow associated with Freud and his followers, a pedestal I do not aspire to. Yet this is an assumption that is hard to shake, and I find it particularly eerie outside the office, when others happily speak German to me, though this is a language my family intentionally avoided teaching me. There is little escape from cultural assumptions.

As a psychoanalyst, however, I have found that embracing my otherness is of enormous help, as I could never assume I knew or understood anything about American culture in all its variations. Growing up without television, I had almost no contact with American popular culture. I had to listen, ask, and learn all that was relevant to my patients. It slowed down the tendency in my own culture to immediately know how a sentence would end, whether accurately or not. Allowing my patients to surprise me was particularly salient when I started my internship in a rural area that was significantly different from what I learned to expect in the American city I came to know. Emotions were the same, but verbal expressions, inhibitions, and the burden of multiple life challenges in addition to my patients' mental-health needs were unique and new. In the same way, the challenges presented by families both in raising their children and dealing with their mental-health needs meant I needed to do some intensive learning about resources and limitations in the context of that particular rural community.

Being parented by parents from multiple cultures

While I could not possibly address all the forms of cross-cultural child-rearing here, I would be remiss if I did not mention that within the United States not all cross-cultural parenting has to do with recent relocation of the parent or the child. Working with mixed-race parents in the United States has taught me that different languages can be spoken even if both parents are native English speakers. Attitudes toward rearing children vary within any culture, but at times with mixed-race couples, assumptions are made about the centrality of the child in the parent's daily life in comparison to the time each parent dedicates to the other. It is easy for a parent to assume that spending most of the time with her child is what is expected from her, and to ignore the fact that this is a choice as well as a duty, while her partner assumes that there will also be some adults-only time. Stress can be reduced if there are conversations about different cultural views.

Wen's parents emigrated from mainland China to England where Wen was born. Later, at age 11, she moved with her family to Singapore from where she, following her older brother's footsteps, ended up in the United States as a young person. She and her husband, David, chose to speak only English in their home, though she grew up speaking Mandarin as her mother tongue and learned English in her first adoptive country. The parents were hoping to provide their two sons with a base from which they could lead a successful life. Wen was working full-time as a physician while David was holding down the fort and raising the boys. Both boys thrived at school, but their oldest son was discontented and angry with his parents, who brought him and his brother up in a society that excludes them. "I look different, no matter how well I do at school," Ty complained to his parents. "You should have moved back to Singapore where everybody is just like me and I do not look weird." Wen says that their sons feel that even though they were born and raised in the United States, the culture around them sees them as Chinese. Both children are in relationships with first-generation cross-cultural partners. Both are successful academically and have high expectations for themselves that influence their attitude toward work and family in different ways. Ty awaits the perfect job, and seems to be unmotivated to take a first job unless it is interesting, while Sam has striven for leadership positions, a characteristic displayed since early childhood. The different attitudes result in dysthymia for Ty, including some anger at his parents for introducing him to a place in which he feels forever different. Sam seems to accept and embrace his life with a force that impresses his parents. He is Chinese-American and that is just fine.

Ty, now a senior in high school, dates a young woman whose parents are also immigrants. Although he loves Anika, he is despondent about the chances of being accepted by her family and becoming part of the American culture. Wen is not sure how to best support her son, as she herself, with all her experience and education, feels that her roots are truly in Singapore. Ty feels isolated, and at times wishes he could crawl out of his skin. He feels that because he is not a proficient Chinese speaker his chances of escaping his destiny vanished at birth. In this situation, Wen's separation from her small family of origin, and her diminished circle of friends, threatens her sense of being right in having chosen the full immersion path for her sons, in light of her sons' disconnection from their family's original culture. Wen feels guilty for Ty's feeling of being limited by his parents' immigration. She is confused, as she thought that she contributed to her child's better circumstances yet now must see that moving away from a family support system left not only her but her son lonely. She is blamed for this, and unable to easily dismiss his now unchangeable course of life.

Recognizing incongruency

Naz, a woman who emigrated from Turkey a decade ago, lamented that her visiting parents could not have meaningful conversations with her sons, as the Turkish language that she speaks to her children is restricted to everyday vocabulary and is also mixed with English, as it is more convenient for both Naz and the children. When her mother spoke about a book by Orhan Pamuk she read recently, and recommended it to her seventeen-year-old grandson, he had a hard time understanding her communication, as it included words that were sophisticated and unfamiliar to him. The patient then had to notice that a live cultural immersion is compromised even when the language is spoken as a mother tongue. The solution was to read an English translation of the Turkish author, which did create a barrier but at least offered access to Turkish literary gems.

Another related difficulty is that however fluent the adolescent is, having a sophisticated conversation is an exceedingly difficult task, and one that is never complete. That can result in a sense of having betrayed the culture of the parents. Guilt can arise for making a choice for the children that no one can now correct, and that forever leaves a sense of non-assimilation in both cultures. In my practice, I have noticed that when parents raise their children cross-culturally, their parents travel from far away to be with the family and often stay for several weeks at a time. Along with the happiness of the reunion and having a temporary live-in set of grandparents, such visits restore old familial ways of being, between grandparents and their own adult child and their grandchildren. This in turn creates a dynamic that invariably raises memories of the now-adult's childhood trauma that influence the present parent-child relational experience, which in turn increases stress on all parties. As these intense visits come to an end, the disappointment of failed expectations, and sorrow and guilt about the upcoming and often long separation, lead to anxiety and depression. This can often give rise to a last-ditch effort to change course, with guilt-producing assertions concerning whose fault it is that the grandparents and their grandchildren do not live near each other. The impact of the physical and emotional distance is most pronounced right before and after a visit. Idealization of the visit, regrets for missed opportunities, high expectations, and concern about each party's well-being are vast, just as the recognition of how limited the ability to help or be helped is. Oftentimes an astute grandchild will raise a question that could not be brought to the table during a deadlock between the grandparents and the adult child. Specifically, because the grandchildren grew up across cultures, they do not abide by the old norms, and can see clearly that there is more than one way to reduce stress in the family during those long visits.

To usher cross-cultural parenting toward a more amiable and successful outcome, the forces from within the parent-child dyad require mental flexibility while negotiating the original and host cultures. Integration seems to work better in helping bridge the different cultures in a relational fashion than does adhering to either a secluded bubble of life to create a mini-homeland in the new land, or dropping all connection to the original culture by manifesting a sort of amnesia that leaves much behind.

Integration clearly may take many different forms, depending on the circumstances and causes of immigration, the age of immigration, and the family status at the time of immigration, along with other factors that actively influence the degree of individuation, and loss and mourning in all the parties.

Because of this irreducible complexity, both parents and therapists should pay special attention to nuances when working with populations that live cross-culturally, even when the original culture is shared by the analyst and patient.

Notes

The statement by Hanoch Levin in the epigraph is from *Hanoch Levin Quotes* (Israel: Hotza'at HaKibbutz Haartzi, 2011), 13.

1 *Hanoch Levin Quotes* (Israel: Hotza'at HaKibbutz Haartzi, 2011), 13. Reprinted as an epigraph in this chapter by kind permission of Kneller Artist Agency Ltd, agents of the Hanoch Levin Estate. Translated from the Hebrew by Jessica Cohen and Evan Fallenberg. All rights reserved.

References

Akhtar, S. (1995). A third individuation: Immigration, identity, and the psychoanalytic process. *Journal of the American Psychoanalytic Association, 43*, 1051–1084.

Akhtar, S. (1999). *Immigration and identity: Turmoil, treatment, and transformation.* Northvale, NJ: Aronson.

Amati-Mehler, J., Argentieri, S., & Canestri, J. (1993). *The babel of the unconscious: Mother tongue and foreign languages in the psychoanalytic dimension.* Madison, CT: International Universities Press.

Arnal, L. H., Flinker, A., Kleinschmidt, A., Giraud, A., & Poeppel, D. (2015). Human screams occupy a privileged niche in the communication soundscape. *Current Biology, 25*(15), 2051–2056.

Berry, J. W. (2007). Acculturation strategies and adaptation. In J. E. Lansford, K. Deater-Deckard, & M. H. Bomstein (Eds.), *Immigrant families in contemporary society* (pp. 69–82). New York: Guilford Press.

Blos, P. (1967). The second individuation process of adolescence. *The Psychoanalytic Study of the Child, 22,* 162–186.

Hogman, F. (1998). Trauma and identity through two generations of the Holocaust. *The Psychoanalytic Review, 85,* 551–578.

Kaplan, J. (2015). *The Jewish agency for Israel.* Retreived January 31, 2017, from www.jewishagency.org/society-and-politics/content/36566

Kwak, K. (2003). Adolescents and their parents: A review of intergenerational family relations for immigrant and non-immigrant families. *Human Development, 46*(2–3), 115–136.

Nesteruk, O., & Marks, L. D. (2011). Parenting in immigration: Experiences of mothers and fathers from Eastern Europe raising children in the United States. *Journal of Comparative Family Studies, 42*(6), 809–825.

Ramírez, N., Ramírez, F., Clarke, M., Taulu, S., & Kuhl, P. (2016). Speech discrimination in 11-month-old bilingual and monolingual infants: A magnetoencephalography study. *Developmental Science,* 1–16. Retrieved February 12, 2016, from http://dx.doi.org/10.1111/desc.12427

Remennick, L. (2009). Exploring intercultural relationships: A study of Russian immigrants married to native Israelis. *Journal of Comparative Family Studies, 40*(5), 719–738.

Tummala-Narra, P. (2004). Mothering in a foreign land. *The American Journal of Psychoanalysis, 64,* 167–182.

12

Book versus booze

Elizabeth Trawick

How often have you read your child to sleep? Sat beside him in his bed, your hand under his small hand under a book, fingers moving together over words? Sat to the end of the story, tucked him in, kissed him, turned off the light and left? A few years later sat beside him as he read to you? Each year a little less until finally he says good night, goes into his room, closes his door, so independently.

I advise this early reading experience: holding the book, looking, hearing, smelling, feeling the pleasure of voice, words, stories together. I advise it because it provided a foundation that has saved my son's life. At a time when he was dangerously addicted to alcohol, we returned to this ritual of daily reading. Not in bed together, of course. He was 30 years old. Not even in the same room together but over the phone. We lived 2,600 miles apart; I in Alabama, he in Los Angeles.

The Christmas before last, Devan, age 33, helped unpack the box of tree ornaments, carefully saved since before he was born. He seemed to be searching for a particular ornament and found it at the bottom. Pulling out a two-inch-by-three-inch book, he held it by its golden string and sighed, "The books." We had hung this miniature copy of *The Night before Christmas* on the tree for his first Christmas. I held the chubby nine-month-old in my arms as he laid the book on a limb. Later he sat on my lap or his father's, as the thick pages of another picture book were turned.

That same Christmas, as my husband and I shared a glass of red wine with dinner, Devan reached his hand for a glass. We laughed and said, "He won't like it," as one of us put a glass to his lips. He wrinkled his nose but swallowed a sip. Soon he grunted for more, grabbed a nearby glass in both hands, and gulped until we pulled the glass away. The thought "My son loves booze" flashed in my mind.

Shocked, I tucked that thought away from consciousness just as Christmas ornaments are tucked away in their boxes. Unlike the ornaments, it was not brought out for annual appreciation and reflection. It was not brought out again for 21 years, when its bright truth horrified me.

That first Christmas, I did not know that a war had begun: book versus booze. I did not know how it would be waged, how close it would be, how long it would last, or for what we fought. I still do not know how long it will last. I do understand something more of how to wage it. I know we fight for my son's life.

I hardly knew my son when we began our daily reading. True, he had grown in my belly, snuggled in my arms, been guided through his education, all the things needed by a modern, cared-for child. All the things I, a divorced working mom, could give. Still, now I know that I hardly knew him. I knew mostly what I needed him to be to refute my fears, hidden but ever-present, of what he might become if he became a "drunk" just like my mother or father or stepfather or brother or Aunt Kat or Uncle Earl.

By the time my son, my first and only child, was born, I was a child psychiatrist with four years of psychoanalytic training. In professional arguments about causation, nature versus nurture, I always came down on the side of nurture. I was sure that with my training and my own analysis, I would nurture well enough to keep addictions at bay. I tried.

But, at 22 years old, home from college, he was unable to function. I really did not know him. I tried, but I could only see my mother, father, stepfather, brother. Especially my brother, who had died of complications from alcohol abuse several years before. All too horrifying, so I recoiled from seeing my six-foot-two-inch, one-hundred-twenty-pound, confused son. My new husband, his stepfather, saw more clearly, saw the impairment, saw the need for structure, and provided it. The first skirmish began with me as a befuddled onlooker.

With Jeff's intervention, Devan made some progress in controlling his alcohol use and found work using his degree in computer science. He continued to drink each night after work and all weekend. No marijuana, just alcohol.

A few years later, we sat in the office of my wise internist. Dr. Seigler said his tremor was not a fatal neurological disorder but rather the result of his alcohol abuse. Moreover, lab work showed that he had liver and heart damage, alcohol related. He would kill himself if he continued to drink. He refused to go to Alcoholics Anonymous as the doctor recommended. He continued to drink.

Sick at heart, I began to unpack the thought, "He loves booze."

A few years later, I arrived from Alabama for a visit to find him terribly ill. He had stopped drinking in preparation for my visit and was in withdrawal – nauseated, shaking, in cold sweats. Withdrawal is more frightening than drunkenness. Death comes during withdrawal. I gave him water and asked if he had taken his thiamine to prevent the cerebellar damage that can occur when alcohol leaves the system. He had, but was vomiting. Had the thiamine stayed down? Should we go to an emergency room? He would not. I stayed, helpless to do much except witness his potential seizure or even death.

The next morning I took Devan to a bed-and-breakfast where we spent the week. For several days, he shook and could not eat. We spent time in silence as he did not feel like talking. We walked when he was able.

In the clean, charming bed-and-breakfast room, my son in the bed next to me became, for me, my brother. They were so much alike: tall dark-haired handsome quiet men. My son, now in his late twenties, seemed on the way to becoming my brother. Each time I called him by my brother's name, I reminded myself that I was with my son, that he was not the same and had not had the same life as my brother. Furthermore, I was not my mother. I was not passed out drunk. More and more I became aware of my confusion of Devan with my family members, of the adult me with the overwhelmed child I had been, of me with my mother, of present with past. I struggled to make separations.

That week was a turning point in the battle. It was the time I surfaced from denial and clearly recognized that Devan could die. As the time came for me to return to Alabama, I wondered how I could leave Los Angeles and expect him to stay alive. As I remember it, I told him he had to talk with me every day or I would get a big man, come to Los Angeles, and bring him back to Alabama, tied up if necessary. As he remembers it, "I begged you to call me every day." I had asked what I could do to help. I knew he wanted help since he had come with me to the bed-and-breakfast and had not had a drink while with me. He did say I could call him. So I suppose both memories are true. I was serious when I said I would tie him up and bring him to Alabama. I lined up two men and made plans to transport him in a van. I could not have a repetition of my father's death from guzzling a fifth of whiskey.

We began daily phone calls, a puny weapon. I could hear his voice and know he was physically alive. But we had little to say to each other. He was dull, without interest in much except computer games. I knew nothing about them and had less interest. The conversations were tedious and disturbing, as he reassured me, "Yeah, I'm ok," with slurred speech. He was not hostile, seemed relieved that I was interested, but was not engaged and was clearly intoxicated. I ended each call feeling relieved. He was alive. At the same time, I was overwhelmed with emotion: hopeless, helpless, and enraged that he could do this, guilty that I had not mothered better.

It occurred to me that I needed to learn more than I knew. In all my training, I had stayed far away from addiction. I could not think well about that subject. I had turned away patients who showed any indication of substance abuse – it was somewhat amazing that I had a practice.

In desperation, I turned to the literature. Most sources are theoretical, offering no guidance in understanding how a parent could step in. There was only advice to seek professional help, rehab, but nothing about how a professional mother should intervene.

My first hope came when I found a book by Gary Winship (2012), an English psychoanalytic therapist, called *Addictive Personalities and Why People Take Drugs*. Winship describes his work as a unit manager and clinical researcher on a drug dependency unit. Using myths and clinical experience, he eloquently asserts that addicts depend on the pleasure they find in the danger of drug use but that this dependency can be replaced by attachment to persons. Furthermore, the attachment occurs without any direct discussion of drug use. In fact such discussion would not only not help, but be a substitute drug.

With this clear model in front of me, I now had a simple way to proceed: form a substantial, trusting relationship with my son. Forget the guilt that came with recognizing that we did not seem to have a relationship that was enlivening to him.

Get on with the future. I would not criticize, direct, demand, or control. I would do what worked in my practice. I would listen to anything he had to say.

Fine – but truly, he had little to say. He did answer the phone every day. "Hey, Dev, how are you?"

"Ooookaaayyy." I hear resentment. I have nothing to say but tell him about the weather, the dogs, some person, ask him about all the same. Get grunted answers. I ask, "What you up to today?"

"Nothing." No questions of me.

And so our conversations go. Often his speech is slurred. I might ask how much he is drinking. "Some." I might ask about work. "Okay."

I feel his suffering. It seems that I have no way to access it and respond. He is not a patient. As I listen to my painfully befuddled self, a moment of his child-hood comes to mind. When he was 3, we saw a pigeon with a broken wing on the steps of a church. Devan said, "Read to it, Mommy. Make it feel better." We took one of his books out of my backpack, sat on the steps, and read to the pigeon. When someone came to take the bird for help, Devan was glad we had made it feel better.

"Dev, what if we read a book together . . . on the phone?" "What book?" Suspicious.

A friend had encouraged me to read the AA *Big Book* with him. That would be a relief, addressing the issue, but it also would be controlling, directing, and criticizing. And, if Winship is correct, it would give pleasure only because the focus would remain on the drug, not on us. Once I had tricked him into an AA meeting – the outcome was not good. I say, "Any book you want."

"*Game of Thrones.*" Was he challenging me? Did I mean what I said?

Yes, I had meant it. I was ready to read whatever would engage him, not realizing that my engagement would be necessary too, or that it would come.

Sometime in the spring four years ago, we began to read one chapter a day, taking turns. I do not think I would have become enthralled with *Game of Thrones* reading it alone. But I became the one to say, "What time tomorrow? We have to see what happens to Danaerys. Oh, what about John Snow?" Devan had read the books before and seen the whole series but would give me no spoilers. Instead he said, "You'll see." Over and over, I was the learner and he was the knower, like a toddler bringing a rock to a curious mother. Slowly, I realized that I was enjoying my son as I had not before. He was teaching me. The trauma of watching him so close to death had stripped my defenses, leaving me open to hearing.

For several years before that, I had struggled to hear my own experience while with him. I recognized that I perceived him through a cloudy lens, mostly traumatic overlays of experiences with intoxicated family members. Transferences. To avoid seeing those overlays, I had looked away from or beyond him to what I wanted, not what was. I recognized how much my looking away blocked knowing him. I didn't mean to block my perception of him – I tried and tried to hear and understand him, and still, without even knowing it, I did not. He knew that I did not.

Not hearing or knowing him was the unknown price I paid in order to avoid reliving my childhood pain. As a therapist I knew that not hearing or mishearing a patient wreaked havoc. At best a patient would act out; at worst, the person would leave without my understanding why. My son could not completely leave. Drinking was a partial exit.

I also knew that I cannot hear my patients well when I am unable to hear something inside myself that has been activated by a patient. Thus, with Devan, I could only know in him what I needed to know in myself. I began to try to listen to myself, when I was with him, as I did with patients – to hear my own internal struggle in relation to hearing him. At the same time, I knew I had to remain a mother, not an interpreting therapist.

I had raised Devan in Los Angeles and moved to Alabama after he was working and had his own apartment, where I visited. I did not intrude. I asked to come, and he accepted. Sometimes he asked me to come. These visits became the stage on which my memory replayed past personal horror shows: my mother passed out, unresponsive; my mother standing before me, thin, disheveled, confused. For the first eleven years of my life, my mother was often passed out or was sick as she sobered up. Because she drank rather than eating, she was thin, malnourished. For years, I had shut these memories away from consciousness. Faced with Devan, they poured forth. The increasing filth in his apartment brought forth memories of the uncleaned houses in which I had lived. An overwhelming sense of helplessness often filled me. Here in Devan's apartment, I relived my childhood fears. The sense of dread that my mother would not awaken. Hunger. Sometimes my stomach had not been fed, but most often my mind and soul had not been fed. I struggled to allow whatever experience came to me to be known. I became aware of a rumbling whine behind my eyes: "Momma, Momma. Move. Don't stop. Don't die." Images began to come with the whine: my mother's matted red hair, slack slobbering jaw, limp arm hanging down from the bed.

I did not tell Devan of these experiences; I just tried to know them for myself. I did not want to be present, with my fears for Devan superimposed on the memories of my childhood, yet I knew I had to. I was sustained in the belief that this kind of hearing would help by my knowledge of Wilfred Bion's (1984a, b) work. While Bion speaks mostly of the communication between mothers and infants, his ideas are true of any time in life when nonverbal communication is used to manage emotional states that are unknown or overwhelming to a personality. For Bion, the mental dynamic of projective identification in which the recipient of the projection feels the emotion is the foundation of normal development, of good-enough mothering. The recipient of the emotion, hopefully a more mature mind, must contain the emotion, reflect on it, and respond with the needed care. For Bion, the emotion is received when the recipient is in a state of reverie and open to communication. Bion labels the raw emotions "beta elements." Emotions that have been contained, changed, and held in thought are "alpha elements."

Until transformed into alpha elements, beta elements continue to impact the being of the person. They may be thought of as "thoughts without a thinker."

These thoughts without a thinker remain out of consciousness but can dominate a person, something like a free radical, a dissociated state. Patients who come for treatment engage in nonverbal communication. Through projective identification, they often fill us with beta elements, raw emotion that they cannot process. As a therapist I try to reach a state of reverie so I can perceive and process the emotion and respond verbally or nonverbally.

As I thought of Devan, I realized that I had often been unable to listen to him, to receive his communications, as my mind was so preoccupied with old and unknown experiences. My memories were shorn of emotion, deadened. The accompanying emotions must have remained beta elements, thoughts without a thinker. Projective identification between parent and child is a two-way street. Children tend to be sensitive to parents. So I reasoned that Devan must be filled with much of me that I had not held in my mind.

Thus, learning Devan meant learning myself, a painful process. It meant learning so much of myself that had not been allowed to cross the barrier of intellectuality. "My parents were alcoholics, severe," I could finally say. "My father killed himself drinking." I could say it openly, defying shame.

I learned Devan when he was killing himself, and only then did I feel this aspect of my life in a way that might be thought of as "suffering," as Bion describes it. I did more than know about it; it became alive with emotion. In moments, lived. I would not have done it, but I knew I must for my son to be free of it.

By the time Devan and I spent the week at the bed and breakfast, I had been listening to myself when I was with him for several years. As I did so, I became able to know him differently, to appreciate that he had suffered from my insensitivity and projections. I also had begun to appreciate that he had his own emotional pain, separate from me. As I heard and contained my own experience, the overlay that had coated my experience of him was pulled away. A space opened for him, and his painful being, to reside within me. The reward is that his loving, playful being came also.

I think Devan sensed this change in me, allowing him to want to talk every day and to put forth a book that was meaningful to him when I suggested reading.

We began *Game of Thrones*. From then on, I have not felt alone in the fight for his life. The part of him that wanted to live joined in. I suggested how we would wage this battle: reading. He brought forth the weapon: his choice of book. Only now that we have finished all five *Game of Thrones* books, moved on and finished his next choice, all seven Harry Potter books, can I reflect on the choices. I see that both series were deeply personal sagas of growth in the face of hostile forces.

When we started our reading, content did not matter. For several years, it was just the connection. Our voices, given reason to exist for the purpose of reading, mattered. For several years Devan was intoxicated. He slurred words and lost his place. When I read, he probably fell asleep. For months, I was enraged. Why didn't he just stay sober? I wondered why I was doing this. It is a substantial commitment to read every day for at least an hour. When he was really drunk, reading could drag on for several hours. The time spent reading was unformed but seemed necessary, so I continued. I became aware that much of the rage I felt was so old, attached mostly to my mother. I came to feel hatred that had lived somewhere in the realm of my dissociations. I did not criticize. I could not have done so without anger flowing from me. Sometime into the second year, I complained that it was too hard to listen when he had drunk so much that he could not talk clearly. By then, I knew the reading was important to him. I knew the reading mattered. Afterward, he could mostly speak clearly.

At no time did I demand he stop drinking. I wanted to so very much. I wanted the power. But I knew the only power I had resided in the connection we were forming with our daily reading.

When I tell people about this, they ask, what it is about these books? Were there themes that we discussed? Did we work through conflicts? Did we discuss the characters? "Well, what did you discuss?" Of course, as I think about it now, these two series of books both have content that is phenomenally relevant to Devan. At their core both are family dramas: in *Game of Thrones*, drunken, crazy parents with damaged, struggling children; in Harry Potter, a child with dead parents growing to manhood. Wars are waged in both. Good versus evil.

In the past, I confessed with embarrassment that Devan and I discussed almost nothing in our phone calls. Now I am able to say with pride that we discussed almost nothing. We, as a child-parent couple, were in no condition to discuss. The language we had was largely based on denial of affect, not containment and representation. What we did as we read all five books of *Game of Thrones* and all seven of Harry Potter was to feel together: horror, fear, love, terror, hate, repulsion, excitement, rage, helplessness, desire, longing, hunger, inadequacy, sorrow, uncertainty. Our discussions consisted of "Oh, how awful!" "What will he do?" "Oh, poor Catelyn." "How can Arya stand that?" "She killed him." "I hate him." "I love her." "Oh, no." "They locked him under the stairs." "No food."

And so much despair when the bad guys seemed to be winning. Rob killed at the "red wedding." Voldemort killed Dumbledore. I cried.

So we experienced these books together. Each of them, bit by bit. I have come to think that the importance of our reading lies in what Winnicott calls the "going-on-being." Of course, we had gone on being for years, but not in the world of affect, feeling – especially not as it connected with the world of early fantasy that is so well represented in these stories. So that is what we did: experience. This was much as it must have been in those early days of reading, of absorbing the experience of being together in loving sensual moments. Much as it was in the early days of life before language.

When I now reflect on this experience, I become more and more aware of the impact on Devan of my blocking my perception of him as he was developing. As painful as it was to urge my "ghosts" to come alive, developing an awareness of how much harm had been done was a thousandfold worse. All I wanted was to love my son, my truly adorable son. I came to realize that I was in many ways what Jeffrey Eaton calls an obstructive object (Eaton, 2005). It has meant knowing the pain I caused, not just the pain I suffered.

Eaton develops Bion's idea of an internal presence that is ego destructive and that rejects projective identification. In plain English, this is saying that what we experience with others is taken into ourselves and becomes a part of us, a presence within. From the beginning of life, the most significant person is the primary caretaker, usually mother. When mother cannot accept the communications of the baby/child, she becomes a presence inside that does not hear the experience of self. Then, that person is hostile to him- or herself and cannot tolerate perception of self. Alcohol is a perfect drug to satisfy this internal state. Ability to perceive is deadened by alcohol, just as mother deadened with her lack of perception.

How painful it has been for me to recognize that my interactions with my son, whom I loved and nurtured, have been so damaging. I had not thought of this when I began sitting in Devan's apartment, inviting my denied traumas to come alive in me, when I began to contain them within myself. I then became receptive to him but only after years of blocking perception and projecting. It seems to have taken these years of my constant, steady accepting presence for him to begin to risk letting me know him without fear that I would refuse to know him, that I would be available to meet what is a most basic need and desire for the infant/child, necessary for development of mind.

We have begun to reread *Game of Thrones*. Maybe this time, we can have the discussions that we seem supposed to have. But I don't know. It may still be long time. There may be more experience to share first.

It was my turn to read. I began the Prologue with only a vague memory of it. Rereading, I see why. It is gruesome. But the themes of the book are presented, and the scene is set for the overarching war of the many wars in the book. The "dead" come back as cold, icy beings who cannot be killed. They come back to kill the living without discrimination between uncivilized "wildings" or "civilized" citizens of the kingdom. As an analyst, I could wax eloquent about the meaning of this as a presentation of a brutal internal drama. The dead: the repressed, the beta elements, the known unknown (Bollas), the dissociated traumatic experience, the projected. All that we cannot tolerate in experience, that we find a way to deaden, comes back to kill us. Not to haunt, but to take us with it, coldly without the warmth of love. Just as it was taken. To come alive is a war with multiple internal and external opponents to life.

I will not speak as a psychoanalyst, theoretically, but instead as a mother who is a psychoanalyst. What I have learned from this experience, this life experience, capped by these last four years of reading is the truth represented in the fantasy of this novel. What we do not know will come back and take the living. My experience of my parents, that which I had refused to know, came back and took my son. Only as I came to know it, and with the knowing warmed it to life, could it cease to live in him.

This sounds mysterious. But if I put on my psychoanalytic cap, it is not so. Isn't this the story of transgenerational trauma? I, a child of alcoholics, raise a son in whom the self-destructiveness is perpetuated? I think of my mother, herself the daughter of an alcoholic father, raised in times much more difficult that any I have known, doing her best to send her children into the life she could not have. I think of other family traumas, too many to be described here, that were not allowed life, never died, and coldly took life from the living. And isn't transgenerational trauma understandable from the perspective of the obstructive object? That which cannot be tolerated in the living mind of a traumatized person is projected onto/into the child, who is not received as a new self but seen as the old. The new self that the child could become has no external home and so cannot grow an internal home.

I will not discuss these theories with Devan, unless he asks. But we will now be able to talk of the characters in this drama.

Our reading has not ended. A few weeks ago, after a summer with a long lapse, we agreed to three regularly scheduled times each week with the agreement that I would be available and he would be sober enough to talk. I asked Devan what his experience had been. He said he could not remember it clearly or how it started, but "we started something good, so I am not worried about the history. . . . I know it started out as a bad part of life but now it's cool, good." He reflected that he knew he had almost destroyed himself with his drinking for a few years, "drinking my breakfast." He still drinks but "not to the point I ever have before. . . . Being hung over is not fun. The cure is not drinking." He speaks now mostly in a deep, strong, clear voice that brings joy to my heart.

In this conversation, he was not defensive, but open and honest. He now drinks mostly on weekends. He was reflective. "It helps to have a job. They care about me from day to day. It helps talking to you day to day. I am an introvert. I want to be left alone from time to time, but I am thinking of another person. It is hard to find the mix." Then came the text, a picture of his cat curled at his feet. "I didn't know I could take care of anything, and I can."

Devan read the last of Harry Potter, the Epilogue. Even on the phone, I heard our smiles. A family goes on. Harry finds and gives love. The generations continue. Life goes on going on. I feel Devan's hope for himself.

We agreed to reread *Game of Thrones* because Devan thought there is a lot to understand when you know the plot. After rereading just the Prologue, I agree. The characters are distinct representations of internal attitudes: three rangers on a scouting expedition – an arrogant young leader, a young but experienced ranger who is discredited, a very experienced older ranger whose knowledge (not completely accurate) is mocked. Because the arrogant leader does not listen, all die when the "others," the dead who have come alive, find them. We will be able to speak of the arrogance of the young leader, the feelings of the rangers when their warnings, which arose from their feelings of eeriness and coldness, were rejected. We can wonder what it was like for them to have to follow someone who did not know what they knew or felt and would not listen.

Indirectly, we will be speaking of Devan's experience with me, and I will know more of my experience with my own mother. A few years ago I could not have had this conversation. Now I can because I have learned that the dead can be warmed.

This last Christmas, Devan rummaged through the gifts until he found "the book." He set it aside to open last. When he did, he looked at me with elfish suspicion. I could see him wondering what it would be this year. Trevor Noah's *Born a Crime*. A real person in a real troubled world struggling through a troubling time. "That will be fun to read."

References

Bion, W. R. (1984a). *Learning from experience*. London: Karnac. (Originally published 1962)

Bion, W. R. (1984b). *Second thoughts: Selected papers on psychoanalysis*. London: Karnac. (Originally published in 1967)

Eaton, J. (2005). The obstructive object. *Psychoanalytic Review, 92*, 355–372.

Winship, G. (2012). *Addictive personalities and why people take drugs: The spike and the moon*. London: Karnac.

13

"Likening" the "other"

Identifying and dis-identifying in adoptive parenting

Billie A. Pivnick

Adoption is a social institution as old as the Bible and as new as the Syrian refugee crisis. Being adopted is known to benefit orphaned children, who fare less well in other institutions, on the streets, or with parents who cannot care for them. However, since adoptive families are formed differently than families in which there is biological similarity between children and parents, they present unique challenges to parents, teachers, and therapists.

Much of the professional adoption literature approaches adoption from the outside in. This empirical approach has led to unexpected insights – such as the finding that parents' behavior is shaped more by their children than the other way around (Reiss, Neiderhiser, Hetherington & Plomin, 2000) – but it fails to account for how that developmental process is shaped by interactions within the family context and between the family and the community (Winnicott, 1957a, 1957b).

There is no single story of adoptive parenting. Adoption is a highly interactive, intersubjective experience for adoptee, adoptive parents, birth parents, and communities. All have their own stories and perspectives that enter the flow of family life. So that adoptees don't feel lost in translation, they must be helped to find themselves in relation to friends and family members, whether present, lost, or imagined. At the same time, attention must be paid to ways that talk alone may lead to misunderstandings and empathic failures. Because adoptees often enact troubling emotions that lack words or seem unrelated to the present context or at unpredictable times, adoptive parents must work to adopt mentalizing conversation to create connection and mutuality (Fonagy, 1996; Nickman, 1985, 2004).

The word "adoption" is synonymous with acceptance and embracing; its antonym is rejection. Choice is implicit in the meaning of the word. In adopting someone, we choose whom we take care of or whom we exclude from care. This social interchange has moral and ethical implications, as well as consequences for our social fabric. In elaborating self-regulatory strategies based on non-genetic similarity, and in developing relational mutuality based on processes that may rely on mirroring somewhat but not solely, adoptees and their adoptive families do not only cope with a sense of "otherness" that most experience frequently and intensely, but also show society a way forward. The solution to reflexive "othering" is something adoptive families learn and practice daily: I call it "likening."

Our ethical sensibility concerning whom we consider "us" and whom we consider "foreign" is at the foundation of Christian religious belief: We are told to love our neighbors as we would ourselves. This religious credo is an interpersonal theory of social regulation, one different from the ancient Greeks' more molar moral motto, "All things in moderation" (Zizek, Santner, & Reinhard, 2005). But exactly who this "neighbor" is appears to be a matter of interpretation (Lacan, 2015). Is it someone other than us who resides within our social/tribal group? Or is it an outsider we do not know? Just how do we come to know someone as one of us? Is this "golden rule" a response to that dilemma, or even a suggested procedure? Or is this rule an injunction to make attachments that enable our safety and security, because in so doing, we create the necessary conditions for living in groups?

Adoptees and their families are typically regarded with some suspicion, if not aspersion. We are different. I am an adoptive mother of two grown, but still developing, sons. I have firsthand knowledge of the struggles for recognition and dread of misrecognition that are part of the adoption experience. These problems do not just face adopted children, but also constitute challenges for adoptive parents, in addition to affecting sibling and marital bonds, extended family ties, and the loyalties of various community institutions such as schools, churches, and sports organizations. I have discovered the loss aversion that is at the core of many of the symptoms that bring adopted children and adults to treatment (Pivnick, 2009). This is because I am also a clinical psychologist who has treated adoptees and their families for nearly 30 years.

After a long period of unsuccessful infertility treatments, my husband and I said, "no more." We had had enough of the dehumanizing medical interventions carried out by well-meaning doctors who sometimes recommended the ludicrous to avoid disappointing us with the futility of our quest. "I could position you upside down when I transfer your embryos," offered one. "You just have to be less stressed out, lose weight," opined another. "I can massage your pelvic floor," offered an alternative healer. Since my fertility problems began with emergency ovarian surgery to treat a cancer scare when I was seventeen, I knew these and other recommendations were mainly in service of mutual denial. I was a tough case – as it turned out, an impossible case.

It was hard to say goodbye to the rounds of medical treatments that acted like an addiction: we'd get high with hope for six weeks of each attempt, only to be dumped flat when we received the pregnancy test results. The only thing to do was to try again. We came to call it "sex for science." When we began to talk to friends, social workers, and lawyers about adoption, our feelings were different, quieter. There were fewer highs, more sighs, but also fewer goodbyes. We began to feel alive again, connected – to one another, and to the many people who understood and offered compassion for our plight. Don't get me wrong, I wept for months before we finalized this decision. But with each new piece of information and each new contact, our trust in ourselves, our marriage, and the goodness of the world increased.

Adopting a child is not an easy process. One is inspected and surveilled for a long time, fingerprinted, interviewed, visited, and evaluated repeatedly. It was sometimes hard not to feel as though we had done something criminal by wanting to take care of a child. We used to joke that one had to be sixteen and making love in the backseat of a car in order to become a parent the "natural" way. Even once we had our babies, we had to undergo further judgment in a court of law before the adoption could be finalized.

But my husband and I had already mourned our imagined genetically related babies. I had miscarried once and failed many IVF attempts. We had already seen a marital therapist for help moving on. Before we got the call that a baby was available and potentially ours, we had purchased an old house. We imagined our life in this big old house, filled with books and art and music, and a fireplace around which we could gather in winter. We had fantasies of cooking, watching movies, and hanging out together. Of course, we would also spend a lot of time attending the kids' sports activities or dance concerts. Our first task, though, would be to fix and feather this sturdy but aged house, so that we wouldn't be too demoralized by our barren nest.

To legally adopt a baby from another state – in this case, Texas – we had to reside there for up to a week. So when we got news of our son's birth, off we went to the airport as quickly as we could. We dropped off our new house keys with our new contractor, saying, "We hope you're honest, because we have to go to Texas to pick up our new baby." We left on a jet plane, humming that Peter, Paul, and Mary song all the way to the hospital.

In deciding to adopt, we'd had to clarify our values. We came to understand that loving people was a choice we could and would make. When people form a family through adoption, as we were about to do, nothing could be clearer. Children and parents were gifts to one another. If treated with wisdom and care, these gifts not only endured as comforts in times of need, but also transformed into a kind of wealth, to be invested wisely and well. When feelings of kinship came not from biological similarity, but from behaving kindly and relating to others as kindred spirits, one realized the power of compassion to create intimacy and growth even in the strange world outside of the family circle. We hoped our family would be a kind of nest, within a larger circle of extended family, which was also within a larger circle of family-like institutions such as school, temple, and team. In turn, our temple, schools, and teams were nested within a community of Americans, and as Americans, we were within a circle of nations. Caring, for us, was not restricted to just the inner circle, though it began there. The value we placed on learning, integrity, generosity, involvement, hard work, play, and laughter flowed from our sense that loving is the core human value. We dreamed that together our family would have many wonderful experiences, but knew they all would begin with home.

We were now far from that home – in Texas. I was about to learn a procedure I would replicate many thousands of times. In medical school, the lore goes, to learn a procedure you watch one, you do one, and you teach one. Standing over the examining table, accompanied by several nurses, I performed my first move. R-r-rip went the first Velcro fastener. R-r-rip went the second Velcro tape. I removed the saturated gauze. The next thing I knew, I was covered with squirting liquid. Blood? No. A geyser of urine had burst forth, hitting me in the face and dripping onto my denim dress. My newborn son smiled – or so it seemed. The nurses and my husband laughed heartily. I had just been initiated not into the medical fraternity but into The Mommy Club, the exclusive sisterhood that had denied me admission for more years than I cared to count.

We had traveled from Brooklyn to Texas on a mission. Our adoption attorney had called to tell us our baby was ready to meet us and that after a few days' stay in Texas, we could bring him home. We dithered a bit over whether it was really okay to show up before the formal consent was signed, but a call from the birth mother's mother put an end to that – come quickly, she commanded. We didn't want to take a chance on losing our new family member, so off we rushed. When there, my husband drove around the parking lot, looking for an appropriate parking space. Our birth mother watched from her hospital window as he chose one spot after another, only to change his mind. How strange we must have looked to her! There were only four spots out of a hundred already occupied. His anxious New York City parking perfectionism was irrelevant in this new place. Strange we looked, too, to the nurses, who told us they had never seen a Texas baby dressed in a cap, even one as cute as the one we'd purchased from the Hanna Andersson catalog, even in the middle of January. They said they'd never met a Jewish couple and were stupefied at the idea that we'd named him Isaac, but, trying to be polite, they assured us that we had a fine healthy boy. When they put him in my arms, I cried. He, on the other hand, was wide-eyed and alert, seemingly ready to sing and dance when he got near me.

We had come unequipped – not just without pulsing hormones, but also without basics like baby blankets and bottles. I hadn't been given any baby showers, and buying stuff seemed like bad luck. The nurses provided formula and bottles, but the only place to buy blankets, diapers, and the like was the local Walmart, a place I had never been. To a girl raised at the JL Hudson Company – a small-scale Macy's-type department store on the wrong side of 8 Mile in Detroit – this huge emporium may as well have been Mars. A store that sold guns and fishing tackle just a few aisles away from baby lotion was not something I could comprehend. But I still have the pastel plaid acrylic blanket we purchased that day – out of the many hand-knit, monogrammed, and designer blankets we eventually received, it held up the best.

My sister lived in Texas at the time with her husband and first daughter, a perky two-year-old. On a map, Austin looked like it was right next to Marshall, where our son was born. In reality, it was an eight-hour drive. But we were fortunate to be able to stay with them while I figured out how to bathe a baby, how to treat a circumcision, and how to walk, talk, and feed a baby without any sleep. Whenever he got fussy, we danced around, he and I, to Bobby McFerrin's "Don't Worry, Be Happy." We took pictures of him on the Texas state flag – the very flag that was flown at the state capitol on the day of his birth. At home, we arrived to find his crib assembled and his room painted a gleaming white, thanks to the kindness of friends – and our new contractor. We drifted to sleep every afternoon and evening to the strains of Daniel Kobialka's lullaby version of "When You Wish upon a Star." We had wished upon one, and we felt like the luckiest people in the world.

Our ideals were soon put to the test. Especially outside our home, life could be stressful. Adoption hearings to finalize family formation are usually joyous occasions, but not always. When we went before a circuit judge in South Carolina to finalize our younger son's adoption, we were asked about our professions and living situation. Again. Then the judge, apparently unimpressed with my Columbia professorship and my husband's usually well-respected legal credentials, asked, "What makes you think you can raise one of our South Carolina boys up there?" He nearly spit his contempt at us Northerners. Worse yet, New Yorkers. And Jewish, oy. Undone by his derisive tone, I unraveled. "We belong to a swim club, Your Honor. We will teach him to swim." The beaches were the only aspect of South Carolina and New York that I could think of that we might have in common.

When my older son was a toddler, fellow shoppers at the local Brooklyn produce market would stop and stare at us. I was a brunette, olive-skinned mom, carrying a platinum blond blue-eyed baby in a pack. "Cute baby. Who does he look like?" Even though I wanted to tell them to mind their own business, I knew they meant well. I had noticed that much of conversation about infants seemed to circle around whose ears they had, or whose toes. If I were honest and mentioned my child was adopted, many, out of ignorance, would say things like "That's the next best thing to having your own child," and I would want to cry – again – or better yet, tell them off. So I learned to smile and instead reply that my grandmother was fair – a truth that was nevertheless completely irrelevant to the matter at hand.

Even in the relatively protected circle of our family, there were differences to be negotiated. "Couldn't you have adopted a child of the rich?" queried one insensitive family member. Another finally accepted our little Carolinian into the family by dubbing him the most articulate of all the grandkids, some of whom were already attending Ivy League colleges. Swimming, meh; words were what counted in my family. My uncle, the rabbi, the family patriarch, adored this placid boy, who would sit still and loved listening to stories, but he had no patience for my hyperactive Texas cowboy older son, who couldn't easily sit quietly through long droning sermons. In my family of origin, it was not normal or desirable to be good at athletics, impulsive, or scrappy, let alone blond. Whereas in the larger society fair skin and hair can confer status, in Jewish circles this is more suspect, approaching as it does the Aryan ideal we learned to fear.

Differences, of course, come in lots of sizes, colors, and orientations. In other families the apparent differences may be between Asian children and Caucasian parents, or Latino parents and African-American children, or Italian parents and African children, or heterosexual children and homosexual parents, or between parents of differing ethnicities and races and their look-alike children.

We all have to live with difference, you may say. Yes, but it is a different difference when it's so apparent to the outside world, rather than existing on the inside as a psychological or cognitive trait. We socialize our children to "fit into" whatever social niche we occupy for good reason – they are going to occupy it too. But we will also have to occupy their social niche, and we are not always prepared for this, especially when our children are in a group that is discriminated against – whether that group consists of Asians, African-Americans, or ADHD sufferers. When children come from a social or ethnic group that experiences the hatred of others for being different, it compounds the rejection sensitivity they can already feel as a result of being adopted (Brodzinsky, 1998). For a number of months or years – sometimes decades – we may wish it were otherwise: it is painful to experience the world from their perspective. But if we let ourselves do so, our children's experiences help us grow in ways we never imagined possible.

Our children's most prevalent fear was of being left – left out, left behind, and left without a word. Like haiku, their life stories left out a lot of supporting detail. Their memories were often experienced as islands of heightened arousal, with no conscious content. Both we and our children sometimes experienced ourselves as talking but not being listened to, while at the same time, neither we nor our children could remember what happened before we met; therefore we could have trouble reading one another's implicit communications (Boston Change Process Study Group, 2008). Our goal became to help ourselves and our children to move from being "lost in translation" to being "found in relation" (Pivnick, 2013).

To do that we had to help them find themselves in relation to all family members, even those lost or imagined. Our children were born to someone else, but now they needed to be borne by us. It was not until they could be accepted by us as both impossible to know and equally impossible not to recognize that our adopted children could truly be borne. Our children, for their part, had to bear (all) their parents – despite our often misguided intentions and sometimes severe misattunements. This drama of "misfitting" played out largely in the implicit realm and thus could at times become a source of great shame. To bear one another we first had to find ways to bear witness to one another's struggles as well as joy. This sometimes required "unthinking" what we thought we already knew.

Andrew Solomon begins his book about parenting challenging children, *Far from the Tree*, in this way:

> There is no such thing as reproduction. When two people decide to have a baby, they engage in an act of production, and the widespread use of the word reproduction for this activity, with its implication that two people are but braiding themselves together, is at best a euphemism to comfort prospective parents before they get in over their heads. In the subconscious fantasies that make conception look so alluring, it is often ourselves that we would like to see live forever, not someone with a personality of his own. Having anticipated the onward march of our selfish genes, many of us are unprepared for children who present unfamiliar needs. Parenthood abruptly catapults us into

a permanent relationship with a stranger, and the more alien the stranger, the stronger the whiff of negativity. We depend on the guarantee in our children's faces that we will not die. Children whose defining quality annihilates that fantasy of immortality are a particular insult; we must love them for themselves, and not for the best of ourselves in them, and that is a great deal harder to do. Loving our own children is an excuse for the imagination."

(Solomon, 2012, p. 1)

He goes on to say: "Our children are not us . . . and yet we are our children." Since we inevitably exist as a unit, internally as well as in appearance, our fates are linked. As a way of sorting out the issues created by parent-child interconnectedness when children are perceived as different or special in some way – and many people see adoptees as both different and special – he wrestles with the issue of identity.

All of us, he asserts, have two kinds of identity. Vertical identities are attributes and values passed down through the generations – by DNA, yes, but also via shared cultural norms. Things like ethnicity, language, religion, and nationality tend to be vertical in transmission. Horizontal identities occur when someone has an inherent or acquired trait that is foreign to his or her parents and must acquire identity from a peer group. These may be a result of recessive genes, random mutations, prenatal influences, or values and preferences that a child does not share with his progenitors. Such traits as being gay, physically disabled, a genius, psychopathic, autistic, intellectually disabled, or a child of rape fall into this category because they involve being part of a subculture that confers identity above and beyond what adheres to the biological origins of the condition.

Being adopted or part of the adoption triad confers on us and our children a horizontal identity. In our family, the problematic differences came down to learning styles. Our kids were smart enough to be admitted to a private school for the gifted. But they both had learning idiosyncrasies that made them feel as if they did not fit in. Teachers criticized Noah, the laconic one, well suited to play Matlock, the attorney in a little Southern town, for not speaking up enough. He told me that by the time he thought of what he wanted to say, the discussion had shifted. Finally, one day he spoke in class. What made the difference, he told me, was the realization that no one else thought about what they were going to say before they said it and that he could do that too. He was also penalized for not wanting to play his bassoon in a group even though he enjoyed playing it on his own. After having him assessed, we learned that his troubles with processing speed made it hard to stay on the same beat with the other kids, and he was trying to avoid embarrassment.

Loss aversion figured in for Isaac too. Sitting for a standardized math exam, he could not tolerate the anxiety of not being sure he knew the answers. Rather than waiting to find out, he left after three minutes – and scored three out of many hundred possible points. By that point, I was actually almost amused. He was the kid who bit another kid in preschool, the one whom all the other kids would get mad at because they had to sit still in a circle for three minutes and he couldn't do it. He couldn't write for long enough either, and forget languages – he couldn't do English grammar, let alone Latin in the fourth grade.

You may wonder what I was thinking by then – as do I. It's just that I had been a spelling bee champion as a kid. I didn't know from learning challenges. It turns out he was a great ice hockey goalie because his reflexes were so quick. I was a poor athlete as a child, and I'm still a dawdler. We were not an easy match. Even when he was an infant, he gulped down his bottle but got stomachaches until I figured out he could only take in little bits at a time. The same is true of words. His birth mother was a slow-talking, fast-riding barrel rider in the rodeo. Me, I'm a fast-talking, slow-moving professorial type.

Not surprisingly, Isaac was ambivalent when approaching his bar mitzvah. He told us that if he had to go through an initiation rite to become a man, he'd rather skin a cheetah than read Torah. He thought long and hard about whether he really wanted to be a member of our tribe, given that it was clear he hadn't started out Jewish. The rabbi modified his Torah portion to make it as small as possible, and he was allowed to memorize it from tape rather than by reading it in Hebrew. Noah, when it came his turn, was paralyzed with fear, literally unable to move, even a few minutes beforehand. Our rabbi normalized this for us by playfully chasing Noah around the sanctuary just before the guests were seated. With the help of our temple community, we normalized for ourselves and our children the experience of difference – we wanted them to feel they belonged.

We enjoyed fostering and observing the interaction of our two sons – brothers not by blood but by bonding. Isaac has always taken it upon himself to help Noah with his athletic development, like a personal trainer, while Noah has frequently functioned as Isaac's conscience in moments of incipient impetuousness. Isaac got Noah to move; Noah got Isaac to think. Isaac was a goalie, Noah was a shooter; Isaac a catcher, Noah a pitcher. Theirs was truly an amazing bond.

Our house was situated in a wonderfully diverse, multi-ethnic neighborhood in the Flatbush section of Brooklyn – featured in the *New York Times* as "Brooklyn's Technicolor Dream Quilt" – and had a living room large enough to contain small community gatherings, like the board meetings of the not-for-profit organizations that my husband, Jay, hosted. In this way, the community came inside our home frequently and in a way that the children could observe, even from a young age. Our children came to expect difference, even to require it.

Of course, one could also take home on the road, and we did. We spent many wonderful summer vacations on Martha's Vineyard, where Noah and Isaac worked on a horse farm, learning about caring for animals and about responsibility. We also traveled frequently to places far from home. Both boys played for an international travel hockey team that took us to places like Finland, Sweden, Italy, Switzerland, and Austria. The boys had a chance to work intensely as part of a team as well as to meet kids their age in each place. Isaac even lived with a Finnish family for a few days. As a result, the Finns came to celebrate Noah's bar mitzvah, forming what we hoped would be a lasting tie between two worlds. I was a high school exchange student who lived in a Japanese family in Tokyo, just after the Japan Olympic Games. Noah, enjoying the Asian-inspired aspects of our life, decided to study Chinese in middle school. We hoped that he would eventually figure out a way to use it in his future endeavors, while temporarily enjoying the musical tones that emanated from his bedroom during homework hours.

As a family, we also adopted others. Noah adopted a kitten he found abandoned in the street, against the initial reservations of my husband, who worried that the cat might carry disease. Defiantly, Noah nursed the kitten to health and saved it from certain death in the busy street. We have donated money and helped spearhead an organization named Project Zawadi that houses and educates Tanzanian orphans. We have been deeply involved in other kinds of community service as well. Jay has nurtured the Flatbush Development Corporation for quite a few years as president of its Board of Directors. He brought together many of the diverse factions of the homeowners within our expansive neighborhood, which represents more ethnicities than anywhere else outside of the United Nations. As a psychologist and professor, I provided counseling services to some of the firefighters in one of the Brooklyn firehouses after 9/11, to help them cope with their bereavement. Noah and Isaac accompanied me on many of my visits and entertained the men with stories, jokes, and silliness, earning coveted spots on the walls for their artwork, and even more coveted rides on the engines. Several of the firefighters even attended Isaac's bar mitzvah; Isaac donated half his gift money to the widows and children of the fallen firefighters. Noah, for his part, decided to help Katrina victims by collecting and donating clothing. The Brooklyn Borough President honored Noah for his donation of much of his bar mitzvah money to Camp Brooklyn, a fund that enables impoverished Brooklyn children to attend summer camp.

We hoped our children learned that giving benefits people. But more than that, we hoped they would discover that giving feels good in and of itself, even without the honors and public displays of admiration. We thought that they would come to feel, as we had, that giving was just a way of life, enriching existence with meaning and purpose. Their birth mothers gave us generous gifts – children to care for. Noah and Isaac in turn brought us much joy. We wanted to enable them to share their gifts with the world as they shared them with us.

But before they could fully embrace belonging to our world, they had to follow their longing to discover the world they had come from. By high school, Isaac wanted out of my perfectionistic way of doing things. I couldn't blame him. Luckily, he was recruited by the hockey coach of the local Catholic school, who had seen him play at the NY State Junior Olympics. Catholic school? My husband asked him, are you sure you want to be the only Jewish kid in a school of Catholic boys? His reply? "You went to Howard University Law School, Dad, so I can go to Xaverian!" End of argument. At Xaverian, he looked and functioned just like the other boys. He did not have to compete with future Supreme Court Justices. And Noah soon followed him there, happy that he could be scrappy with the other boys in the halls. This is the child who told me, when his hockey team was finally old enough to hit each other defensively, "I live to check!"

Isaac faced his first challenge in his mandatory religion class. His first assignment was to come up with an advertising slogan version of why he loved Jesus – using metaphor – and to draw it! He was stumped and came to us for help. We suggested a number of ideas that he rejected – including talking to his teacher about why this assignment was so inappropriate for him. He didn't want to make his differences an issue – he just wanted to feel normal. He came up with a clever idea, playing off the Snickers campaign that was riding around the city on top of the taxis that year. His slogan: "Christopia: Like a candy bar, He's always in your pocket when you need Him." His religion teacher loved him until he refused to teach an entire class on the Jewish High Holidays because he didn't like being singled out.

When he was small, however, he liked being chosen. For several years, Isaac played a game of his own invention in which he was a kitten or puppy left in a basket on the orphanage steps. I would open the box and exclaim, "Oh, what a cute little kitten! I am so happy to have found you! You're just what I wanted. Now I can take care of you!" This game's repetitiveness revealed its traumatic origins and the need to repair a deep wound to the self that is thought to characterize many adopted children (Verrier, 1997). It is in relation with us, their parents – and their larger world, in part mediated for them by us – that they are found to be whole, not full of "holes." So we play – over and over if necessary.

In some settings adoption is considered a disadvantage, so many adoptees have emotional problems, we're told, or learning challenges. Yet if we follow Solomon's paradigm, we see that a condition often characterized as a disability is also a way of being, an identity. But, like wave and particle, these two views often can't be seen as coexistent: to the extent we think about adoption in terms of identity politics and affirm our children's differences, we help them and us fight against the idea that they and we are "ill" in any way; when we treat our kids' differences as disabilities, we can ameliorate some of their more challenging differences – but does that come at the cost of diminishing their pride? For instance, if we had squelched our son's wish to play varsity hockey and sent him instead to a Jewish Day School, would he have become "more like us" or just more unhappy? There is no glib answer – for many families the Jewish Day School would have been the correct answer, not Catholic school.

Solomon asserts that we need to reconcile the contrast between pathology (illness) and identity – that we need to see these categories not as opposites but as compatible aspects of a condition. Without that ability to see identity as simultaneously multiple, we cannot change how we value our children, nor help them counter what they encounter in others' attitudes.

Based on my experience with my patients, with adoption research, and with my own family, I'm going to suggest some new concepts that can help us embrace the complexity of our new identities.

First, though we all tend to think that children are who they are because of how they are raised by their parents, research (cf., Reiss, Neiderhiser, Hetherington, & Plomin, 2000) now tells us that we are who we are by virtue of how our children shape us!

Second, we're told that adoptees have trouble mourning what they've lost because they've never known it. It's like trying to grieve a hole (Quinodoz, 1996). While that can be true in later stages of development, young children are more likely to suffer from loss aversion. In other words, they try to avoid feeling disappointment, because for them, often beginning at birth, disappointment is like a repetitive stress injury. It is often the things they do to avoid being disappointed that make them appear to others to be "ill" or pathologically different in some way.

Third, adoptees and their families tend to inhibit their curiosity about many things (Pivnick, 2009). After he flunked history, one adoptee I know told his school, "Who cares about history? Knowing about the past is unimportant." It was his own history that he didn't want to learn.

Fourth, adoptees and their families suffer from a lot of shame over perceived differences. It is our role as parents to be proud of our families, and this is especially important for dads, whose roles outside the family sometimes can confer a bit more detachment (Flynn, 2004). Prideful acceptance helps counteract the shaming messages our children pick up in social settings. I was raised by a gay uncle almost as much as I was raised by my mom and dad. He was publicly pilloried for many of my teen years, a time when being different is difficult. But my family and I stood by him, no matter what, and that helped him do great things in his life. I internalized that familial loyalty and expect it in my life too.

Fifth, the reasons we don't feel more pride at times probably relate to what we don't know about our own histories. Psychotherapy and support groups can be useful to parents. Child adoptees seeking treatment commonly complain of middle-childhood behavioral and learning challenges, life-threatening acting out in adolescence, early abandonment by the adoptive father, maternal rejection and/ or depression, parental discord, and divorce. Sometimes, too, the wish to initiate a search for the birth parents creates a crisis in the adoptive family. Because of difficulties in middle childhood with creating coherent family narratives, adoptees and their parents hold multiple, often contradictory, stories about themselves (Pivnick, 2009; Steele & Steele, 2005). These conflicting stories about self and other, if held in unconsciously compartmentalized fashion, can lead to confusion and problematic communication patterns.[1]

Learning attachment rhythms, rhymes, and reasons takes time, and must be responded to in an embodied way. Despite usually secure attachments to their adoptive parents, adoptees may have unconscious memories of multiple prenatal and postnatal attachment experiences that lead to contradictory expectations of adoptive caregivers, which are often enacted and misunderstood. These need to be observed, matched, better understood, and gradually left behind in favor of more symbolic means of connection (in non-adoptees, accomplished in infancy and again in middle childhood with the construction of a coherent family narrative). Until then adoptees can have great difficulty with ego functions such as impulse control and self-soothing, and therefore often experience delays in traversing expected developmental milestones. In adoption, this is reflected in the disproportionate number of adoptees who are diagnosed with learning disabilities. The father, with his natural affinity for socializing risk assessment, can either hinder or help in significant ways (Fonagy et al., 2002; Pivnick, 2009). One worried father of a particularly impulsive son wanted to help him better anticipate the consequences of his actions. He decided to switch their bedtime reading material from Harry Potter to the New York State Penal Code for a time during his son's preadolescent years. Another father helped his particularly restless son channel some of his energy through taking long nightly walks and weekend bike rides together.

For some adoptees, individual treatment raises the risk of forming yet another attachment – in this case with the therapist. Although an attachment can be created to help the child mourn the attachments that were lost, the loss of the new attachment when therapy ends can reinforce loss aversion rather than attenuate it. On the other hand, family therapy alone can fail to get at unconscious or unformulated determinants of individual maladaptive functioning. I have found that treating the child through the parents is an arrangement that works best for young children.

Sixth, despite the aforementioned difficulties in coping, adoption is a process and an identity, as well as an act: born of the intent to care. It is not inherently psychopathological (Pivnick, 2013). While the birth parents set in motion a process through which the child is *born*, adoptive parents and maturing adoptees must together find ways to manage *being borne* by one another. Often distressed and disoriented by the sense that they were "left without a word," adoptees can enact unexpectedly disruptive feelings that lack words (Pivnick, 2009). Because the sense of dislocation in adoption packs the shock of trauma while evoking the chronic sadness of bereavement, an important function of the parent is to bear witness effectively to our children's suffering and successes so that predictable interpersonal ruptures can be repaired. We facilitate exploration of these feelings to help our kids grow, but we also have to build emotional scaffolding to create continuity, bridging occasional gaps in self-experience that otherwise lead to inhibited curiosity or calamitous enactments of disorienting, unexpected behavior. Our goal is to help our children move from being "lost in translation" to being "found in relation" (Pivnick, 2013).

The old adage "the apple doesn't fall far from the tree" inspired Solomon's title for his book, *Far from the Tree*, because some children do fall far from where their parents expected. As long as we're fighting to be "normal," we must devote enormous effort to parenting the child who is not quite whom we expected. And yet, when people say things like "Oh, that happens to non-adopted children too," we feel terribly unrecognized. The lives of each of us are utterly unlike anyone else's, and trying to normalize adoption in that way can do us and our kids a disservice. We are unique and have much to teach the world about the richness that comes from our sustaining non-conventional worldviews.

Solomon again: "Having exceptional children exaggerates parental tendencies – those who would be bad parents become awful parents; but those who would be good parents become extraordinary" (Solomon, 2012, p. 6). We do so by embracing our new identities – we are parents who have been transformed by our experience of straddling two or more worlds. Because we have children who are different, we are forever different too. I, for one, am far more compassionate with people with learning challenges and so-called attention deficits.

When my children were young, I felt as if I had a second full-time job – fielding calls from their school was a nearly daily occurrence. When I felt our differences from other families stemmed from our inferiority, I couldn't help but be more critical of us. This created more unhappiness, not only because my husband and kids could sense my disapproval, but because they in turn became critical of me. Sending my kids to a less demanding school not only helped them accommodate to living in Brooklyn rather than the ranges of Texas or the beaches of the Carolinas, but also helped me get used to relaxing about academic achievement. I had to remind myself that we sent them there less to achieve than to belong. That was our priority. And if they felt they belonged, they would probably achieve.

We finally realized that we ourselves didn't belong in our achievement-at-any-cost upper-middle-class intellectual world anymore. We had changed our opinion of many people we had once admired, because they weren't tolerant, compassionate, or did not appreciate life's humor. And, as the years have passed and we've continued to learn to love our kids for teaching us the value of togetherness over individuality, the happier we've become. By virtue of loving our children we have acquired an entirely new status – as caregivers and care recipients. We have also been enriched by their caregiving. Both have become first responders. Our older son, Isaac, is a sergeant in the National Guard, on full-time active duty, patrolling our airports and train stations. Our younger son, Noah, now married to an adoptee also raised Jewish, is father to our adorable two-year-old grandson. He trained to be an emergency medical technician, but finding the work too stressful, he now breeds dogs while attending a technical college in a rural area.

A number of years after these decisions were made, they decided to search for their birth parents. As they set their life course, we had encouraged them to trust their intuitions and be guided by their strengths while being mindful of their limitations and our values. Perhaps, then, it was less than ironic that Isaac discovered his birth grandfather had been a Vietnam War hero and Noah found he had come from a long line of farmers. Getting to know themselves by acquainting themselves with the "ghost kingdoms" (Lifton, 1988; Gunsberg, 2009) derived from their birth families helped them understand their choices in a deeper way, while helping them consolidate their identities. For a time, however, this knowledge was also destabilizing.

Of course, it is not enough to become self-accepting; social and familial acceptance is also crucial to managing the cruelty and unfairness to which people who are different are subjected. Solomon (2012, p. 6) has something to say about this, too: "To look deep into your child's eyes and see in him both yourself and something utterly strange, and then to develop a zealous attachment to every aspect of him, is to achieve parenthood's self-regarding, yet unselfish, abandon." This requires more than just "getting used to it"; it requires compassion and mutuality. Because of our capacity for parental love, Solomon (p. 697) concludes, "the tree doesn't grow far from the apple." I couldn't agree more.

Note

1 These are described in greater detail for clinicians in Pivnick (2009) and Pivnick (2012).

References

Boston Change Process Study Group (BCPSG). (2008). Forms of relational meaning: Issues in the relations between the implicit and reflective – verbal domains. *Psychoanalytic Dialogues*, *18*(2), 125–148.

Brodzinsky, D., Smith, D., & Brodzinsky, A. (1998). *Children's adjustment to adoption: Developmental and clinical issues*. London: Sage.

Flynn, D. (2004). The adoptive father. In D. Flynn (Ed.), *Severe emotional disturbance in children and adolescents: Psychotherapy in applied contexts* (pp. 131–152). New York: Taylor and Francis.

Fonagy, P. (1996). The significance of the development of meta-cognitive control over mental representations in parenting and infant development. *Journal of Clinical Psychoanalysis*, *5*, 67–86.

Fonagy, P., Gergely, G., Jurist, E., & Target, M. (2002). *Affect regulation, mentalization, and the development of the self*. New York: Other Press.

Gunsberg, L. (2009). An invitation into the ghost kingdom. *Psychoanalytic Inquiry*, *30*(1), 102–110.

Lacan, J. (2015). *The seminar of Jacques Lacan: Book VIII: Transference: 1960–1961*. (J.-A. Miller, Ed. & B. Fink, Trans.). Cambridge, MA: Polity Press.

Lifton, B. J. (1988). *Journey of the adopted self: A quest for wholeness*. New York: Basic Books.

Nickman, S. (1985). Losses in adoption: The need for dialogue. *Psychoanalytic Study of the Child*, *40*, 365–398.

———. (2004). The holding environment in adoption. *Journal of Infant Child Adolescent Psychotherapy*, *3*(3), 329–341.

Pivnick, B. A. (2009). Left without a word: Learning rhythms, rhymes, and reasons in adoption. *Psychoanalytic Inquiry*, *30*(1), 3–24.

———. (2012). Being borne: Contextualizing loss in adoption. *Psychoanalytic Perspectives*, *10*, 42–64.

Pivnick, B. A. (2013). *Lost in translation, found in relation: Treating adoptees and their families*. Workshop conducted on April 6, 2013, National Institute for the Psychotherapies, New York.

Quinodoz, D. (1996). An adopted analysand's transference of a "hole object." *International Journal of Psychoanalysis*, *77*, 323–336.

Reiss, D., Neiderhiser, J., Hetherington, E. M., & Plomin, R. (2000). *The relationship code: Deciphering genetic and social influences on adolescent development*. Cambridge, MA: Harvard University Press.

Solomon, A. (2012). *Far from the tree: Parents, children, and the search for identity*. New York: Scribner.

Steele, H., & Steele, M. (2005). The construct of coherence as an indicator of attachment ecurity in middle childhood: The friends and family interview. In K. Kerns & R. Richardson (Eds.), *Attachment in middle childhood* (pp. 137–160). New York: Guilford Press.

Verrier, N. (1997). *The primal wound*. Baltimore, MD: Gateway Press.

Winnicott, D. W. (1957a). Two adopted children. In *The child and the outside world* (pp. 52–65). London: Tavistock.

———. (1969). The use of an object. *International Journal of Psycho-Analysis, 50,* 711–716.

Zizek, S., Santner, E., & Reinhard, K. (2005). *The neighbor: Three inquiries in political theology.* Chicago: University of Chicago Press.

Part V

Building resilience

In this final section, we explore contemporary notions about building resilience in the face of loss or grief. While the concept of resilience is not new, how we think about it today is very different from how we thought about it in the past. Neuroscience has revealed that the brain has a profound ability to develop new neuronal pathways and to rewire itself to promote adaptation and healing in the aftermath of overwhelming circumstances. We understand resilience in the context of the individual's capacity to promote the establishment of new strategies for coping and for adapting to novel and often adverse circumstances.

Kerry Leddy Malawista's chapter describes how loss and grief can be transformed across the span of generations. She writes about the intergenerational bonds that reach across time and space, linking her daughter to herself and to her mother, who died when she was a child. In sharing a meaningful exchange with her daughter, she discovers that through familial attachments and intimate relationships across generations, old wounds can begin to heal in unexpected ways. She movingly describes her efforts as a young child to restore her mother by trying to transform herself into her mother – using her lipstick, a spritz of perfume, and a touch of her mother's fox stole, she tries to glimpse her mother's image reflected back at her as she gazes in the mirror. Ultimately, she truly reclaims her mother when she discovers her mother's legacy of curiosity, playfulness, and determination alive in her own now-adult daughter.

Finally, in Ann V. Klotz's chapter, the author presents an exploration of an entire community's efforts to cope with a sudden and unexpected loss. When a student at the school where she is headmaster dies in an accident, the whole school is in shock. Klotz shows how grief expands and folds back on itself. She describes her own experience balancing multiple roles, as the head of school, the mother of the deceased girl's best friend, and a friend of the deceased girl's mother – and as a mourner herself, now re-experiencing the early loss of her beloved sibling. In the course of leading the school community through communal and individual grief, Klotz begins to understand more deeply how to build resilience in adolescence, and learns to develop steps toward fostering a sense of hopefulness and resilience in her community through the use of ritual, attachment, and bonding.

14

Personal essay

Shining through

Kerry Leddy Malawista

My daughter arrived home for college, dropped her backpack, and immediately began telling me about her work splicing worm DNA. Worms, tinier than a comma, with a lovely sounding name – *C. elegans*.

Anna explained how she'd carefully removed DNA from one worm, combined it with whatever substance it is that makes jellyfish fluorescent, and then transferred this new concoction into another worm. She showed me an image on her iPhone – a luminous creature caught in the midst of an eerily glowing dance. I was captivated by her passion and her facility with scientific terminology – a language completely foreign to me; amazed that my daughter – my child – had grown into an adult who could bring me along into this new world of genetics.

As I was admiring this glowing creature, Anna suddenly shifted the conversation, and with her utterly green eyes looked up at me and said, "Oh, yeah, Mom. I was in this store near school and saw this vest I thought would look really good on you."

This switch didn't surprise me. With her eye for fashion and love of YouTube videos on style, Anna often advised me on my choice of clothes. In her teens she knew exactly what colors complimented my skin tone.

"Oh, yeah? What did it look like?" I asked, interested to learn a new tidbit of what was currently in vogue.

"No, I bought it for you," she said as she pulled a plastic shopping bag from her backpack and handed it to me. She continued on casually, as if buying me a vest was something she did all the time.

"I thought it would look good on you. It's your color – purple."

In that instant Anna had stepped over a doorstep, a threshold she had previously straddled, from a child who receives to an adult who gives as well as receives.

As I opened the bag I thanked her, again and again. Here was a gift from Anna, and it wasn't my birthday. As quickly as this thought formed in my mind, I realized that it wasn't true: In childhood Anna had brought me gifts almost daily – a poem that she wrote about me being like a circle with no sharp edges, a dandelion that she plucked from the yard, and endless kisses at bedtime.

I recalled an early evening during Anna's first month at college when my cell phone rang. Looking at the caller ID, I saw an unfamiliar number.

I picked up.

"Hi Mom, it's me."

"Oh, hi, Sweet Pea. I didn't recognize the number."

"Yeah, it's Kenzie's phone. I can't stay on right now. We're running into town to get a few things. I forgot my cell phone, and I remembered we had planned to talk. I didn't want you to worry. I'll call you soon. Love you." That too was a gift.

Now we were in new territory. Anna's generosity had a different flavor. She had bought me a gift with money she could have spent on herself simply because she wanted to. On one level I knew this passage was to be expected, a normal part of growing up, and yet this new reciprocity astonished me.

Her gift brought to mind the times in the past that I had arrived home with a package of her favorite Pepperidge Farm cookies, a new type of Rubik's cube, gifts purchased for no reason other than to please her.

"I love it!" I said as I slipped the vest over my shirt. Anna was right; it fit me perfectly, as if it had been made with me in mind.

Trying on the vest transported me back to my mother's closet. She had died in a car accident just before my tenth birthday. Her fox stole snaps at my memory, as lucid as in my childhood imagination – its jaws opening and closing, biting his own tail to clasp around her shoulders. When his beady eyes stared right at me, I could almost imagine he was alive, that I was his prey, and yet somehow I could see to the bottom of his little fox soul.

Mom's fox had come out of hiding when she would go out for dinner and dancing with my dad. Even though they had five kids under the age of nine at that point, they still made time for each other, which even back then I recognized as beautifully romantic. On those nights I would sit on the countertop next to the bathroom sink and watch Mom get ready. I knew her routine – first, face cream, followed by eye shadow – my eyes tracing each of her movements.

"What color do you like best, Mom?" I asked. She said, "the blue" as she swept the brush along the crease, concentrating.

"It brings out the blue in my eyes," she added, "don't you think?"

Next, she put on eyeliner, and if it was an extra special night, false eyelashes. I focused on her reflection in the mirror: fair, creamy skin, and a slightly crooked smile.

She let me try on a little of her coral lipstick, which she said was "the finishing touch." I watched as she opened her mouth like one of my goldfish being fed, as she put on her lipstick.

For me, sitting there was like watching magic happen. She looked just like a movie star on the silver screen – immortal. Time would never change it.

After her accident I would return to her closet and look through her clothes. I'd open the hatbox where the fox stole was stored and try it on. Wrapping the fur around my neck, I'd sit in front of her vanity with the three-way mirror. For the longest time all her makeup and brushes remained on the counter top. I'd put on her lipstick. I'd spritz myself with a bit of her perfume, smelling a mix of flowers and something fruity. Like Mom. I'd adjust the fox this way and that across my shoulders. I was looking for something; I just didn't know what it was. Yet, when I stood up, my head no longer appearing in the mirror, I could for a moment imagine it was she whom I saw.

After giving me the vest, Anna returned to talking about the *C. elegans*, her eyes alight with the buzz of discovery. She described the scientific process, how she used a glass needle to insert the DNA into the next generation of worms, repeating and failing at these microinjections, day after day, worried it would never work, until finally she saw the glow. Her pleasure continued, as she showed me the drawings she had rendered of the worms in motion. It was then that I caught a glimpse of the two of us in her wall-sized ballet mirror. It surprised me how similar we looked. While our resemblance is often remarked on, in that moment I saw that it wasn't just our physical likeness that so powerfully merged, but that it was something subtler that Anna and I shared; something that came from my mother, her generosity, curiosity, and perseverance.

If my mother had an idea, she was all in, never doubting that if she worked hard enough, she would succeed.

There was the dollhouse she designed. Unlike the homes of my friends, with the standard two floors and the back of the house exposed so you could peer in, ours was made from one large sheet of plywood, about four feet by four feet. Open from above, you could look down and see the entire floor plan. The walls of the eight rooms were divided by thin pieces of wood. It was set up for a family like ours: a family with a mom, a dad, four girls, and a boy.

Some of the furniture had been bought, but most of the pieces she had made herself, out of balsa wood. All tiny and delicate. From scraps of fabric she had sewed bedspreads, curtains, and upholstery for the furniture. She used rug remnants to cover the floors and applied a different pattern of wallpaper to each room. The wallpaper on my dollhouse bedroom matched the tiny flowers of my actual bedroom. My mother was an avid wallpaper hanger. Around the entranceway, she added little potted plants. When you looked inside, it was almost like seeing a mini version of our house.

She always told us nothing was impossible if you set your mind to it. My father knew this about her too. If my mother had a brainstorm before he left for work in the morning, there was a very good chance the venture would be well under way before he got home that night. Once as he headed out the door my mother mentioned that if they took down the wall in the entryway, it might open things up a bit and give a better view of the living room. That night my dad came home to find my mom had taken a sledgehammer to the wall.

"You're right, Helen. It does make the room look a lot bigger," Dad said with a smile.

So her idea for a completely cement backyard was no surprise.

"Bob," I heard her say to my dad, "think of all the time you'll save never having to mow the lawn. And the kids wouldn't have to roller skate in the street."

She poured the concrete herself.

Now, watching Anna, I saw that the link between my mother and daughter had been there all along. In contrast to Anna's deliberate insertion of DNA from one being to another, my mother's gifts of generosity, curiosity, and determination had been passed on to me and her granddaughter naturally, no outside intervention necessary. This understanding of my mother's legacy – the knowledge that the three of us were indelibly entwined, connected in essential ways, had been Anna's true gift to me. While she still looked just like herself, with the same long, thick wavy brown hair, the same milky white skin, I now saw her differently. Like my mother, Anna shone, maybe even glowed.

15

No going back to before

Ann V. Klotz

Irrevocable, the death of a close family member or friend is a slash that divides lives into before and after. In our swiftly moving culture, while adolescents are continuously exposed to horrific events, typically, it is easy enough to click to another screen when they confront unwanted information or headlines. Death's permanence, however, requires young people to reinterpret their world as they struggle to integrate a permanent loss. The process of grief and mourning is antithetical to all they know: grief takes time – a long time. There is no going back to how we were before a significant loss. One loss inevitably recalls other losses – grief piles up. As a teenager, I lost my older brother in a car accident; six years ago, my second daughter stood by my side when her grandmother, my mother, died. Then, a year and a half later, when that same daughter was a junior in the school I lead, her dear friend and classmate died in a sledding accident.

In leading a school through tragedy and in comforting a grieving daughter, I've learned more about the way sorrow spools out and about how to help teenagers move forward into a new normal after the sudden death of a peer.

In the play *Our Town*, Emily, returning to Grover's Corners after her own death, asks the Stage Manager, "Do any human beings ever realize life while they live it? – every, every minute?" He answers that few people do. But for a few months in 2012, after one of my students died in a tubing accident, we did. Every minute, we realized that we were living. Every minute, too, we realized how much we had to lose.

***

It was the middle of the night when my daughter shook me awake.

"They can't wake up Jessica, Mommy."

"What?" I murmured, having trouble following her, struggling to rouse myself.

"There was some kind of accident in Utah. They can't wake her up."

Frantic, Cordelia told the story in bits. She learned on Facebook that there had been an accident. Her dear friend, Jessica, and another classmate, Janet, had been terribly injured. Jessica lay in a coma in Utah. I looked at the clock – after midnight. My husband was still downstairs watching a movie, no doubt.

"Mom, do something," Cordelia implored.

"Do you have her mom's number on your phone?" I asked groggily.

"Only her dad."

"I'll call."

As I dialed, Cordelia, stricken, held her laptop open, as if Jessica might miraculously communicate through the screen.

When Jessica arrived in eighth grade at Laurel School in Shaker Heights, Ohio, where I was headmistress, Cordelia found a friend. Heads bowed over schoolwork, one golden and one dark, the two were thick as thieves. United by a love of gymnastics, they were math buddies – Jessica, more confident, a patient teacher. Jess was an easy friend – level, smart, loyal to Cordelia. Because I wasn't Jewish and Seth had not grown up with formal religion as a part of his life, Jessica was our guide to all things Jewish the year Cordelia became a bat mitzvah. I remember her at Cordelia's party wearing a black feathered mask, glamorous but girlish, too, and giddy.

Cordelia loved Lori, Jess's mom, loved hanging out at their house. In the center of teenage girl drama, it was Jessica who stood by Cordelia, listening, affirming, a steady friend. Jess was a fashionista, un-self-conscious, true to her own style. In tenth grade, when Jess had surgery to repair her ACL, Cordelia went to her house to do math, day after day, buoying up her friend.

But the girls hadn't seen each other for any length of time since spring. In the fall of their junior year, Cordelia, eager for a respite from being the headmistress's daughter, headed for a semester away at The Mountain School. We collected her in mid-December, but Jess had already left for her family's vacation home.

"Sometimes these things sound much worse than they are, honey," I soothed as the phone rang far away in Deer Valley.

A young voice answered. It was Marc, Jessica's younger brother.

"Is Mr. Frankel available?" I inquired. "It's Ms. Klotz, the Head at Laurel."

"No, he can't talk now."

"Could you tell him I called? Tell him we are thinking about Jessica, about all of you; if there's anything at all we can do . . ." I trailed off. What could I possibly do so many states away? Fleetingly, I wondered if I should take Cordelia to Utah. I hung up, suddenly catching Cordelia's despair as if it were a contractible disease.

"Try to sleep," I said, walking her to her bedroom. "We'll know more tomorrow."

Perhaps the situation was not as grim as Cordelia's white face suggested. Maybe the kids were fueling the drama? I lay down with her on her bed, my mind far away, replaying my older brother's death when I was fourteen. I remember hoping we would wake to discover it had all been a bad dream, my brother grinning at the prank he had played. "Please, no," I prayed silently. "Please let her be okay," I rubbed Cordelia's back, knowing I did not have enough information to be reassuring, hoping my physical presence might bring some comfort.

In the morning, Jessica's desperate friends tried to use Facebook to contact Robert Pattinson, the star of the film *Twilight*. Jessica adored him; perhaps the sound of his voice would wake her? I did not understand how they intended to reach him, but I recognized that it was good for all of them to have something to do.

Later in the day, still with no news about Jessica, I found myself at the mall. Why was I there? Perhaps because Christmas was only a few days off. Perhaps I was at the Lego store for my son Atticus, who was six years old. I'm not sure, but what I haven't forgotten was the sensation of my phone buzzing in my pocket. Amid the crush of holiday shoppers and piped-in Christmas music, a parent in my school confided, "It's bad, Ann, really bad." She was friendly with Janet's family. They were hopeful about Janet's recovery, but not about Jessica. "She may not ever wake up." My heart dropped. I swallowed hard, gripped the bannister of the balcony, floated away for a few seconds to the kitchen of my grandmother's house, thirty-five years earlier, when my mother and I had answered the phone and learned that Rod had been killed in a car accident.

"Thank you for letting me know," I managed, hanging up, trying to inhale and exhale rather than scream outside of Abercrombie & Fitch. I knew, with excruciating familiarity, what lay ahead. Always good in a crisis, I began to make a list of all we would need to do to prepare.

I called Lisa, our school's consulting psychologist, and Kathryn and Liz, the Upper School directors. We made a plan to invite the Upper School girls to gather at school the next morning. Though winter break had started, many were nearby. I wrote to the girls – the first of many emails I would send them about Jess and Janet – reminding them that we were holding both girls in our hearts, counseling them to resist feeding the rumor mill, and requesting that they not to speak with the media, whose cars were already parked across the street from our lovely school.

At home, I tried to warn Cordelia, gently, gently, that the news would not be good. She sat, huddled into an armchair in our living room, still and silent, as her older sister, Miranda, home from college, mechanically hung ornaments on the Christmas tree. Miranda glanced worriedly at her younger sister.

"Want to help?" she asked, tentatively.

Cordelia shook her head. Our minds hovered over a hospital bed in Utah, where Jess lay, un-wakable. My husband had gone off to a massage; my father-in-law, visiting for Hannukah, sat with Atticus, six, in the TV room, the Disney channel blaring.

The phone rang. Cordelia recoiled, as if her body could shield itself from the coming blow.

"Yes," I murmured, "I'm so sorry. Whatever we can do. Would you like me to tell her classmates? I can do that." I hung up gently, as if my care could matter to Jessica's unmoored father.

I didn't need to tell Cordelia what I'd just been told. She knew and she began to keen. Atticus ran in from the TV room as Cordelia slid, fetal, to the floor.

In the doorway, Atticus asked softly, "Did Jess die, Mommy?"

"Yes, my love."

"Could I get Cordelia a glass of water?" he offered, his brown eyes fearful.

"Good idea, Atticus," Miranda answered calmly. "We'll go together."

I sat on the floor next to my stunned younger daughter, stroking her long dark hair. I knew I had no magic to mend her grief, no charm to salve her sorrow. I recalled being beyond speech at fourteen, stuck in a mute agony that could not be mitigated.

The twinkle lights on the tree blurred.

What next? My father-in-law came in to share that he, too, had lost a close friend when he was sixteen. He meant well, but in the shock that follows sudden death, no one else's sorrow feels relevant. As a mother, I had rarely felt as powerless as I did that night. Miranda, sad, too, but focused on her sister's grief, distracted her little brother with a video, made me a cup of tea. Seth arrived home, enfolding Cordelia in his arms, then taking Atticus off to bed. A little later, both daughters, tears spilling, sat with me at the dining room table, while, as headmistress, I called the homes of Jessica's classmates, one by one. Most parents seemed to have been sitting by the phone. A mother claimed Jessica had been dead for hours. I wanted to correct her, explain to her that I had just spoken with Jess' dad, but why argue? A fight wouldn't bring Jess back. The calls were brief, supercharged with sorrow.

***

I remembered the clumsiness of death from my own adolescence. People didn't know what to say. They muttered platitudes, eager to flee the scene of the sorrow. Again and again, I answered the doorbell, finding neighbors or people from our church clutching casseroles and cakes, awkwardly stuttering through rehearsed condolences. I offered polite, if listless, thanks and carried each new dish to the kitchen, placing it next to other items that sat uneaten. Carefully, I'd record in a notebook that mysteriously appeared who had brought what. I remember coffee-flavored Jello that Aunt Vi made, smothered with fresh whipped cream, as the single food I could choke down.

***

The next morning, I woke with the lines of an Emily Dickinson poem (known as 'After great pain a formal feeling comes' or number 341) pounding in my brain, of feet numbed and mind dulled by the pain of loss. I swung my feet out of bed, tears sliding from my eyes. My muscles ached, as sore as if I had worked out. I was not fourteen, but my body remembered what it was to forget for a moment, to surrender to the oblivion sleep offered, only to wake and recall tragedy. My eyelids were swollen. No point in putting on mascara. I wept for Jessica's family, for my own children, for my young self. The possibility of losing my own child brushed against me, insistent as the cat demanding breakfast. My breath caught. Seth, tender, wrapped his arms around me, held me until I pushed away. His own experience of death was, mercifully, limited – both his parents were still alive; he had his brother and sister. It was tempting to remain in the circle of his quiet, constant care, but I knew I had to put away my own sadness to care for others, to get on with the busy-ness of death. So, into the chilly light I went. There were media statements to write, words to consider for the girls who would assemble in a few hours.

***

My brother died in the era of "Stiff upper lip," "Don't wallow," and "God must have wanted it this way." There were few opportunities to speak of unspeakable sorrow. Mrs. Goppelt, a remarkable English teacher in the girls' school I attended, encouraged me to write, gave me permission to howl onto the page, suggested I audition for a production of *Our Town* at the boys' school, where my grief was unremarkable, in keeping with the play's themes. She knew, better than I could, what might help me begin to integrate Rod's death into my life. I found a way to creep forward. I wanted to give the girls in my school permission to mourn in whatever ways they needed, to be their Mrs. Goppelt, an unassuming shepherd.

***

In the Alumnae Room, a large group of girls – pale and shaken – gathered. When we ran out of chairs, they sat on the carpet, leaning against one another, as if they could not sit up straight any longer. Adolescents are hard-wired to reject mortality, to believe they will live forever. We explained the ways in which shock protects us from absorbing too much horror at one time; it's actually essential. We answered questions; we told them however they were feeling was okay, that there were no rules about how to grieve. "No," we said, "she would not have suffered; she would not have been in pain." Jessica had possessed a spirit of adventure, relished physical challenges. We reminded them that she had gone tubing many times. There would have been no reason for her to be afraid. We emphasized the fact that this had been an accident. There was no one to blame, no way to have prevented it or predicted it. Our presence and tone mattered more than the words we said.

In the following days, I wrote to the Upper School girls often. I used my words as a way of wrapping my arms around each of them. Writing, the practice that started formally in the months after my brother died, was my go-to comfort strategy. I offered details about the funeral, explained that the TV stations parked outside the school were simply doing their jobs (though the sight of them enraged me), demystified how to pay a *shiva* call, tried to reassure them that they would not always feel this bad. Writing felt like something I could do.

More than a thousand people gathered to say goodbye to Jessica, but the temple felt eerily still. The girls sat among their families, tucked next to one another, shoulders shaking with silent sobs. Seth and I put our two daughters between us, as if we could protect them. I kept my composure knowing all the girls needed me to be strong. My falling apart would have scared them. Perhaps that sense of obligation was how my own parents got through my brother's funeral. I don't have many memories of that day – still gripped by shock, I remember sucking on a Crist-o-Mint Lifesaver and watching tears trace tiny lines down my mother's powdered face as we sang, "O God Our Help in Ages Past." I remember Rod's classmates, the girls in muted shifts, the boys in coats and ties in pews in the back of the church, a summer tragedy, not this winter one.

Jessica's rabbi reminded us that it was hard to fathom why Jessica had been taken from us – that our job was to hold onto two opposing realities: there is tragedy in the world and we must see the good and work for good. He told us that Jessica was on her way, that she was safe from pain, that we carried her with us. He exhorted her parents to live – for Jessica, for their son, for themselves. Finally, he asked that we move from strength to strength together, one breath at a time.

Afterwards, I stood on the temple steps, hugging my Laurel girls – one after the next, the reverse of a wedding receiving line. I watched one of our students, with enormous dignity, rebuff a reporter, murmuring: "Thank you for understanding that this is a private time." I could not go to the burial – some part of me balked at the idea of laying her in the "cold, cold ground" – but Cordelia, stoical, attended with another classmate's family and went to sit *shiva* with Jess's family.

It was my birthday, but I could not summon joy. Losing Jessica over the holidays, a time associated with family and celebration, felt ironic. Would we ever enjoy these rituals again? We invited the junior class to our home to light Hanukkah candles. Parents sent cookies and pretzels and chips. Girls crowded into our living room, again sitting on the floor when we ran out of seats. Christian girls lit candles, sang Hebrew blessings, thought about their precious classmates. I told them I had spoken with Janet. I did not tell them that Janet did not yet know that Jessica had died. We shared funny stories about Jessica. It was a wake of sorts, and it felt good to laugh, to have permission not to be so sad for a bit. My mom, I recalled, never forgot Rod, always made it safe to speak about him, to include him in our stories. As I looked at the candles glowing in the menorahs, I saw Jessica's bright eyes. At her classmates' request, we re-lit our gaudy lawn display of holiday blow ups – in sorrow must come brightness, too, and Jessica had loved the tackiness of my husband's over-the-top inflatables.

***

The holidays continued – slushy, grey. Cordelia was with us, but far away. Bad dreams woke her – jagged sobs and a version of the night terrors she had occasionally suffered as a little girl. Nights were the worst. I often lay with her, humming lullabies from her childhood, so grateful and so guilty that she had not gone to Utah with Jess, a plan we had discussed from time to time. My parents must have felt the same way – grateful that I had not been in the car with my brother when he died. But in the months after his death, I wondered whether he would have stayed awake if I'd been in the car? Or, would my parents have lost two children if I'd been there? To feel both glad and guilty was a familiar state.

As was our custom, we went to New York City after Christmas. Perhaps a different but familiar landscape would help us all. Walking into a shop in Manhattan, I saw a pin in the shape of a dragonfly. Jess's bedroom had been papered in dragonflies. The dragonfly in the display case felt like a talisman. I bought it.

Then, it was time to return to school, to pick up our lives again. I spent a long time thinking about how to start the semester. While I often speak extemporaneously to the girls, I did not trust myself to improvise. With the dragonfly pinned above my heart, I began with Houseman's "To an Athlete Dying Young" because Jess had been a runner, because the formality of verse helped anchor me as I began. I smiled out at the girls:

"So, here we are in a new year, and two of our own are not among us. Janet will return in time; she is making a tremendous recovery. Jessica, as her rabbi told many of us, is on her way.

"And whether or not you were close to Jess or not; whether you ran with her or did math homework with her or went to temple with her or barely knew her, we are all affected by her loss.

"Nobody deserves to die. There is no one to blame. It was an accident, but even that can make us mad. Many of us in this room have done things that were not particularly safe, but we didn't die. If we blame her for going down the ski run in a tube, we don't have to wrestle with the pain we feel at her death.

"We won't erase her; we will carry her with us in a new way. I've marked her seat with a rosemary plant. Rosemary, you may know, is an herb we associate with remembrance."

I explained the custom of *shloshim*, the thirty-day ritual of mourning, following *shiva*, which we would observe by creating a mural of thoughts and photos of Jess to give to her family.

And then we went back to school. We knew how to go to school, and the routine was useful for many of us – girls and grown-ups.

***

As I started Julia Alvarez's novel *In the Time of the Butterflies* with my ninth grade English class a few days later, my voice trembled. Loss upon loss. My eyes filled with tears for the Mirabal sisters, who died, martyrs to social justice; for Dede, the one sister who lived, having to bear witness for years and years. I was conscious of loss all around me – in school, at home with my grieving daughter, in the seasons of my own life – my brother, five miscarriages, the deaths of both my parents only a year earlier. I was a mess and embarrassed to be weeping. I hated the idea of children having to caretake adults. The girls in my class did not really know Jessica unless they had run cross-country with her, but they did understand the wound in our community. They watched me, quietly, perhaps a little frightened that their teacher, their headmistress, was struggling. And then one said, "It's okay, Ms. Klotz; we know you're sad." And I smiled and said, "I am, girls. I am so sad. Thank you." In my students' generosity in witnessing my sorrow, I corrected a piece of my own childhood.

***

Some months after Rod's death I had come downstairs in the middle of the night. Hearing an unfamiliar hoarse sound, I stepped to the door of the dining room, where my mother was sobbing, her head cradled in her arms, leaning on the table – raw, desperate, unguarded sobs. Her grief was immense and intimate, hers alone, unable to be shared. I crept away. We never spoke of it. In public, she remained in control because it was expected of her; it was what she thought I needed. I wish I had put my arms around her, held her, but I did not know how to intrude on her privacy. Decades later, my own ninth graders helped me by sitting with me, acknowledging our collective sorrow.

***

An art teacher at school offered to help the girls make pendants, each etched with a dragonfly. The dragonfly, a symbol of transformation and adaptation, was apt for those of us deep in mourning. Neither Cordelia nor Jess's mother nor I can exactly recollect how or why it began, but we researched the symbolism associated with dragonflies and, gradually, the dragonfly took on totemic qualities. Most of Jessica's classmates wore their pendants, strung on a silken cord, until they graduated; some still wear it at their throats, their own pulses warming the silver disc. Two girls took one to the cemetery; they wanted Jess to have one, too. I wore one as well.

***

We are a culture focused on acquiring and achieving; none of us likes losing – state championships or friends. Accepting loss feels too passive. Most in our community had little experience with letting go permanently; many struggled even to let go of a grudge. No wonder letting go of Jess felt tremendously hard.

There was a generational difference, too. I had grown up familiar with the rituals of death – grandparents laid out in the living room, funerals for obscure aunts and cousins. Death was an expected part of my childhood, at least for the elderly. But for many girls, Jess' death was an uncomfortable first. Parents asked if we could help their daughters draft sympathy notes, run a parent grief group. We did. We became experts in the etiquette of death, trying to make sure that no question was taboo, trying to anticipate what people, of all ages, needed.

Marcia, mother of a ninth grader, came to a meeting of our parent group. Parents of girls of all ages filled the room, grown-ups grieving for their grieving children, grown-ups suffering private griefs, grown-ups needing to be together – who could help being frightened when catastrophe had intruded? We went around the circle sharing what had brought us to the conversation, and Marcia quietly explained that she had lost her son, Daniel, in an ATV accident two years earlier. Her generosity, wisdom, and compassion moved me hugely – that she would join us to offer her perspective, to see if she could help us help the girls and Jessica's family, felt like a gift.

Some girls wondered how the rest of the world could continue when their world had tilted out of control.

We pivoted between the philosophical and the practical. I reminded the juniors that it was not selfish to pay attention to what they needed. We urged sleep, water, exercise, bubble baths, small rituals that would make them happy, even if only for a moment. It was not disloyal to Jess, I explained, to play basketball or to audition for the play. We ate a lot of chocolate. Jessica had loved Hershey Kisses and Swedish Fish. I kept the candy jar in my office stocked, some girls stopping by for candy daily. Cordelia, it seemed to me, was wasting away, eating only chocolate.

Cordelia and her old friend, Katie, on the outs for almost a year, found their way back to one another; sorrow ebbed and flowed, but we worked to be kinder than we had been. I worried about several classmates who had had a quarrel with Jess before she died. "Lay that down," I commanded. "It would have all been fixed by now; you don't need to carry that." Life is too short, as Thornton Wilder knew, to nurse grudges. My parents had been fighting with my brother when he died. I saw the weight of carrying that knowledge on top of his sudden ending. Though I have no credentials as a member of any sort of clergy, I granted absolution left and right.

Janet returned; her injuries had been significant and she had always been intensely private. Her friends encircled her, knew they could never understand all she had suffered, but did the best they could. With grace and courage, she moved forward.

We reminded the girls that we were with them on this journey for as long as it took. We tried to create safe spaces and the girls, themselves, created a culture of care. "Check in on so and so," one would tell me quietly, "She's really sad."

I mentioned to the small groups who haunted my office the fact that grief can sneak up on us, that grief is often in the details. It might be months from now when sadness surged, triggered by someone tossing her hair the way Jess did, a fragrance, a memory that came floating back. "And that is normal," I said over and over again. The juniors made a memory book full of photographs and anecdotes to share with Jessica's family.

***

Tragedy leaves in its wake disorder and chaos – that's how school felt. Jess's inexplicable death brought up all the past deaths everyone had experienced or that we all feared. It was tempting to let fear win, allow fear to control us, force us away from doing what we loved. Alternately, we could proceed with courage, as Jess, herself, would have done. Every day offered us the choice.

Atticus asked to go sledding that winter, and Cordelia insisted he wear a helmet; Miranda didn't want him to go at all. Our rational selves warred with our frailties, with our impulse to catastrophize, to flee and avoid any kind of risk.

We felt, as a school, as if we were living inside a snow-globe. People on the outside looked in curiously, oblivious to the effect of their casual insensitivity. Beyond Laurel, the gruesome details of the girls' accident obsessed strangers, who made up details in the absence of facts. In Starbucks, a junior, wearing a Laurel sweatshirt, overheard some women speculating about the accident. Had the girls been drinking? Furious that they were gossiping, she wheeled on them, sputtering, "You are talking about my friends," and fled without her coffee, to my office, where she wept and worried that she had been rude. I explained that a lowest common denominator of human behavior has long been the desire to place blame, to be a know-it-all.

In the ice cream store, Miranda and Cordelia stood in line with two other Laurel girls and heard more gossip about Jessica. One of their friends burst into the Laurel Alma Mater at full volume; Cordelia burst into tears. Miranda hurried them all from the store. In the same way that the adults in our community sought to care for the girls, the girls, themselves, cared for one another with enormous skill.

I told the girls that I, too, felt angry with those who sensationalized the accident, feasting on the drama. I was angry at reporters still circling, hoping one of the girls would give them the "inside scoop" on private school girls run amok in Utah. I felt protective of Jess and Janet, of all the girls. I admitted to myself that I was even angry with beloved Jess, so often in our home. I was angry that she had died. And angry that my brother had left us, too, so long ago.

At home, Cordelia's heart broke over and over again. One evening, I came back from work late, and Cordelia was bent over the dining room table, weeping. She had, by accident, picked up her phone and phoned Jess for help with math, forgetting that Jess could not answer. One spring morning, in math class, Mr. Hassel counted the girls and he said, "We're missing someone." The girls all looked around, and, as a moment ticked by, they realized it was Jessica who was missing. Then, one day, Lori sent Cordelia a funny photo of Jess and Cordelia doing math together – it was a small comfort, a moment captured that she had forgotten, confirmation of what they had shared. Cordelia made it the background for her phone.

***

When I was a little girl, Mom often took me to tend the graves of her family in the churchyard. We weeded, planted bulbs, trimmed ivy; it was a companionable time, but my own parents and Rod were buried in Eagles Mere, Pennsylvania, where we spent the summers. I found myself often driving to the cemetery where Jessica was buried, offering Hershey Kisses, pebbles. But I never stayed long. She was not there. I left the car running and walked to the grave, bending, noting all the gifts that had been left, girls bewildered that their lively friend rested here now. It defied understanding. I worried that I would bump into her mother.

I worried I wouldn't. Leaving the cemetery, I thought more than once, "I am not okay." One grief begets another, and in losing Jessica, I lost my own brother over and over again, moving through loss as if it were a thick, swampy fog and trying to pull the whole school community through the thickness with me. I felt inadequate, raw, ill-equipped. Grief is fundamentally lonely.

***

Even in the midst of sorrow, our high-achieving, intensely motivated Upper School girls were conscious of the potential impact of their sorrow on their grades and on standardized test scores. They were managing more stress than we wanted them to have to cope with, but were there things that could help, that we could offer? Our thinking coalesced around identifying five components of resilience: creativity, growth mindset, self-care; purpose and relationships. When we offered resources, some girls felt less stuck, comforted to have tools or strategies. We could not eliminate the stress of Jess's death, but we could teach the girls to develop resources to manage this stress as well as the other stresses they would inevitably face throughout their lives. Laurel's Center for Research on Girls began to develop and implement curricula around the five components. We defined creativity as finding another path, getting unstuck, trying a different approach. Growth mindset was already well established at Laurel, but we reminded girls that hard work and perseverance could improve outcomes, even in this tough time. We had long used the word "yet" as shorthand for maintaining growth mindset. We tweaked "yet" for the juniors and adopted it in terms of feeling better: "You don't feel better yet, but someday, you will." "Yet" offered hope and optimism. Self-care centered on adequate sleep – never easy for adolescents – and self-soothing strategies – yoga, running, coloring, knitting – rituals girls knew would help them feel calmer. Purpose helped mitigate the senselessness of Jess's accident. If a girl has a purpose larger than herself, she often feels better about herself, less self-absorbed, more connected to someone or something else. Gradually, more girls began to volunteer, started a club, got involved in a cause; it helped. Relationships, of course, were already part of the fabric of our school community, but we encouraged the girls to connect with one another and with adults who mattered to them. All five components had a rich research base, which helped us to demonstrate their validity to parents and teachers. The girls seemed grateful for this new language of help, for tiny strategies to help them feel less paralyzed.

***

For a long time, I could not get out of my head an image of Jessica in a white parka with a fur ruff, smiling. Finally, I told Cordelia and she explained Jessica actually had such a white parka. That relieved me – I wasn't insane.

***

I thought about Jessica's brother often; I wanted him to know that it gets better, but it will never be okay. I wanted him to understand he will never forget his sister but that thinking about her won't always be painful. That was my experience.

***

Grief in the age of social media was daunting and inescapable. I had asked the girls to stay off of Facebook and Twitter as the details of the accident unfolded, but afterwards, many were drawn to two Facebook pages. One was a memorial page and the other was Jess's own profile page – girls would log on and see Jessica's little green dot, suggesting she was online as well, but it was her brother, Marc, who was her administrator. Many girls wrote to her there, publicly expressing their grief. Sometimes, it seemed almost competitive: "Who loved her more?" "Who misses her the most?" Some wanted to deify Jessica, to make her into a saint rather than preserve her as real with strengths and quirks. Cordelia raged against it all, her own love and grief finding no outlet in such public expression. Several classmates confided that they continued texting Jessica out of both habit and longing. I imagined their texts wafting into cyber-space. Later, I imagined them arriving in a stranger's phone. No one wanted to delete her phone number. We hold onto what we can keep.

***

Some months after Jessica's death, a classmate sat in my office.

"Sometimes, I think I'm going crazy, Ms. K. Sometimes I imagine she's just away, that she'll come back." She blinked back tears.

"I know," I murmured, thinking, *Me too*.

As a group of girls trooped out of our house to go to the prom at the boys' school in May, I thought, "Where's Jess?" and when I remembered that she was not among them, I put my head down on the dining room table and sobbed, furious that I had forgotten.

***

Grief takes more time than we want it to. It cannot be hurried though we feel impatient with ourselves, with the ungainly process. We want to feel better faster.

It's always been my habit to look to words for consolation – in poetry, in books. As the months passed, I often felt like a mole, blind, trying to feel my way forward by instinct. But my wise therapist reminded me that I, more than many others, did know how to do this work, was, in fact, a kind of expert. I set myself free of trying to fix it; that was beyond my power. To forget was never the goal. What I could do was inch forward, demonstrating to all the girls that the agony of grief's gash lessens imperceptibly – so subtly that we hardly notice.

***

The summer after Jess' death, our family took an RV trip out West. At Crater Lake, magnificent dragonflies skittered, perched, danced. "Hello, Jess," I thought to myself. "Hello." Dragonflies fly and perch on water, inviting us to dive into feeling, adapt, move. Breathe in. Breathe out. Live.

***

For months after Jessica's death, Cordelia's anger was adamantine, her aloofness and isolation complex and off-putting. It frustrated me that other girls sought comfort from me, but my own daughter couldn't be comforted. Right before we celebrated Jessica's life at school in September, my husband decided to foster a desperately sick rescue dog. The puppy was ill with mange – oozing sores, matted tufts of fur. She was grotesque and Cordelia was furious. Her sorrow was too big to allow a more pathetic being to join our family. But Seth brought the black and white puppy home. A few days later, I discovered Cordelia on the floor of the kitchen with the mangy little creature, crooning to it, stroking with her finger a single patch of fur. Watching her tenderness, I understood that though Cordelia's heart had been fractured, she would come back to us – eventually. This small wretched dog saw right through her defenses and knew she could be trusted to return love with love. Much later, Cordelia told me that her own memory of the events surrounding the months after Jess's death were vague, blurred by shock. But once the puppy arrived, she began to remember events again. Who rescued whom?

***

With the gifts sent to the school in Jessica's memory, we built a roof garden. Jess loved the outdoors and mountains. We thought she would like the idea of being up high. Her parents, intensely practical, wanted a gift that would have meaning long after those girls who knew Jess had been graduated, so we made a contemplative space – first open only to her class, now open to the whole Upper School. Donald, her father, supervised construction. Each time he came to school, he opened the candy jar in my office, searching for a piece of chocolate. Like daughter, like father. The garden features a small fountain, trees planted in pots, and a sculpture of a gymnast on the bars, dressed in a red leotard, with a purple dragonfly adorning the frame. Benches given by family members and friends are arranged around beds of sedum, lovely. Hydrangeas climb lattice. It is beautiful year round.

On a sunny Sunday afternoon, we gathered to dedicate the garden. The seniors (now they were seniors) and I had planned the ceremony, checking in with Jessica's parents at every step. The garden had a plaque at its doorway, with a dragonfly on it and a QR code with more about Jessica. "You read, Ms. K.," her classmates had decided, "we don't trust ourselves." Our Chapel was full. Again, I stood at the podium. Time had passed. In the front row sat Jess's family, her mother, elegant, composed, face still, as if carved from alabaster. "How can she do this?" I wondered silently, "Be in this room with these girls who are all alive?"

The seniors sang Ingrid Michaelson's song, *Everybody*, upbeat, melodious. They knew Mrs. Frankel didn't want anything lugubrious. Only when they returned to their seats could we hear them crying. I left the stage and walked a box of Kleenex over to them.

I started with a passage from *Jeremy Thatcher, Dragon Catcher*, a children's book Atticus and I had read. Jeremy, sad about losing his beloved dragon, talks to the librarian, who asks him why he is sad to let his dragon go. He explains he does not want to lose the dragon, and the wise librarian reminds him that nothing we love can ever be truly lost.

Nothing we love is lost. We hold in our hearts those who leave us.

***

Both daughters asked me, months later, separately, if, after my brother died, I ever felt happy again.

"Of course I did," I responded, and in that moment, I knew that it was true. "There was a long stretch of numb," I explained, "A long time where all our feelings were rubbed down like the nub of an eraser, but when enough time passed, we found a path forward. And the sting lessened eventually – more of an ache than a fracture."

"Do you still miss him?" Miranda asked.

"Yes. Not all the time, but unexpectedly – your little brother's big front teeth remind me of him. Or that time last summer, when Atticus wore his bangs shoved over to the side as Rod did." My son had looked, in that second, so much like my brother that I had gasped. I still missed the idea of Rod, but I had carried on. There is no getting over death, but there is getting on with it, carrying on.

***

The musical the year after Jessica's death was *Little Women* and Cordelia was Jo. When Beth died, Jo's grief was exquisite, real tears falling. In the back of the theatre, I wept as Claire, who played Marmee, comforted Jo:

So believe that she matters.
And believe that she always will.
She will always be with you.
She'll be part of the days you've yet to fill.
She will live in your bounty.
She will live as you carry on your life.
So carry on,
Full of hope,
She'll be there
For all your days of plenty.[1]

Beth and Jo. Jess and Cordelia. Onstage and off, we were thinking of Jessica. Marmee's reminder to Jo to carry her sister Beth with her echoed Jessica's rabbi's insistence that we live ourselves and live for her, too.

***

Commencement. Sixty-one girls in white robes. I began the ceremony by acknowledging the girls' beloved missing sister, Jessica Frankel. On my pinky glowed the Laurel School class ring that the seniors had given me the day before. We had walked a long road together. I was theirs. Diplomas given, hugs exchanged, we sent the Laurel School Class of 2013 off into the world. Our family enjoyed a graduation luncheon to celebrate Cordelia. When lunch concluded, I laid a program from Commencement on Jess' grave.

***

How mysterious that the experience of death brings moments of startling clarity and moments that are forgotten altogether. Cordelia remembers interactions I don't recall; Miranda remembers other pieces. I suspect my sister has a whole host of memories around the time that Rod died that I don't share. Grief is individual, personal, even when we mourn together.

***

Almost five years after Jessica's accident, I ran into her mom in a parking lot one summer morning. She had become a good friend – walking buddy, irreverent, gorgeous, funny, authentic – she reminded me of her daughter. And she has been extraordinarily kind to my own daughter when she could so easily have turned away.

"Lori!" I called, clambering from the car. She squinted, smiled.

"It's Ann." I tossed my keys into my purse and moved to hug her.

"What are you doing here?" she asked.

I shrugged, "Therapy."

"Therapy?" she giggled.

"Yep," I rolled my eyes. She, impeccably dressed and coiffed, was headed to Pilates.

"So, how was drop-off?" I inquired. Her son, Marc, had recently left for college. Cordelia had returned to Maine for her own senior year.

"Okay, okay," she assured me. Of course, it was, I thought to myself. It's only college.

Reading my mind, she added, "He'll be back."

"Yes," I murmured. "In the new house yet?" I inquired. They had designed and built a new home, sold the old one, the one so full of memories of their girl, a home I'd envied.

"Not yet." She explained they'd been to a *bris* the night before.

"Who was born?" I asked. A little boy, obviously.

"With the middle name Judah. For Jess," she said, eyes bright. I nodded.

"Rabbi Skoff was great," she says. "He talked about addition and subtraction in families." We embraced again and headed in different directions.

"I want to walk with you soon," she called. I nodded, smiled, walked up the stairs considering this idea of addition and subtraction. When we dedicated Jessica's garden, Gadi, Jess's religion teacher, had allowed me to join her family in the garden for a prayer. He had spoken about the branches of a family, how roots grow down for the tree to stretch up, how some limbs fall away and others grow.

***

On Labor Day, almost five years after Jessica died, I stood on the hillside in a cemetery in Pennsylvania where my brother's grave lies in between my mother and my father. I thought about the wildness of grief quieting down in the Grover's Corners cemetery and about my own wild grief quieting and resurging. I had forgotten the bouquet of wild phlox I'd cut the night before for my mom; it would wither on the dining room table of our summer house, closed up now for the fall. By now accustomed to leaving some token at a grave, I arranged tiny pinecones on the flat stones.

Sun warm on my hair, I wondered what Jess would look like now: a senior in college, confident, poised for her next chapter. In the funny kaleidoscope of possibility, I saw her at her wedding, cradling an infant; instantly, I recalled her in eighth grade – sparkling, alive.

Since her death, we have developed robust programming around resilience. We teach girls that the components of resilience can be helpful when we confront stresses, both large and small. We have presented on this topic, taking this work into the world through Laurel School's Center for Research on Girls. This work is part of Jessica's legacy and continues to shape the experiences of girls she never knew. When we speak of her, we keep her with us.

With sudden death, the event itself occurs in real time. After that, time is no longer reliable. We benchmark our grief against might-have-beens. We replay moments we remember. In my mind's eye, I see my family before my brother died; in my young son's smile, I see the ghost of my brother. In the faces of my brother's contemporaries, whom I see most often in this small summer community, I contemplate what Rod might have looked like in middle age.

We who remember look through a telescope in both directions, backward in memory, forward in anguish.

Standing in front of the graves of my brother and parents, I think grief, perhaps, is the cost of life, of love, of loss. It's a huge price to pay and there's no going back to before. Yet in the breeze ruffling the pine trees, I smelled summer. In this place associated with death and memory, I still felt alive, grateful.

Note

1 From the song "Days of Plenty," lyrics by Mindi Dickstein and music by Jason Howland, from *Little Women: The Musical*. Reprinted by kind permission of Kate Bussart, Literary Department, Bret Adams Ltd., literary agent to Mindi Dickstein.

Concluding remarks

Anne J. Adelman

In our day-to-day lives, we often use the expression "free time" ironically or wistfully. "I'll get to that in my free time," we might say breezily, knowing full well it will never happen, or "If only I had more free time. . . " We are all yearning for a way to escape the confines of our ordered days. Adolescents and adults alike maintain frenetic schedules, with no reprieve from the press of what is yet to be done or the worry about what must remain unfinished or fall by the wayside. We are at risk of losing the space for calm and reverie.

Time is one of the few things we are granted for free, on par with oxygen, sunlight, and water – and even those aren't necessarily free. Yet inevitably we wrestle with time. Noted on calendars, memorialized on holidays and anniversaries, pinned down by historical facts, the passage of time marks the progression of our lives. We map our lives in moments, anchored between what has just been and what is about to be. But try as we may, we cannot control time – it eludes our grasp. We think of it as an imperious tyrant, indifferent to our needs and wishes – we imagine time "marching on," "flying by," "waiting for no man."

Time is the one asset we have that we are destined to deplete. We waste it, we lose it, we forget the past, and we fail to plan adequately for the future. Ultimately, we all run out of time.

In the digital age, our sense of time has been altered in profound ways – everything can be reworked, embellished, amplified, or deleted. On the one hand, whatever we capture digitally can be preserved indefinitely, while on the other hand it is subject to infinite revision. Either way, it can never be quite the same as it was in its original – real time – version.

As our sense of permanence has changed, so too has our tolerance for expectancy. We measure the future in milliseconds, with the notion that what we want can be obtained instantaneously – information accessed, questions answered, responses received in the blink of an eye. Conversely, we can be absorbed for hours in the virtual world, one click leading to another until we fall into a virtual time vortex. The digital world has simultaneously sped up and collapsed our experience of time.

I wonder, have we gained time or lost it in the digital age?

For many, the Internet and the digital world have generated a new space for play. Composers, writers, and artists revel in the creative spaces that digital media make possible, by opening up a new virtual dimension where creativity can grow exponentially. Podcasts, blogs, digitized music, and multimedia expositions, among other possibilities, expand the realm of self-expression, communication, and connectivity. For young people coming of age alongside these technological advances, it has changed the shape of their futures, the arc of their life narratives, and probably the neurocircuitry of their brains.

Still, as we have seen, these same technological advances have robbed young people of time on their own to connect deeply with others, to be alone with their thoughts, to engage in the natural world and disengage with the virtual one.

Yet the digital world has not altered the rhythms of developmental time. As we have explored throughout this book, young adults need to be granted the slow, steady pace of maturation, to consolidate earlier developmental achievements, and to prepare for what lies ahead. Thus, they need their parents to hold open the time and space for the gradual unfolding of emotional and psychological maturation, while coming to terms with the magnified tempos of digital time. It is similar in this sense to studying a new language – we may readily learn the vocabulary and decipher the rules of grammar, but it takes us longer to become proficient in speaking the language in real time.

As for the parents of today's young adults, maybe we feel as though time has pulled a fast one on us too. Wasn't it only a few years ago – a couple of decades, no more – that we held our infants in our arms, soothing them with the whispers of our hopes and dreams for their futures? Now, here they are on that threshold, ready to step into a future far beyond the scope of what we may have envisioned. But no matter where they are headed, we cannot stand in the way of the developmental imperative. The best we can hope for is that they move forward with the breath of our whispers sealed on their hearts.

Index

acculturation strategies 136–137
action echolalia 60–61
addiction: alcohol abuse 31, 149–155; cell phones and 31; treatment of 149, 158
Addictive Personalities and Why People Take Drugs (Winship) 149
Adelman, A. 7
Adelstein, D. 40
adolescence: identity conflicts in 44; secrecy in 17–18, 27–28; separation and individuation in 17, 25, 29–31, 44, 84
adolescents: cell phones and 19–21; death and 179–193; grief of 183, 186–188; loneliness and 13–15; parenting 10–11, 39–40; sense of self 15; social life of 13, 19, 21; social media and 7, 13–14, 19
adoptees: attachment experiences of 167; curiosity and 167; emotional problems and 166; identity and 163–164, 166, 168; loss aversion and 163, 167; perceived differences and 167; rejection sensitivity of 162; therapy and 167–168
adoption: birth parents and 167, 169; challenges of 157–158; difference and 161–165, 167–169; family reverie and 118–119, 122; by gay men 118–119; identity and 163–164, 166, 168; internal mother and 119; kinship relations 159; likening and 157; primal wound narrative in 118; process of 159–161, 168
adult children living at home: adulthood and 42; clinical example 47–49; increase in 41–42; oedipal issues in 46–47; psychological considerations of 43–44; rates of 51n1; separation and

individuation in 44–47; socioeconomic reasons for 43; therapy and 50–51; value of 51
adulthood: adult children and 42; disabilities and 74–75, 80; emerging 44; gay men and 119; transitioning to 18, 22, 29, 46, 74
"adultlescence" 42, 47
Ainsworth, M. 25
Akhtar, S. 132, 136
alcohol abuse 148–155
Aleichem, Sholem 10
Alone Together (Turkle) 14
alpha elements 151
Althusser, L. 113
ambiguous loss 106
anti-LGBT legislation 110
Arad, H. 127
Arnett, J. J. 44
attachment styles 25, 44–45
autism parenting: challenges of 53–54, 56–57; mentalizing and 57–58; sensory dysfunction and 55; transitional experience and 60–61
autism spectrum disorders: context blindness and 59; defining 54; echolalia and 60; neuro-biological nature of 57; psychoanalysts and 61–62; sensory dysfunction and 54–62; theory of mind and 56–57; understanding and 53, 57; weak central coherence and 58–59
Ayres, A. J. 60

Bernfeld, S. 42
Berry, J. W. 136
beta elements 151–152
bilingualism 131–132
Bion, W. 151–152, 154